ONE Country,
TWO International Legal Personalities

The Case of Hong Kong

Roda Mushkat

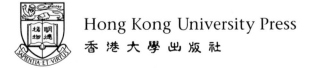

Hong Kong University Press
香港大學出版社

Hong Kong University Press
The University of Hong Kong
Pokfulam Road, Hong Kong

© Hong Kong University Press 1997
First published 1997
Reprinted 1997

ISBN 962 209 427 9

Printed in Hong Kong by Prosperous Printing Co., Ltd.

Contents

Foreword

China's resumption of sovereignty over Hong Kong is a unique and important event in world affairs. It has already spawned a large body of literature in China, as well as elsewhere. If handled well, the reintegration of the British colony into the People's Republic will have a strong positive impact upon both international relations and China's modernization. Whatever the outcome, the implications of the daring 'one country, two systems' formula will be profound for every area of Chinese life, not only in Hong Kong but also in the mainland. 1997 marks the start of the PRC's experimentation with federalism.

Law — domestic and international — will play a critical role in the process. Yet nothing could be more different than the conceptions of law and legitimacy implicit in the colonial common law system that has been belatedly democratizing and liberalizing in hasty preparation for the transition, on the one hand, and the Chinese socialist/traditional legal system that has been belatedly promulgating and institutionalizing in hasty mobilization for economic development, on the other.

The differences between these two systems in assumptions, values, customs, experiences and underlying philosophy have infused each of the debates that has occurred over the implementation of the PRC-UK Joint Declaration of 1984 and the PRC Basic Law of the Hong Kong Special Administrative Region. The determination of what provisions should govern the selection and powers of Hong Kong's chief executive, its legislature and its Court of Final Appeal, the interactions of these institutions among themselves and with China's central authorities and the arrangements for interpreting these provisions, involve the application of basic constitutional principles.

Moreover, in the particular context of Hong Kong, PRC-UK treaty relations and the political-economic-social interdependence of the contemporary world, the line between domestic law and international law, which has everywhere become increasingly blurry, is often, but not always, difficult to discern.

In these circumstances, Professor Roda Mushkat's new book 'One Country, Two International Legal Personalities: The Case of Hong Kong' is especially timely. It demonstrates the very great relevance of international law to virtually all of the public questions that have arisen in Hong Kong since the signing of the Joint Declaration a dozen years ago and that still need to be addressed in the post-97 era. In spirited, analytical and yet scholarly style, Professor Mushkat takes on one controversy after another, summarizing much of the academic, professional and journalistic opinion on each topic and presenting her own views in clear-cut and courageous fashion.

Whatever the subject — prospects for international enforcement of the Joint Declaration, the competence of the Standing Committee of the National People's Congress to control Hong Kong's judiciary, the nationality of local residents, human rights or Hong Kong's international obligations for the protection of the environment or the treatment of migrants — this book will be the place to begin one's quest for enlightenment about law's impact on Hong Kong's future.

Hong Kong University Press and the University's lively Law Faculty, which has done so much to promote public understanding about the need for law reform, can be proud of this newest contribution.

Jerome A. Cohen
Professor, New York University School of Law
Formerly, Director of East Asian Legal Studies at Harvard Law School
Partner, international law firm of Paul, Weiss, Rifkind, Wharton & Garrison

Preface

Hong Kong, a community traditionally preoccupied with the maximization of economic value and shunning international political attention, has found itself since the early 1980s in the centre of events of a distinctly transnational character. Whether deliberately or unintentionally, China has decided, with Britain's 'active acquiescence', to assert its sovereignty over the territory, thrusting it into a position of international prominence and spawning a host of complex questions regarding its new legal status and obligations and rights arising therefrom.

While some of these questions may not elicit a consensual response or one grounded in traditional concepts, they should be explored in a systematic fashion given the fact that they pertain to the future of 5.8 million people who have developed an unmistakable sense of identity and who have come to be perceived by others as international actors in their own right. Further, those people seem to have aspirations which transcend the confines of the Chinese body-politic and the legitimacy of these aspirations is apparently recognized by other relevant parties.

The international legal aspects of Hong Kong's predicament are also of considerable academic interest. The concept of 'one country-two systems' is without direct parallel in international law and there is an obvious need to determine its formal parameters and examine its practical implications. The study of this original concept may also highlight its potential contribution as an institutional vehicle for dispute resolution and as a possible model for the management of territorial entities which either claim or enjoy a high degree of autonomy.

The international legal dimension of the territory's evolution from a British dependency to a Special Administrative Region of the People's Republic of China [HKSAR] may be worth analysing for the benefit of its commercial partners as well, both actual and prospective. Hong Kong, its relatively small size notwithstanding, has extensive trade links, and those engaged in business relationships with it, or contemplating such ties, may no longer be able to operate effectively on the basis of historical images. To achieve their objectives at a reasonable cost, they should aim to acquire an understanding of the local situation which is grounded in the emerging reality.

Hong Kong's external relationships are not limited to commercial interactions alone. It is both a source and a target of substantial people flows (for example, tourists) and other less tangible forms of communication (for example, cultural exchanges). The non-commercial agents who forge contacts with the territory, or envisage such connection, may also wish to develop a better appreciation of the 'new international law of Hong Kong'.

This book aims to serve the needs of the academic and non-academic, commercial and non-commercial, specialized and general, market segments by highlighting facets of the territory's international legal configuration which either relate to its transition from one historical state to another or reflect its growing visibility as a global player. As a result, it is selective in nature and does not purport to serve as a comprehensive introduction to the international law of Hong Kong.

The specific topic addressed in the first chapter is the territory's status in international law, embracing Hong Kong's claim to 'international personality' as well as the content and extent of its international personality — with regard to 'right to life', 'high degree of autonomy', internal self-determination, succession, capacity to bear international responsibility and capacity to bring international claims. The discussion in this chapter draws upon Mushkat, 'Hong Kong as an International Legal Person' (1992) 6 *Emory International Law Review* 105-170, and passages are reproduced here with permission of Emory University School of Law.

The following three chapters focus upon, respectively, the scope of the territory's jurisdiction (specifically, territorial and extraterritorial jurisdiction, personal jurisdiction, exceptions from jurisdiction, extradition, and jurisdiction in civil matters); some of its key international legal obligations (in the areas of treatment of aliens and the protection of the environment); and human rights concerns of local significance (in particular nationality and avenues of international redress). Chapter 2 includes substantial parts of Mushkat, 'Jurisdictional Issues in a "Highly Autonomous Region" — the Case of Hong Kong' (1993) 42 *International and Comparative Law Quarterly* 11-47, and appear here with permission of the British Institute of International and Comparative Law.

The penultimate chapters may display a more theoretical bias but are an essential ingredient of any attempt to examine Hong Kong in an international legal context. Thus, Chapter 5 examines problems of treaty law which arise in the Hong Kong context (for example, 'inequality' of treaties, validity and binding nature of the Sino-British Joint Declaration, and the implementation and breach of international agreements), while Chapter 6 explores the interrelationship between international law and the domestic law (with special reference to customary international law and treaties, the status of international human rights law in the Hong Kong legal system, and post-1997 predictions).

Given the dynamic nature of the situation, and the consequently changing relations between the principal protagonists, some issues may not be effectively accommodated within the framework governing the flow of the analytical/normative argument. On the other hand, these issues cannot be overlooked, and thus, in order to maximize flexibility, they have been relegated to the Epilogue.

In the light of the rather mixed record of modern international legal institutions, the author approaches her task with a degree of humility. Nonetheless, it could be argued that Hong Kong faces such great challenges in the years ahead that international law must be considered as one of the policy tools that should be resorted to in the quest for a prosperous and stable future for the territory. The book is intended as a modest contribution to this process.

Chapter 1

Hong Kong's Status in International Law

HONG KONG'S CLAIM TO 'INTERNATIONAL LEGAL PERSONALITY'[1]

Can it be substantiated?

Defining Hong Kong's international legal status poses a daunting challenge to an international lawyer confronted with an entity which is not a 'state' — yet possessing 'stately attributes'; not 'sovereign' — yet 'highly autonomous'; not a 'conventional' member of the international community — yet a most respectable 'actor' on the international stage. Further, the validity of traditional notions of 'statehood' and 'sovereignty' is increasingly questioned in light of fundamental continuing changes in the structure of international relations. The traditional focus is particularly difficult to reconcile with the emerging pattern of shifting alliances, proliferation of new forms of identity, multiple tiers of jurisdiction, and escalation in the volume of transnational interactions on the part of a variety of non-state actors.

More specifically, commonly accepted criteria of statehood[2] — a permanent population; a defined territory; government; and capacity to enter into relations with other states' — cannot be held to represent sufficient[3] or

---

[1] International legal personality denotes the ability to act (exercise rights, bear duties) within the system of international law; entities possessing international legal personality are 'subjects' of international law.

[2] See Art I, 1933 Montevideo Convention on Rights and Duties of States which is regarded as 'customary international law' ('general practice accepted as law').

[3] Query, for example, whether the independent principality of Sealand (a steel-and-concrete second-world war anti-aircraft tower governed, since they liberated it in 1967 by Major/

even necessary[4] qualifications. Obviously, the less legalistic symbols of statehood, such as kings/presidents, armies, central banks, currency, or passports, offer no reliable yardsticks.[5] It is equally evident that UN [inconsistent] admission practices[6] or its current membership[7] are not particularly instructive in respect of the key distinguishing attributes of statehood.

Nor would the international lawyer's quest for indices of 'international legal personality' be advanced by adopting the 'sovereignty' test. As amply documented by theorists of widely diverging ideological persuasions, the position of the state as the central actor in the international community is being eroded, while 'non-sovereign' actors are increasingly assuming a prominent role in shaping the norms that order and maintain the international community. Analysts of contemporary global politics invariably note that the inefficacy of states to manage grave problems with ramifications beyond national frontiers (e.g. pollution), as well as formidable scientific and technological developments, have forced states to concede power to

---

Prince Roy and Mrs/Princess Joan Bates) — which has its own constitution, flag, coat of arms, stamps, currency, and passport — is a 'state'. At a more scholarly level, it has been argued that *the method by which a 'state' comes into existence* is of crucial importance, and that entities that owe their existence to a use of force by one state against another, originate in interference with the exercise of the right of self-determination, or are created in violation of the principle of non-racial discrimination are a 'nullity' under international law (even if they satisfy the four 'traditional requirements'). See John Dugard, *Recognition and the United Nations* (Cambridge: Grotius Publications, 1987).

4   Note, for example, that Ukraine and Byelorussia were admitted as members of the UN — whose membership is confined to 'states' — for decades before they became independent states.

5   The European Community/Union, for example, has no king or army but its Ecu is a recognized, if unminted, currency; it also has its own diplomats, and holders of the standardized passports issued by its members enjoy 'citizen' status everywhere in the EC. The Community is also a member of several international organizations and a party to major international treaties.

6   Significant inconsistencies have been displayed particularly with regard to enforcement of requirements stipulated under Art 4 of the UN Charter:'Membership in the United Nations is open to all other *peace-loving* states which *accept the obligations contained in the present Charter* and, in the judgment of the Organization, are *able and willing to carry out these obligations.*' [emphasis added]

7   Members include Caribbean pinpoints such as Saint Christopher and Nevis or Saint Lucia, as well as other microentities like Vanuatu in the Pacific or San Marino in Europe — but not Taiwan (which has a population of 20 million and boasts 'the world's 25th highest per capita income; 20th largest gross national product; 15th biggest overseas trade volume; and the largest foreign-exchange reserve holdings in the world' — see Fredrick F. Chien, 'UN Should Welcome Taiwan' *Far Eastern Economic Review*, 5 August 1993, 23).

international regulatory organs and surrender to regional organizations control over numerous areas previously within the exclusive domain of individual states.[8] It is also clear, in the light of an extensive body of human rights law, that states can no longer erect barriers in the name of sovereign/domestic jurisdiction and are subject to international scrutiny and judgement.

The inadequacy of concepts such as 'statehood' and 'sovereignty' should not, however, hinder the task of determining who is a 'subject' of international law or whether an entity possesses an 'international legal personality'. Rather, the inference to be drawn is that restrictive yardsticks of an older political space must be replaced with more flexible perspectives and way given to more expansive pluralistic frameworks able to accommodate the progressive requirements of a 'diffuse multi-centric world'.[9] It may be further observed that 'international legal personality' is a relative and open-textured concept which may depict different characteristics in different circumstances. Thus, states may be said to possess the fullest measure of international personality, international organizations are endowed only with the degree of personality that enables them to discharge their functions effectively, whereas the extent of personality enjoyed by other subjects of international law depends on various factors such as a constitutent treaty or constitution and recognition.

Consequently, an assessment of international legal status/personality should be conducted with reference to a *range* of factors, including: factual 'stately' attributes (such as permanent population, defined territory, government); international recognition and 'legitimacy'; international legal entitlements (e.g. right to self-determination); membership in the 'international civil society';[10] and *sui generis* qualities. It is within such a structure that the following analysis of Hong Kong's international legal status is undertaken.

---

[8] Including [the generally well-guarded sovereign] border control, as exemplified in the 1985 Schengen Agreement, implemented on 26 March 1995.

[9] Term borrowed from James N. Rosenau, 'Patterned Chaos in Global Life: Structure and Process in the Two Worlds of World Politics' (1988) *International Political Science Review* 9. For the link between international legal personality and the 'needs of the [international] Community'/'requirements of international life' see: *Reparations for Injuries Suffered in the Service of the United Nations*, Advisory Opinion [1949] ICJ Reports 174,178.

[10] The 'international civil society' consists of international/regional organizations, multilateral conventions and intergovernmental associations. See C.N. Murphy & E. Augelli, 'International Institutions, Decolonization, and Development' (1993) 14 *International Political Science Review* 71.

Factual 'stately' attributes

Its portable[11] dimensions notwithstanding, Hong Kong exhibits essential factual 'stately' attributes: it is populated by a community of permanent inhabitants whose ordinary place of residence is Hong Kong. Its physical existence as a distinct territorial unit within coherent frontiers is well established both in fact and in law. It is effectively ruled by a local government which exercises jurisdiction over the population and territory, and is endowed with the necessary legislative and administrative competence in respect of what is recognized as fundamental government functions (that is, promulgation of laws, maintenance of order, collection of taxes, dispensation of justice, and conduct of social affairs).

Furthermore, while lacking formal/'juridicial' sovereignty (in the sense of legal entitlement to constitutional independence), Hong Kong possesses a degree of latitude to engage in international action autonomously, said to be matched by no other non-sovereign government in the contemporary international system. Indeed, the territory's considerable international capacity — which is 'further enhanced by its economic strength and extensive involvement in the global economy' — and the extent of its 'empirical'/ 'positive' sovereignty (in the sense of ability to provide political goods for its citizens, collaborate with other governments in international arrangements and reciprocate in international commerce and finance) have led one political analyst to conclude that Hong Kong is well-qualified to be a 'quasi-state'.[12]

International recognition and 'legitimacy'

Amidst a continuing debate among international lawyers regarding the 'constitutive'[13] or 'declaratory'[14] nature of recognition, the practical relevance of the 'recognition factor' in the calculus of international legal personality is rarely disputed. Although it is widely conceded that according a political act a decisive force in the determination of international personality is

---

[11] Note that 'minuteness of territory and population . . . does not constitute bar to statehood' — Ira A. Shearer, *Starke's International Law* (London: Butterworths, 1994) 89 (citing, e.g. the independent state of Nauru which has a territory of 8.25 square miles and an indigenous population of about 3000 persons).

[12] See James T.H. Tang, 'Hong Kong's International Status' (1993) 6 *The Pacific Review* 205.

[13] Under the 'constitutive' theory, the act of recognition establishes ('constitutes') the legal personality of the entity in question.

[14] Under the 'declaratory' theory, recognition is merely a formal acknowledgement of an already existing state of circumstances, indicating willingness to treat the entity as an international person.

undesirable (as well as theoretically unsound), recent events attest to the importance of recognition, particularly when collectively granted.[15] It also appears that some element of 'legitimacy' is sought to be appended to the award of recognition. An implied condition of this nature has arguably underscored UN decisions condemning and urging denial of recognition to entities created in violation of fundamental principles of international law, such as aggression, non-racial discrimination and self-determination.[16] In a more current context, 'legitimacy' has been translated into a requirement of respect for the 'rule of law, democracy and human rights'.[17] While not firmly established as a prerequisite of international legal personality,[18] it is nonetheless evident that the international community expects its members to abide by this trinity of governing norms.[19]

At the same time, given proclivity of domination of pragmatic considerations over principles and legal doctrines, different patterns of interaction are developed among the various actors in the international arena and new norms of behaviour are formed to cope with the emerging vicissitudes of international law. 'Recognition' may thus be inferred from treaty relationships, ministerial visits, formal communications, technical, cultural, or other exchanges. In a similar vein, memberships in international organizations and associations may be taken to imply (at the very least) an acknowledgement of the entity's ability to carry out the essential obligations of membership.

As will be elaborated later, Hong Kong has received a considerable measure of recognition as an autonomous entity by virtue of its extensive involvement in international activities, whether as member of international organizations or as party to multilateral treaties. Of recent significance in

---

[15] Note, for example, the admission to the UN of former Yugoslav republics and the apparent acceptance of the statehood of Bosnia-Herzegovina by the ICJ [*Prevention of Genocide Case* (1993) 32 *International Legal Materials* 888], notwithstanding lack of factual prerequisites such as an effective government, and regardless of 'legality' of creation.

[16] Examples often cited by textbooks are, respectively, the Turkish Republic of Northern Cyprus; Southern Rhodesia; and the so-called 'Black homelands' of South Africa — Venda, Ciskei, Transkei, and Bophuthatswana. See Shearer, op.cit., at 87.

[17] See Council of European Community, *Guidelines on the Recognition of New States in Eastern Europe and in the Soviet Union* (16 December 1991).

[18] Note that the 'Guidelines' have been stipulated by the European Council in the context of a *discretionary* act of recognition (rather than as prerequisites for statehood/international legal personality). It has been observed, however, that '[a]lthough by their terms [the Guidelines are] confined to Europe, and to a particular period of history, it is likely that these guidelines will be influential in shaping future state practice more widely, with necessary adaptations. At the very least they demonstrate that the Montevideo criteria of statehood . . . are no longer considered in practice a sufficient basis for decision.' Shearer, op.cit., at 125.

[19] See later for a discussion on the right to democratic governance under international law.

this context is the '*de jure*' recognition extended to the territory under the US-Hong Kong Policy Act of 1992, whereby the United States 'should continue to treat Hong Kong as a territory which is fully autonomous from the United Kingdom and after June 30, 1997, should treat Hong Kong as a territory which is fully autonomous from the People's Republic of China'[20] in accordance with the provisions of the Sino-British Joint Declaration. Other less explicit[21] 'acts of recognition' by states include the acceptance of Hong Kong's official representatives and Government Offices overseas as well as its permanent missions in major cities such as Brussels, Geneva, London, Tokyo, Toronto,[22] San Francisco and Washington.

Hong Kong may further assert a claim to 'international legitimacy' founded on the territory's general adherence to relevant international norms. Notwithstanding the 'democratic deficit'[23] of its institutions or the flaws in its human rights system,[24] 'Hong Kong is a free society with most individual freedoms and rights protected by law and custom.'[25] It enjoys a well-entrenched tradition of rule of law — backed by 'democratic oversight from Westminister'[26] — an independent judiciary and a free press. The HKSAR is equally posed to make a similar claim to international legitimacy. Indeed, its case is bolstered by the 'internationalization' — through a legally binding international treaty — of respective guarantees for the maintenance in the territory of the rule of law and the integrity of the legal system; local governance in accordance with democratic principles; and protection of universally recognized human rights and fundamental freedoms.

---

[20] Sec. 103(3), United States-Hong Kong Policy Act of 1992, repr. in (1993) 32 *International Legal Materials* 545.

[21] As noted by the Commissioner for Canada in Hong Kong, no special legislation was considered necessary in order to treat Hong Kong as a separate entity, given established bilateral ties and accords between Canada and the territory. See Susan Furlong, 'Canada Ties "Not Affected by 1997" ' *South China Morning Post*, 2 November 1992, at 2.

[22] Note that, backed by an amended Foreign Missions and International Organizations Act 1991, the Canadian government has 'upgraded' the Hong Kong Office in Toronto, granting it 'quasi-consular' status. See 'New Diplomatic Status' *South China Morning Post*, 8 December 1991, at 2.

[23] See International Commission of Jurists, *Countdown to 1997. Report of a Mission to Hong Kong* (Geneva: ICJ, 1992) 68–77.

[24] See Amnesty International, *Hong Kong and Human Rights: Flaws in the System. A Call for Institutional Reform to Protect Human Rights* (London: International Secretariat, April 1994).

[25] *Report to Congress on Conditions in Hong Kong as of March 31, 1995 As Requested by Section 301 of the United States-Hong Kong Policy Act of 1992* (Hong Kong: Consulate General of the USA, 31 March 1995) 12.

[26] Christopher Patten, 'Why We Need a Rule of Law' *South China Morning Post*, 23 November 1993, at 17.

International legal entitlements

Hong Kong's claim to international legal personality is further substantiated by its right in international law to self-determination.[27] As a 'people' so entitled, the territory enjoys under the UN Charter a 'separate and distinct'[28] status (not to be equated with independent statehood). Its international personality by virtue of a right to self-determination should find additional support in international judicial decisions, most notably the International Court of Justice's Advisory Opinions concerning South West Africa.[29]

More specifically, Hong Kong's case as a 'self-determination unit' may be grounded on its status as a 'colony' or 'non-self-governing territory'. It is indisputable that Hong Kong came into being and has functioned as a British colony since 1842. To a certain extent, the territory's colonial status was acknowledged internationally when it was placed on the agenda of the UN Special Committee on Decolonization in 1961. Although — following a request by the PRC — Hong Kong was subsequently removed from the colonial territories listed by the UN under the Declaration on the Granting Independence to Colonial Territories and Peoples, no substantive decision has been rendered negating Hong Kong's status as a non-governing (colonial) territory. Nor did the action of the Decolonization committee have the 'effect in international law of removing from the people of Hong Kong (who had not been consulted on the Chinese request) their right to self-determination'.[30]

While it is generally accepted that the inhabitants of any non-self-governing colonial territory — being 'separate and distinct' — are 'peoples' for the purpose of the right of self-determination,[31] further enhancement for local 'national selfhood' could be provided. Hong Kong satisfies suggested

---

[27] For the conclusion 'without hesitation, that the people of Hong Kong are entitled to the right of self-determination under international law' see: International Commission of Jurists' Report, op.cit., at 49.

[28] As 'solemnly declared' in the 1970 Declaration on Principles of International Law Concerning Friendly Relations and Co-operation Among States in Accordance with the Charter of the United Nations [GA Res 2625, UN GAOR, 25th Sess Supp No 28, at 12, 124 UN Doc A/8028)]: 'The territory of a colony or other Non-Self-Governing Territory has, under the Charter, a status separate and distinct from the territory of the State administering it; and such separate and distinct status under the Charter shall exist until the people of the colony or Non-Self-Governing Territory have exercised their right to self-determination in accordance with the Charter . . .'

[29] See *Western Sahara Case* [1975] ICJ Reports 12; *Legal Consequences for States of the Continued Presence of South Africa in Namibia (South West Africa) Notwithstanding Security Council Resolution 276* [1971] ICJ Reports 16.

[30] International Commission of Jurists Report, supra (note 23) at 50.

[31] See ibid., at 47, 50.

UN criteria[32] as a 'social entity possessing a clear identity [at least, 'profoundly different from that of mainland China'[33]] and its own characteristics [including distinct legal and economic systems]' as well as 'a relationship with a territory'. Undoubtedly, it qualifies as a self-determination unit under British 'working definition or rule of thumb' which attaches importance to 'whether the people in a particular territory constitutes a settled and self-sustaining community with its own institutions and civil administration'.[34]

At the same time, it is evident that neither party to the Sino-British Joint Declaration has accepted self-determination for Hong Kong as a viable option;[35] that no international forum is likely to collectively sanction any 'decolonization' attempt;[36] and that 'in present circumstances a meaningful exercise of the right of self-determination is impractical.'[37] Yet, the inability to enforce its right to self-determination should not detract from the territory's legitimate claim to international legal personality based on such a right. Nor should support be withheld for international personhood, given the limited nature of the claim and the fact that no threats to the integrity, organic structure, or vital interests of any state are posed. Reliance on the right of 'peoples' should, moreover, be favourably regarded in the context of a world community that is increasingly embracing human rights, minority rights, and indigenous rights.

Membership in the 'international civil society'

The relevance of international relationships and associations to the assessment of an entity's 'subjecthood' in international law requires little elaboration. It is also clear that in this regard, Hong Kong's claim to international legal personality is particularly strong. Hong Kong participates — either as a full member in its own right, associate member or a non-member participant —

---

[32] See Aureliu Cristescu, *The Right to Self-Determination: Historical and Current Development on the Basis of United Nations Instruments* (New York: United Nations, 1981), para 279.

[33] International Commission of Jurists Report, supra (note 23) at 49.

[34] See Sir Ian Sinclair, Legal Adviser, Foreign and Commonwealth Office, in the course of evidence to the Foreign Affairs Committee of the House of Commons on 17 January 1983, as repr. in (1983) 54 *British Yearbook of International Law* 398–400.

[35] For a description of China's 'uncompromising' views and the British 'non-view' attitude, see: International Commission of Jurists Report, supra (note 23) at 48–49.

[36] The UN has been radically inconsistent in articulating the norm of self-determination and selective in enforcing it, especially with respect to small or strategic places.

[37] International Commission of Jurists Report, supra (note 23) at 56.

in more than forty international organizations and associations.[38] Particularly noteworthy is the territory's membership in UN 'Specialized Agencies',[39] key international trade and financial institutions,[40] and in regional economic associations.[41]

Hong Kong is also under the regime of over two hundred multilateral treaties in fields such as customs, conservation, health, trade, transport, marine pollution, drugs, international crime, science and technology and private international law.[42] A similar number of bilateral agreements have also been extended to the territory. In addition, observers have pointed to the remarkably wide participation of Hong Kong in non-governmental organizations[43] as well as the fact the territory serves as a 'regional headquarters to close to one thousand multinational corporations'.[44]

Hong Kong's high profile as a member of the 'international civil society' is postulated — both internationally (under the Sino-British Joint Declaration) and constitutionally (under the Basic Law) to be preserved beyond 1997. Thus,

> The Hong Kong Special Administrative Region may on its own, using the name "Hong Kong, China", maintain and develop relations and conclude and implement agreements with states, regions and relevant international organizations in the appropriate fields, including the

---

[38] See Appendix A.

[39] Including the ILO [International Labour Organization]; ICAO [International Civil Aviation Organization]; WHO [World Health Organization]; UNEF [United Nations Environment Programme] UNDP [United Nations Development Programme]; IAEA [International Atomic Energy Agency]; UPU [Universal Postal Union]; ITU [International Telecommunication Union; ITSO [International Telecommunications Satellite Organization]; WMO [World Meteorological Organization]; IMO [International Maritime Organization]. Note also that Hong Kong is an associate member of ESCAP [Economic and Social Commission for Asia and the Pacific] which is one of the regional organizations of ECOSOC [UN Economic and Social Commission].

[40] Including membership in the World Bank [International Bank for Reconstruction and Development], IMF [International Monetary Fund], ADB [Asia Development Bank] and GATT [General Agreement on Tariffs and Trade]/WTO [World Trade Organization].

[41] Including PECC [Pacific Economic Cooperation Conference]; APEC [Asia-Pacific Economic Cooperation.

[42] Attorney General's Chambers, *Multilateral Treaties Applicable to Hong Kong* (Hong Kong: AG's Chambers, 1990); *International Labour Conventions Applicable to Hong Kong* (1985).

[43] Hong Kong participates in 884 non-governmental organizations; see (1992/93) 2 *Yearbook of International Organizations* 1613.

[44] See Anthony C. Chan, *Hong Kong of 1997 Responding to Uncertainty* (Hong Kong: Business International, 1992) 41, 42, 49.

> economic, trade, financial and monetary, shipping, communications,
> touristic, cultural and sporting fields. Representatives of the Hong Kong
> Special Administrative Region Government may participate, as members
> of delegations of the Government of the People's Republic of China, in
> international organizations or conferences in appropriate fields limited to
> states and affecting the Hong Kong Special Administrative Region, or
> may attend in such other capacity as may be permitted by the Central
> People's Government . . . , and may express their views in the name of
> "Hong Kong, China". The Hong Kong Special Administrative Region
> may, using the name "Hong Kong, China", participate in international
> organizations and conferences not limited to states.

Indeed, the attitude of the 'international civil society' — as reflected in the securing of Hong Kong's continued participation in key international organizations and multilateral treaties,[45] as well as the forging of bilateral agreements with post-1997 effect[46] — should serve to reinforce the territory's claim to international legal personality.

Sui generis qualities

That legal personality may be extended to entities professing unique qualities which are appropriately valued by the international community is commonly acknowledged in treatises on international law. Examples cited invariably include the Order of Malta (for its dedication to the assistance of the world's sick and poor), the Holy See (for leading the Catholic Church), and, occasionally, national liberation movements (for their purported aim to combat colonialism). While it cannot claim to have made significant contribution to global religious, spiritual, or social well-being, Hong Kong may nonetheless ground its case for international legal personhood, alternatively, on the unique characteristics it possesses.

In particular, Hong Kong could rely on its existence as a semi-autonomous/'quasi-state' entity for over 150 years, its unprecedented capacity for international action, its prominent position as a global economic actor,[47]

---

[45] See *Achievements of the Joint Liaison Group and its Sub-Group on International Rights and Obligations, 1985 – May 1990* (Hong Kong: Government Printer, 1990).

[46] See Constitutional Affairs Branch, *List of Bilateral Treaties Which Will Continue to Apply in Hong Kong After 30 June 1997 (Agreed in the JLG)* (5 June 1995), including investment protection and promotion agreements, surrender of fugitive offenders agreements, and air services agreements.

[47] See Miron Mushkat, *The Economic Future of Hong Kong* (Boulder & London: Lynne Reinner Publishing, 1990).

and the respect it is accorded by the world's governing institutions.[48] Evidently, the British and Chinese governments have recognized Hong Kong's special qualities and — using the highest form of international legal expression (an internationally binding accord) — have signalled to the international community their determination to preserve the territory's distinct personality and the pivotal role it plays in both regional and global economies. The parties have conferred on the HKSAR express functions and powers that imply possession of international personality, including the maintenance and development of relations with states, regions, and international organizations as well as the conclusion and implementation of international and regional agreements; the issuing of its own passports and travel documents; regulation of immigration to the territory; and the establishment of official and semi-official economic and trade missions in foreign countries. The agreement also reflects the reality that in order to enable the territory to continue to operate effectively, in light of the difficulties involved in assimilating two vastly different cultures and divergent economic systems, Hong Kong's distinctly separate personality must be secured.

THE CONTENT AND EXTENT OF HONG KONG'S INTERNATIONAL PERSONALITY

'Right to life'

Can Hong Kong expect international 'intervention' should the need arise to defend its autonomous political structure and the free choice of its people?

Whereas a state's 'right to life' is safeguarded under international legal rules prohibiting aggression, the applicability of these rules to nonstate legal entities is rather more ambiguous. In Hong Kong's case, can the territory be, for instance, devolved out of existence at the whim of Britain or China? In the event of a military occupation by the PRC, might Hong Kong legitimately expect to benefit from a supportive international response of the kind offered to Kuwait when faced with the Iraqi challenge?

---

[48] See 'World Bank Praise for Hong Kong' *South China Morning Post*, 23 January 1995, at 1; 'Territory Hailed as Dynamic in GATT Report' *South China Morning Post*, 7 October 1994, at 12.

Clearly, as a 'separate and distinct' people, regardless of its lack of statehood, the territory's inhabitants may claim international protection on the basis of their right to self-determination. Under general international law, a forcible deprivation of such a right entitles the people of Hong Kong to seek political or judicial[49] remedies as well as to receive international assistance 'in accordance with the purposes and principles of the Charter of the UN'.[50] Nor is foreign intervention in such circumstances to be confined to struggles for external self-determination but is said to embrace 'efforts by outside forces to give a voice to the people' who have been prevented from exercising their right to internal self-determination or to a democratic order.[51] Indeed, one may query whether the United States' doctrine of 'intervention for democracy' — used to justify Operation Just Cause in Panama and the Grenada invasion — would also be adopted in relation to Hong Kong, given large American humanitarian and commercial stakes in the territory. Furthermore, since the right to self-determination — in the sense of the right of individuals and groups to participate in the creation and recreation of an internal social order — is continuous, neither the right nor any claim based on it should be affected by the transfer of administration over the territory in 1997.

Viewed in purely legal terms, an encroachment upon Hong Kong's territorial integrity before the 1997 handover would also be sufficient to justify an action in self-defence by the United Kingdom. Notwithstanding its reluctance to formally acknowledge Hong Kong's colonial status, China has nonetheless accepted British responsibility for Hong Kong, and hence

---

[49] For support of an *actio popularis* in these circumstances, see *Barcelona Traction, Light & Power Co.*, Second Phase (Belgium v Spain) 1970 ICJ Reports 304 (Feb 5) (separate opinion of Judge Ammoun). Note also that an adjudication clause (Art 22) is incorporated into the 1966 International Convention on the Elimination of All Forms of Racial Discrimination, to which the PRC is a party (subject, however, to reservations including in respect of Art 22). Note, nonetheless, the recent dictum by the International Court of Justice in the *Case Concerning East Timor* (Portugal v Australia) [reprinted in (1995) 34 *International Legal Materials* 1581, 1589) that although the right of peoples to self determination has an *erga omnes* character, the Court could not rule on the lawfulness of a conduct of state in the absence of the state's consent to jurisdiction.

[50] See G.A. Res. 2625 (XXV), 1970 Declaration on Principles of International Law Concerning Friendly Relations and Co-operation Among States in Accordance with the Charter of the United Nations ('The Principle of Equal Rights and Self-Determination of People').

[51] See Kevin Ryan, 'Right, Intervention and Self-Determination' (1991) 20 *Denver Journal of International Law and Policy* 55, 65; See Also Malvina Halberstam, 'The Copenhagen Document: Intervention in Support of Democracy' (1993) 34 *Harvard International Law Journal* 163–175.

has waived sovereign claims with respect to the territory.[52] Taken a step further, the recognition of Britain's right to govern Hong Kong is clearly implied in the Sino-British Joint Declaration and its British Implementing Act which stipulate, respectively, that the government of the PRC 'has decided to resume the exercise of sovereignty over Hong Kong with effect from 1 July 1997'[53] and that the United Kingdom will relinquish sovereignty over Hong Kong at midnight, 30 June 1997.[54]

At the same time, while the maintenance of Hong Kong as an autonomous entity is explicitly guaranteed for a period of fifty years from 1 July 1997, in substance, the object of this protection is the territory's internal structure. Notwithstanding recent acknowledgements by the British Prime Minister that, as a signatory to the Sino-British Joint Declaration, Britain will have 'continuing [legal][55] responsibilities' towards Hong Kong and that 'Hong Kong will never have to walk alone',[56] the transfer of sovereignty over Hong Kong will be total and complete, allowing the United Kingdom no right to recover sovereignty should the Sino-British Joint Declaration be abrogated. In contrast with the United States-Taiwan position as reflected in the Taiwan Relations Act of 1979, Britain did not express an intention to 'maintain the capacity . . . to resist any resort to force or other forms of coercion that would jeopardize the security, or the social or economic system, of the people . . .'[57] of Hong Kong.

The prospects of a more global involvement hinge to a certain degree on whether the 'Hong Kong question' (conditions for coming into effect, existence/extinction and identity) is recognized as an 'international problem' governed by international rules and principles. Arguably, an entity 'created by international law' and possessing state-like characteristics of territory, population and government, should be internationally protected. It may be

---

[52] The PRC has not directly challenged or expressed any misgivings about Britain's conclusion of bilateral and multilateral agreements on behalf of Hong Kong, or the fact that Britain has represented the territory and its inhabitants in relation to third states. Furthermore, the PRC has extended recognition to foreign consular representatives accredited by the British government in Hong Kong. Moreover, China has also accepted the right of the United Kingdom to issue currency in Hong Kong; currency being one of the most important attributes of sovereignty.

[53] JD, Art 1.

[54] Hong Kong Act of 1985, Public General Acts and Measures, Eliz. II, Ch. 15 (Eng) ('[a]n Act to make provision for and in connection with the ending of British sovereignty and jurisdiction over Hong Kong').

[55] '. . . not just a moral responsibility as the former colonial power, and as staunch friends of Hong Kong.' See extract from John Major's speech to business leaders in Hong Kong, reprinted in *South China Morning Post*, 5 March 1996, at 19.

[56] Loc. cit.

[57] Taiwan Relations Act, 22 USC 3301(2)(b)(6) (1979).

further contended that an infringement of the territorial integrity and autonomous existence of such an international person constitutes a violation of the world's public order, or *jus cogens*, which could be vindicated by any member of the international community in an *actio popularis*.[58]

It is, however, unrealistic to ignore doubts as to whether the Hong Kong issue would indeed be viewed as a matter of concern for all states, whether the international community would assert the collective legal right to proceed against the sovereign power involved, and whether the exclusivity of domestic jurisdiction would no longer be deemed a legitimate defence when invoked by this sovereign. The Chinese government, on its part, has lent a high profile to its objections over 'internationalizing' or what it considers 'interfering'.[59] Yet, as noted by one observer, the registration of the Sino-British Joint Declaration with the UN is 'surely an invitation to the whole world to monitor the situation in Hong Kong'.[60]

Since the main concern of the United Nations is the maintenance of peace, an intervention by that organization is not likely in the absence of a determination of a perceived threat to international peaceful relations. At the same time, the world's responses (based on 'humanitarian grounds'[61]) in

---

[58] On the notion of *actio popularis* see Kenneth C. Randall, 'Universal Jurisdiction Under International Law' (1988) 66 *Texas Law Review* 785, 831–32.

[59] See, for example, Commentary in the People's Daily, 19 December 1989, cited in Chris Yeung and Shirley Yam, 'China Repeats Reform Warning' *South China Morning Post*, 20 December 1989, at 4. The article branded as hegemony the view that foreign countries would naturally have an interest in the political development of Hong Kong because of their economic interests in the territory. It charged '[t]hose who advocate internationalizing the question of Hong Kong' with 'attempting to create a situation in which international forces will gradually and politically interfere in the affairs of Hong Kong. They are actually trying to muster the international anti-Communist and anti-China forces to obstruct China from resuming its sovereignty over Hong Kong.' Earlier, in a statement quoted on state radio and television on 25 October 1989, Beijing said that Hong Kong's future was a matter between Britain and China, and the '[o]ther countries or international organizations have no right to interfere in it.' Ibid. The statement followed the issuing of a communique by the Commonwealth Heads of Government Meeting in Malaysia which had called for the restoration of confidence in Hong Kong. 'Beijing Attacks UK Leaders Over Stance on Territory' *South China Morning Post*, 26 October 1989, at 7. Chinese authorities protested strongly against US legislation of the United States-Hong Kong Policy Act 1992, which they deemed an 'unjustified interference in China's internal affairs' and a 'violation of universally acknowledged norms governing international relations.' See *A Report to Congress on Conditions in Hong Kong as of March 31, 1993* (Hong Kong: Consulate General of the United States of America, 31 March 1993), 4.

[60] Frank Ching, 'Calling a Spade a Club in Dealing Out Criticism' *South China Morning Post*, 22 December 1989, at 12.

[61] Including what was set out as a 'goal of the international community' – 'restoration of democracy;' see Resolution 940 on Haiti, adopted by the Security Council on 30 July 1994.

Haiti, Rwanda and Somalia should not be disregarded. UN member states appear to be increasingly aware that the distinction between internal and international conflicts is breaking down, and conflicts that begin within a state's border, such as human rights violations or struggles for self-determination, may ultimately pose a threat to international peace and security subject to international response.[62] Although the notion of a 'global neighbourhood'[63] appears as yet utopic, some progress could be said to have been made towards defining new principles for international action based on concerns for the 'security of people'[64] transcending state boundaries. Nor need 'intervention' necessarily take the form of a despatch of troops or military invasion, and other channels of 'indirect' international protective action may be available to Hong Kong through its membership in international and regional organizations (utilizing pressure-exerting devices such as fact-finding, reporting and inquiry). Indeed, in this respect, the territory's continued participation in international organizations and its international exposure might well prove to be imperative in forestalling potential dangers to Hong Kong's security and independence.

'High degree of autonomy'

How 'high' is HKSAR's 'high degree of autonomy'?[65]

Notwithstanding its prominence in both policy and academic discourse, the concept of 'autonomy' has not been authoritatively defined in international

---

[62] See Jane E. Stromseth, 'Iraq's Repression of its Civilian Population: Collective Responses and Continuing Challenges' in Lori Fisler Damrosch, ed., *Enforcing Restraint: Collective Intervention in Internal Conflicts* (New York: Council on Foreign Relations Press, 1993) pp. 97–8.

[63] See Ingvar Carlsson, 'The World Needs A Humanitarian Right to Intervene' *International Herald Tribune*, 25 January 1995, at 9 (the writer, Sweden's prime minister and co-chairman of the Commission on Global Governance, discusses a report entitled 'Our Global Neighbourhood' submitted to the UN Secretary-General).

[64] See ibid. The concept of 'security of people' underlies a proposed amendment to the UN Charter, submitted by the Commission on Global Governance, that would permit international action in cases which, in the judgment of the Security Council, constitute such a gross violation of the security of people that an international response is required on humanitarian grounds.

[65] JD, Art 3(2) ('The Hong Kong Special Administrative Region will enjoy a high degree of autonomy, except in foreign and defence affairs which are the responsibilities of the Central People's Government.') Although Hong Kong is currently enjoying an 'autonomous' position, the first official reference to the phrase was made in the Sino-British Joint Declaration. The following analysis, therefore, focuses on the HKSAR.

law. Indeed, it was submitted by the authors of a comprehensive study on the subject that, given the broad array of recognized 'autonomous' entities and the divergence of relevant practices, a 'firm definition that is appropriate in all cases' could not be formulated.[66] By extension, constructing a scale for determining the degree to which autonomy may manifest itself in practice is fraught with considerable difficulties. Yet, since an essential component of autonomy is the non-interference by the principal government in areas within the sphere of competence of the secondary entity, some element of measurability is afforded by reference to the insularity of the latter from potential central control.[67]

At a minimum, an autonomous entity is expected to possess the following powers:[68] 'a locally selected chief executive [with general responsibility for administration and execution of local laws] who may be subject to approval by the central government'; 'a locally elected legislative body with some independent legislative authority [in areas of local concern] limited by a constituent document [and subject to no veto by the principal or sovereign government unless it exceeds its competence as defined in the constituent document]'; 'an independent local judiciary with full responsibility for interpreting local law'; and joint authority in areas of concern to both the autonomous and central governments.

As originally conceived, the HKSAR appears to meet these minimal requirements. In general, it will be vested with 'executive, legislative and independent judicial power, including that of final adjudication'.[69] More specifically, the HKSAR will be headed and represented by a chief executive 'selected by election or through consultations held locally and . . . appointed by the Central People's Government'.[70] The Region's legislature — which is to be 'constituted by election'[71] — 'may on its own authority enact laws in accordance with the provisions of the Basic Law and legal procedures'.[72] Judicial power (including that of final adjudication) in the HKSAR is to be

---

[66] Hurst Annum & Richard B. Lillich, 'The Concept of Autonomy in International Law' in Yoram Dinstein, ed., *Models of Autonomy* (New Brunswick: Transaction Books, 1981) 215, 250.

[67] For an attempt of evaluation along these lines, see Brian Z. Tamanaha, 'Post-1997 Hong Kong: A Comparative Study of the Meaning of "High Degree of Autonomy"' (1989) 20 *California Western International Law Journal* 41.

[68] See Hurst Hannum, *Autonomy, Sovereignty, and Self-Determination: The Accommodation of Conflicting Rights* (Philadelphia: University of Pennsylvania Press, 1990) 467–8.

[69] JD, Art 3(3); see also BL, Art 2.

[70] JD, Annex I, art I, para 3; BL, Art 45.

[71] Loc. cit. Note further elaboration in BL, Art 68 that '[t]he ultimate aim in the election of all the members of the Legislative Council by universal suffrage.'

[72] JD, Annex I, art II, para 2.

exercised by the local courts 'independently and free from any interference;'[73] the independence of members of the judiciary would be closely guarded in accordance with detailed provisions[74] pertaining to their appointment, removal from office and immunity from legal action in respect of judicial functions.

Edging towards the 'higher' end of the autonomy scale — and geared to the preservation of the territory's social system and lifestyle[75] — are the self-governing powers and independent decision-making capacity to be enjoyed by the HKSAR in respect of a wide-range of fields, including education, science, culture, sports, religion, labour, and social services.[76] Especially important to the maintenance of the Hong Kong's separate economic identity, is the extensive (near-total) control granted to the HKSAR over the economy: The local government is empowered to decide its own economic and trade policies,[77] develop its own economic and trade relations with other states and regions,[78] formulate its own monetary and financial policies,[79] and determine its own excise and taxation policies.[80] HKSAR's status as a separate customs territory — entitled to its own export quotas, tariff preferences and other similar arrangements — is to be retained.[81] Additionally, the Region will continue to have a separate shipping register[82] and be responsible for its civil aviation management.[83] Also to be maintained are Hong Kong's distinct 'capitalist economic and trade systems'[84] — as reflected in its status as a free port,[85] its policy of free trade, free movement of goods and capital,[86] and a freely convertible currency.[87] Ranking even 'higher' in the context of autonomous entity/central authority relationship, is the lack of formal financial ties between the HKSAR and the Central People's government:[88] The HKSAR is to have independent finances, to be used exclusively for its own purposes. No funds will be channelled to the

---

[73] JD, Annex I, art III, para 2; BL, Art 85.
[74] See JD, Annex I, art III, para 3; BL, Arts 88, 89, 85.
[75] JD, Art 3(5).
[76] See details of implementation in BL, Chap VI.
[77] JD, Annex I, art VI, para 1.
[78] Ibid., para 2.
[79] JD, Annex I, art VII, para 2.
[80] JD, Annex I, art VI, para 3.
[81] Loc. cit.
[82] JD, Annex I, art VIII, para 2.
[83] JD, Annex I, art IX, para 1.
[84] JD, Annex I, art VI, para 1; BL, Art 5.
[85] JD, Annex I, Art VI, para 2; BL, Art 114.
[86] JD, ibid; BL, Art 115.
[87] JD, Annex I, Art VII, para 1.
[88] See JD, Art V; BL, Arts 106, 108.

Central People's government, nor will the CPG be permitted to levy any taxes in the territory.

Perhaps, given its significance to the latter's 'international personality', most weight on the autonomy scale should be assigned to the considerable powers vested in the HKSAR regarding external affairs. The Region 'may on its own, using the name "Hong Kong, China" maintain and develop relations and conclude and implement agreements with states, regions and relevant international organizations in the appropriate fields, including the economic, trade, financial and monetary, shipping communications, touristic, cultural and sporting fields'.[89] In addition,

> [r]epresentatives of the Hong Kong Special Administrative may participate, as members of the delegations of the Government of the People's Republic of China, in international organizations or conferences in appropriate fields limited to states and affecting the Hong Kong Special Administrative Region, or may attend in such other capacity as may be permitted by the Central People's Government and the organization or conference concerned, and may express their views in the name of "Hong Kong, China".[90]

The Special Administrative Region, in its role as an autonomous entity, may also take part in international organizations and conferences not limited to states. Indeed, under the Joint Declaration, China has agreed 'to ensure that the Hong Kong Special Administrative Region shall continue to retain its status in an appropriate capacity in those international organizations of which the People's Republic of China is a member and in which Hong Kong participates in one capacity or another.[91] The PRC has also undertaken to facilitate the 'continued participation of the Hong Kong Special Administrative Region in an appropriate capacity in those international organizations in which Hong Kong is a participant in one capacity or another, but of which the People's Republic is not a member'.[92]

Consistent with the emphasis on the development of external ties by the territory, the Sino-British Accord stipulates the establishment, with the approval of the Central People's Government, of consular and other official or semi-official missions in the SAR.[93] The Accord also provides for official and semi-official SAR economic and trade missions in foreign countries.[94] The SAR's external relations capacity is further enhanced by the authority

---

[89] JD, Annex I, art XI, para 1; BL, Art 151.
[90] JD, ibid; BL, Art 152.
[91] JD, Annex I, Art XI, para 2; see also BL, Art 152.
[92] Loc. cit.
[93] JD, Annex I, Art XI, para 3.
[94] JD, Annex I, Art VI, para 4.

granted to it by the PRC to issue passports and travel documents,[95] as well as to conclude agreements for the mutual abolition of visa requirements.[96]

Finally, to buttress the territory's autonomous status, the Basic Law expressly stipulates[97] that '[n]o department of the Central People's Government and no province, autonomous region, or municipality directly under the Central Government may interfere in the affairs which Hong Kong Special Administrative Region administers on its own in accordance with [the Basic] Law.' Consent for the setting-up of any Central Government's offices in the HKSAR must be obtained from the government of the Region, and the personnel of such offices 'shall abide by the laws of the Region'.

In contrast to the high level of non-subordination described above, several conceivable sources of central government's interference as well as apparent curbs on HKSAR's powers appear to be pulling the autonomy scales downwards. Noted, in particular is the wide scope for indirect control through the appointment of a power-wielding Chief Executive, who is to be 'accountable'[98] to the Central People's government. Regarding the legislative powers with which the HKSAR is endowed, three potential constraints have been highlighted: (a) laws enacted by the local legislature are subject to invalidation by the Standing Committee of the National People's Congress [SC-NPC];[99] (b) PRC legislation — beyond that envisaged in the Sino-British Joint Declaration[100] — may be applicable in Hong Kong;[101] and (c) the power to amend the Region's 'constitution' (the Basic Law) is vested in the NPC.[102] The power of the National People's Congress to interpret the Basic Law (and its assumed derivative power of 'disallowance' of locally enacted legislation) underscores perceived derogation from the Region's autonomous judicial competence and the 'final adjudication' to be exercised by HKSAR's courts. Additional concerns arise from the ousting of the courts' jurisdiction

---

[95] JD, Annex I, Art XIV, para 2.

[96] Ibid., para 7.

[97] BL, Art 22.

[98] See BL, Art 43. The Chief Executive is expected, *inter alia*, to 'implement the directives issued by the Central People's government in respect of the relevant matters provided for in [the Basic] Law' — Art 48(8).

[99] See BL, Art 17.

[100] See JD, Annex I, art I, para 2.

[101] Under BL, Art 18 laws 'relating to defence and foreign affairs *as well as other matters outside the limits of the autonomy of the Region as specified by [the Basic] Law*' [emphasis added] may be applied in the HKSAR. Additionally, '[i]n the event that the Standing Committee of the National People's Congress decides to declare a state of war or, by reason of turmoil within the Hong Kong Special Administrative Region is in a state of emergency, the Central People's government may issue an order applying the relevant national laws in the Region.'

[102] See BL, Art 159.

over undefined 'affairs which are the responsibility of the Central People's Government'[103] and 'acts of state, such as defence and foreign affairs.'[104] Apart from 'legalistic' sources of encroachment, more concrete intervention is also feared as a result of an undemarcated allocation to the Central government of responsibility over foreign affairs and defence, especially in the light of the stationing in the HKSAR of Chinese military forces (which may be mobilized under the pretext of responding to a 'foreign affairs' crisis or upon a declaration of a 'state of emergency' by the SC-NPC).

To shift the pendulum towards the higher end of the autonomy scale, some counterweights can be employed (with varying degrees of force) to moderate the autonomy-diluting currents. Thus, China's power of 'appointment' of a democratically-selected[105] Chief Executive ought not to be interpreted to mean that approval can be withheld at will by the PRC.[106] Nor should 'accountability' imply compliance with orders violating the autonomy guaranteed under the Basic Law.[107] The available 'checks and balances' — such as the Chief Executive's duty to consult the Executive Council before dissolving the Legislative Council,[108] the Legislative Council's power to impeach the Chief Executive,[109] and the requirement that judges' appointment be based on the recommendation of an independent commission[110] — may also serve to allay concerns over compromises in the independence of the legislative and judicial branches of the HKSAR

[103] BL, Art 158.

[104] BL, Art 19.

[105] Under BL, Art 45, '[t]he Chief Executive of the Hong Kong Special Administrative Region shall be selected by election or through consultations held locally . . . The method for selecting the Chief Executive shall be specified in the light of the actual situation in the Hong Kong Administrative Region and in accordance with the principle of gradual and orderly progress. The ultimate aim is the selection of the Chief Executive by universal suffrage upon nomination by a broadly representative nominating committee in accordance with democratic procedures.'

[106] A local commentator speculated that the appointment will be a 'mere formality' to demonstrate China's sovereignty over Hong Kong. He suggested that if the Central government refused to appoint the Chief Executive elected by the local authorities, a constitutional crisis would follow with a serious adverse impact on the stability and prosperity of the territory. See Joseph Y.S. Cheng, 'Looking at the Other Options' *South China Morning Post*, 2 March 1986.

[107] Under BL, Art 43, the Chief Executive 'shall be accountable to the Central People's Government and the Hong Kong Special Administrative Region *in accordance with the provisions of [the Basic] Law* [emphasis added].'

[108] BL, Art 50.

[109] BL, Art 73(9).

[110] BL, Art 88; the Commission is to be 'composed of local judges, persons from the legal profession, and eminent persons from other sectors'.

government by a Chief Executive 'with divided loyalties' who is empowered to dissolve the legislature[111] and appoint/remove judges of the courts.[112]

Potential 'infiltration' of HKSAR's legislative autonomy may be countered (with somewhat limited force) by emphasizing, *inter alia*, the restraints embedded in assurances provided by the Basic Law; the confinement of the SC-NPC's review powers to the 'constitutionality' of HKSAR laws (i.e. whether 'regarding affairs within the responsibility of the Central Authorities or regarding the relationship between the Central Authorities and the Region'[113]); and the explicit stipulation that '[n]o amendment to [the Basic] Law shall contravene the established basic policies of the People's Republic of China regarding Hong Kong'[114] which 'have been elaborated by [the Chinese Government] in the Sino-British Joint Declaration'.[115]

With respect to the SAR's judicial autonomy, it may be observed that — although judicial review of legislation ought to reside in the Region — '[i]n virtually all the autonomous entities, the central government has final jurisdiction, whether appellate or original, for judicial decisions regarding the relationship between it and the secondary entity, and exclusively controls decisions relating to its power over foreign affairs and defence matters'.[116] Arguably, the local courts would be able to exercise an incidental, interpretative function — including the classification of issues — and defer to the SC-NPC, when considered necessary, the interpretation of Basic Law provisions 'concerning affairs which are the responsibility of the Central People's Government, or concerning the relationship between the Central Authorities and the Region'.[117] The SC-NPC, in turn, is obliged to consult the Hong Kong Basic Law Committee before giving an interpretation, and while their interpretation is binding on the courts, 'judgments previously rendered shall not be affected'.[118]

The danger of physical invasion — presently less feared than more subtle forms of intervention — might be mollified by the pledges in both the Sino-British Joint Declaration and the Basic Law that '[t]he maintenance of public order in the Hong Kong Special Administrative Region shall be the responsibility of the Hong Kong Special Administrative Region Government'

---

[111] BL, Art 50.

[112] BL, Art 48(6).

[113] BL, Art 17.

[114] BL, Art 159.

[115] BL, Preamble.

[116] Tamanaha, supra (note 64), at 54–5.

[117] BL, Art 158.

[118] Ibid.

and that '[m]ilitary forces sent by the Central People's Government for the purpose of defence shall not interfere in the internal affairs of the Hong Kong Special Administrative Region.'[119] It may also be noted that under an agreement signed between Britain and China, PLA troops stationed in the territory would be subject to HKSAR law.[120]

On balance — from a purely international legal perspective, and assuming the narrowest construction of potential constraints — the HKSAR appears to have been endowed with a 'high degree of autonomy'.

Internal self-determination

A 'right to democracy'?

While it 'cannot be said to vest in any fragment of a territorially defined national community' nor, as yet, 'entail obligations *erga omnes* of governments of the world that may be universally enforced as a matter of *jus cogens*'[121] — the right to 'internal self-determination'[122] arguably embodies a right of people to 'be able to have a full voice within the legal system of the nation-state, control over its natural resources, appropriate ways of preserving and protection their culture, and generally to be a partner or participant with equal powers within the overall national polity'.[123] There is moreover strong support for the contention that a 'right to democracy' (in the sense of relatively full, free and equal participation in the political process) has evolved as a normative and customary rule of the international system.[124]

Thus, the right of every person to participate in one's government is recognized and guaranteed in all major human rights instruments. It is

---

[119] JD, Annex I, Art XII; BL, Art 14.

[120] See 'Britain and China Agree Military Land Transfer' *Financial Times*, 1 July 1994, at 1.

[121] J.D. van der Vyver, 'Sovereignty and Human Rights in Constitutional and International Law' (1991) 5 *Emory International Law Review* 321, 416.

[122] The right to self-determination has been interpreted as pertaining to two aspects: external — alluding to the achievement of independence or other appropriate legal status by peoples under colonial and alien domination; and internal — which refers to the right of citizens to 'maintain, assure and perfect their full legal, political and cultural sovereignty.' See H. Gros Espiell, 'The Right to Self-determination: Implementation of United Nations Resolutions' UN Doc. E/CN.4/Sub.2/405, para 47.

[123] William S. Grodinsky, 'Remarks' (1992) *American Society of International Law Proceedings* 394, 395.

[124] See Thomas M. Franck, 'The Emerging Right to Democratic Governance' (1992) 86 *American Journal of International Law* 46. See also Gregory H. Fox, 'The Right to Political Participation in International Law' (1992) *Yale Journal of International Law* 539.

enunciated in the Universal Declaration of Human Rights,[125] the International Covenant on Civil and Political Rights,[126] as well as the American,[127] European[128] and African[129] Conventions on Human Rights. It is further affirmed and reinforced in General Assembly Resolution on Enhancing the Effectiveness of the Principle of Periodic and Genuine Elections,[130] which 'stresses' the member nations' 'conviction that . . . the right of everyone to take part in the government of his or her country is a crucial factor in the effective enjoyment by all of a wide range of human rights and fundamental freedoms, embracing political, economic, social and cultural rights. Clearly, the most comprehensive prescription of the 'democratic entitlement' is contained in the documents[131] generated by the thirty-four members[132] of the Conference on Security and Co-operation in Europe [CSCE].[133]

---

[125] UNGA Res 217A(III) 1948, Art 21. That the Universal Declaration has acquired the force of customary international law is amply evidenced by subsequent events and the practice of states during the past forty-seven years. See John P. Humphrey, 'The Universal Declaration of Human Rights: Its History, Impact and Judicial Character' in B.G. Ramcharan, ed., *Human Rights — Thirty Years After the Universal Declaration* (The Hague: Nijhoff, 1979) 33. See also Richard L. Lillich, 'Civil Rights' in Theodore Meron, ed., *Human Rights in International Law — Legal and Policy Issues* (Oxford: Clarendon Press, 1984) 116–117. Some authors have suggested that the Universal Declaration has in fact the 'attributes of *jus cogens*'. See Myres M. McDougal, Harold D. Lasswell and Lung-chu Chen, *Human Rights and World Order* (New Haven: Yale University Press, 1980) 274.

[126] Repr. in (1967) 6 *International Legal Materials* 368. Article 25 extends to every citizen the right (a) to take part in the conduct of public affairs directly or through freely chosen representatives; (b) to vote and be elected at genuine elections which shall be by universal and equal suffrage and shall be held by secret ballot, guaranteeing the free expression of the will of the electors. With a 'balance heavily tilting towards the substantial new majority of states actually practising a reasonably credible version of electoral democracy', the legal obligations contained in the Covenant (now binding on more than two-thirds of all states) may be held to be 'stating what is becoming a customary legal norm applicable to all'. Franck, supra (note 124), 64.

[127] Repr. in (1970) 9 *International Legal Materials 673, 682; Art 23.*

[128] First Protocol to the European Convention on Human Rights, European Treaty Series No 9, 213 UNTS 262,264 (1952); Art 3.

[129] African Charter on Human and Peoples' Rights, repr. in Malcolm Evans, ed., *Blackstone's International Law Documents*, 2nd ed. (London: Blackstone Press, 1994) 251; Art 13.

[130] G.A. Res. 45/150 (21 Feb. 1991).

[131] See Document of the Copenhagen Meeting of the Conference on the Human Dimension, repr. in (1990) 29 *International Legal Materials* 1305, 1308 (para. 5); Charter of Paris for a New Europe, repr. in (1991) 30 *International Legal Materials* 190,194; Document of the Moscow Meeting of the Conference on the Human Dimension of the CSCE, repr. in (1991) 30 *International Legal Materials* 1670; and most recently, The Budapest Summit — Declaration on Genuine Partnership in a New Era, repr. in (1995) 34 *International Legal Materials* 764.

[132] Including Canada, the US and the nations of Eastern Europe.

[133] Renamed the Organization for Security and Co-operation in Europe [OSCE].

Apart from an international normative framework, progress towards what has been termed 'collective democratic security'[134] can be discerned at the international institutional level. Most significant in this respect is the developing practice of election monitoring (including the formulation of relevant guiding rules) under the auspices of international and regional organizations such as the UN, the Organization of American States (OAS), the CSCE and the Commonwealth.[135] A greater willingness to 'intervene' — both 'judicially' (by international human rights courts and commissions)[136] and 'materially' (through the imposition of sanctions or military action)[137] to promote and protect democratic values and principles is also evident.

By the same token, the emerging norm of democracy has found expression in 'state practice'. As amply supported by contemporary studies, the world is undergoing 'democratic globalization'[138] and [a 'third wave' of] 'democratic expansion'.[139] Indeed, even Asia's traditionally authoritarian regimes have gradually embraced democratic ideas and opened the governmental process to grass-root elements.[140]

Leaving aside debates[141] regarding issues such as the universality of western/Westminster model of democracies, the emphasis of elections as the most crucial element of the democratic process or whether democracy is always the 'people's choice/interest' — Hong Kong satisfies the general requirements of democracy.[142] It features an increasingly politicized active

---

[134] See James Crawford, 'Democracy and International Law' (1993) *British Yearbook of International Law* 113.

[135] See elaboration in Crawford, ibid., at 123–5.

[136] See Crawford, ibid., at 125–6.

[137] Most recently the UN authorized [under SC Resolution 940 (30 July 1994)] a mission to restore to power the democratically elected president in Haiti.

[138] See Larry Diamond, *The Globalisation of Democracy* (Boulder, Col.: Lynne Rienner Publishers, 1993).

[139] See Samuel D Huntingon, *The Third Wave: Democratization in the Late Twentieth Century* (Oklahoma: University of Oklahoma Press, 1991).

[140] See Diane Stormont, 'Democracy Creeps Across Asia — An Analysis' *South China Morning Post*, 22 December 1992, at 5; 'Suharto Calls for More Democracy' *South China Morning Post*, 2 March 1993; Jonathan Braude, 'Leading Asian Slams Autocracy' *South China Morning Post*, 3 December 1994 (referring to a speech by the Malaysian Deputy Prime Minister, Dr Anwar Ibrahim, in which he urged Asian governments to eradicate the vestiges of what he called "oriental despotism" by "enhanc[ing] the workings of truly representative, participatory governments, promot[ing] the rule of laws rather than men, and foster[ing] the cultivation of a free and responsible press").

[141] See, for example, Thomas Carothers, 'Empirical Perspectives on the Emerging Norm of Democracy in International Law' (1992) *American Society of International Law Proceedings* 261.

[142] See Mason Hills, 'The Rule of Law and Democracy in Hong Kong — Comparative Analysis of British Liberalism and Chinese Socialism' (1994) 1 *E Law — Murdoch University Electronic Journal of Law*.

population, freedom of speech, potentially capable political leaders, belief in democratic principles and individual rights, high level of literacy and education, a pluralistic social order, lack of extreme inequalities among the politically relevant strata, an advanced system of law and regulation of executive and administrative action, as well as a political system which is influenced by a large number of interest groups none of which has absolute control of resources and outcomes.

At the same time, it is evident that the 'democratization' of Hong Kong has not progressed in accordance with local expectations, and falls short of internationally postulated norms (at least in terms of erecting the necessary formal structures). Notwithstanding expressions of the public desire for a faster pace and the consensus advice given by the Office of Members of the Executive and Legislative Councils [OMELCO] on the need for an accelerated timetable to full democracy, the British government resolved to open only 18 of the sixty seats in the Legislative Council for direct elections in 1991 and 20 in 1995 (the last elections due under British rule).[143]

Although a set of reform proposals — introduced by Hong Kong's Governor (Mr Patten)[144] with the aim of expanding the voting franchise in the territory and broadening other democratic initiatives[145] — has recently (30 June 1994) been passed into law, it is viewed by democratically inclined observers as a 'small and belated steps towards the fully democratic political system for which Hong Kong has long been ready'.[146] Indeed, the Governor

---

[143] See White Paper on the Annual Report on Hong Kong 1989 to Parliament (Hong Kong: Government Printer, 18 April 1990) para. 29. It may be noted that until 1985 all members of the Legislative Council were either government officials or appointed by the Governor. In 1985 a system of indirect elections was instituted whereby 12 members (out of 57) were elected by functional constituencies (e.g. commercial, financial, education and other professions) and another 12 by an electoral college. First direct elections were held in 1991.

[144] See Governor's Address at the Opening of the Hong Kong Legislative Council, *Our Next Five Years, The Agenda for Hong Kong* (7 October 1992), paras. 101–147 ('The Constitutional Package').

[145] The proposals are: to lower the voting age from 21 to 18; to replace the 1991 system of double member constituencies which are directly elected with single seat constituencies; to replace the corporate voting in existing functional constituencies by individual votes; to make all District Board members elected and to abolish appointed members of Municipal Councils; to give District Boards responsibility for local public work projects and other local activities; to increase their funding; to establish an independent Boundary and Election Commission; to draw all or most of the members of the 1995 Election Committee (which will select Hong Kong's Chief Executive) from the elected membership of the District Boards.

[146] Christine Loh, 'Not Far Enough' *Far Eastern Economic Review* (8 April 1993) 24. Note that under the new system, only 20 LegCo members (out of 60) are elected by universal suffrage.

himself has admitted that the fierce row between Britain and China, triggered by the proposals, was not about whether Hong Kong would soon become a democracy but over 'greater or lesser degrees of semi-autonomy'.[147]

Post-1997 prospects for the implementation of the right of Hong Kong people to internal self-determination do not appear encouraging.[148] As pointed out by one commentator, the Basic Law 'accepts democracy as a long term principle (BL 45 and 68) but does not provide it. Neither the first Chief Executive nor the majority of the legislature to take office in July 1997 will be directly elected . . . No significant change in the method of selecting the Chief Executive is contemplated until 2007 (that is, after two terms of office) nor is it intended that the legislature would have a majority of directly elected representatives until at least after that date (annexes I and II). Thereafter, the system may be altered, but only with the support of two-thirds of the members of the legislature, the chief minister, and the Standing Committee of the National People's Congress . . .'[149]

Yet, as emphasized by the same observer,[150] 'the participation of the Hong Kong people in the autonomous political processes of the SAR immediately on the termination of colonial rule not only underlies the Basic Law, but is central to its success. The denial of that opportunity would confuse and demoralize the community of Hong Kong, sap the vitality of its public life, upset the balance of political forces through outside intervention and destroy the status of the Basic Law. Many other negative consequences would follow, inconsistent with the goal of the stability and prosperity of Hong Kong proclaimed in the Joint Declaration and the Basic Law.'

Succession

Will the HKSAR succeed to existing memberships in international organizations and associations and to rights currently enjoyed by Hong Kong under international agreements?

Given the importance of international links to the maintenance of Hong Kong's status as a major international commercial centre, questions of

---

[147] Cited in 'Patten's Next Stand' *The Economist* (2 July 1994).

[148] Apart from ongoing Chinese threats to dismantle Hong Kong's political institutions in 1997.

[149] Yash Ghai, 'A Comparative Perspective' in Peter Wesley-Smith, ed., *Hong Kong's Basic Law Problems & Prospects* (Hong Kong: Faculty of Law University of Hong Kong, 1990) 11.

[150] See Yash Ghai, 'Basic Flaws in China's Thinking' *South China Morning Post*, 14 December 1994, at 21.

succession loom large on the agenda of the transfer of sovereignty in 1997. Although some international rules governing the subject of 'state succession'[151] have emerged, they are yet to be crystallized as customary international law. As observed by international jurists, the practice of states in this area has been largely based on political expediency, pragmatic solutions and on power relationships between the states involved, resulting in 'an abundance of contradictory and conflicting trends upon which no coherent theory and principles can be built'.[152]

By the same token, 'a tendency' has been discerned 'to pay regard to the question whether it is just, reasonable, equitable, or in the interests of the international community that rights or obligations should pass upon external changes of sovereignty over territory ... Moreover, treaties providing *expressis verbis* for the transfer of certain obligations upon changes of sovereignty have generally been interpreted by international tribunals in the light of considerations of reason and justice'.[153]

Yet, insofar as specific provisions are concerned, state practice has remained 'unsettled and full of inconsistencies',[154] notwithstanding the conclusion of the 1978 Vienna Convention on the Succession of States in Respect of Treaties[155] and the 1983 Vienna Convention on Succession of States in Respect of State Property, Archives and Debts.[156] Indeed, while the subject as a whole appears unsuited for doctrinal solution, it is clear that the issue of succession to membership in international organizations cannot be resolved effectively by uniform rules.[157]

---

[151] Despite China's contention that no transfer of sovereignty is to take place, since it will merely 'resume' the exercise of sovereignty over Hong Kong, the situation falls within the definition of 'state succession' given that the responsibility for the foreign relations of the territory is passed from one sovereign to another.

[152] See D.P. O'Connell, *State Succession in Municipal and International Law* (Cambridge: Cambridge University Press, 1967), 490.

[153] Ivor A. Shearer, *Starke's International Law*, 11th ed. (London: Butterworths, 1994), 293.

[154] Loc.cit.

[155] Repr. in (1978) 17 *International Legal Materials* 1488.

[156] Repr. in (1983) 22 *International Legal Materials* 306.

[157] 'It has long been recognized that succession to international organization membership is a different question from succession to treaty rights and obligations, even though such membership is often derived from the terms of a multilateral agreement. This difference exists because membership in an international organization creates multiple rights and obligations that extend beyond the comparatively limited and explicit obligations found in most treaties. As such ... international organization issues need to be considered more on a case-by-case basis in light of the specified conditions of membership.' Edwin D. Williamson, 'Remarks' *American Society of International Law Proceedings*, 1992, at 13–14.

Nor for that matter are any of the few formulated theories commonly associated with state succession strictly appropriate in the unique circumstances of Hong Kong, which is not gaining full independence yet vested with a high degree of autonomy, including extensive powers of external relations. Thus, for example, the 'clean slate' theory advocating the right of newly independent states to decide which bilateral and multilateral treaties will remain in force, has no direct relevance. By the same token, the 'moving treaty frontiers rule' — which provides that a territory undergoing a change of sovereignty passes from the treaty regime of the preceding state directly to that of the acquiring one — is not applicable in light of Hong Kong's special autonomous status (distinguished from complete submergence/integration with another state). In addition to defying easy categorization, Hong Kong's succession problems are further compounded by the fact that the successor sovereign, the PRC is not a party to many of the international agreements presently extending to the territory and is not a member of all the international organizations of which Hong Kong is a member.

It is not surprising, therefore, that the sides to the Sino-British Joint Declaration have opted for a pragmatic formula whereby international agreements implemented in Hong Kong remain in force, even if the PRC is not a party to the agreement, while international agreements to which the PRC is a party (but not Hong Kong) would apply to the territory by the Central People's government only after seeking the views of the SAR government.[158] Additionally, the Chinese government 'shall, as necessary, authorize or assist the government of the Region to make appropriate arrangements for the application to the Region of other relevant international agreements'.[159] Special attention is accorded to agreements regarding Hong Kong's international air transport relations, in order to ensure the maintenance of the territory's status as 'a centre of international and regional aviation'.[160] Thus, the HKSAR, acting under authorization from China, may 'renew or amend Air Service Agreements and arrangements previously in force . . .'[161]

The reasonableness of the Hong Kong succession formula apart, third party states must consent to the arrangements postulated since they are not obliged to accept new parties within their treaty relations. Endorsement must

---

[158] JD, Annex I, art XI, para. 1. See also BL, Art 153.

[159] Loc.cit.

[160] JD, Annex I, art IX, para. 1. See also BL, Art 128.

[161] JD, Annex I, art IX, para. 3; BL, Art 128. In fact, not only will the HKSAR succeed to aviation related rights currently enjoyed by Hong Kong, but it may also assume additional international responsibilities with respect to the management of civil aviation. These responsibilities include the negotiation and conclusion of new Air Services Agreements (ASAs). JD, Annex I, art IX, para. 3; BL, Art 128.

also be gained from the members of the relevant international organizations for the succession of the territory's membership in these organizations. The tasks of procuring the necessary acceptances and working out the technical details of treaty succession have been assigned to the Sino-British Joint Liaison Group [JLG],[162] which lists amongst its 'achievements' securing Hong Kong's continued participation in thirty international organizations[163] as well as preserving the application to the territory of about half of the multilateral agreements currently in force in Hong Kong.[164] Noted in this regard is the approval obtained for Hong Kong's preservation of its own GATT (General Agreement for Trade and Tariffs) membership[165] and the related capacity to enter in its own right into bilateral fibre export restraint agreements under the Multi-Fibre Arrangement.

Of particular significance among treaties to be succeeded to by the HKSAR are the International Covenant on Civil and Political Rights and the International Covenant on Economic, Social and Cultural Rights whose continuance has been specifically guaranteed under the Sino-British Joint Declaration.[166] In fact, it is arguable that even in the absence of an express provision, a presumption operates in favour of continued application of multilateral conventions pertaining to human rights (as well as health, narcotics, and similar matters), which are regarded as 'universal' in nature and hence should not be deemed inapplicable by reason of changes of sovereignty.[167] Such a perception has been recently acknowledged in respect of succession to human rights treaties by former Yugoslavian republics. Looking into this issue, the UN Human Rights Committee took the view

---

[162] JD, Annex II.

[163] See *Achievements of the Joint Liaison Group*, supra (note 45); agreement for continued participation in three additional organizations was secured since 1990. For the position in respect of specific organizations as of 31 March 1996 see *United States-Hong Kong Policy Act Report* (1 April 1996), pp. 24–26.

[164] See Constitutional Affairs Branch, *List of Agreed Multilateral Treaties* (5 June 1995). See also Joint Liaison Group *Joint Communique*, 35th Meeting (6, 7, 9 February 1996), announcing that the parties 'reached an agreement in principle on the mechanism for giving legal form to all the agreements on international rights and obligations reached so far by the IRO [International Rights & Obligations] Sub-Group.'

[165] Hong Kong became a separate contracting party to GATT in 1986. See Accession of Hong Kong, Succession, GATT Doc. L/5976 (Apr 23, 1986), repr. in 4 *GATT: Basic Instruments and Selected Documents* 27 (34th Supp 1988).

[166] JD, Annex I, sec. XIII, para. 4.

[167] See Shearer, supra (note 153), at 295. Moreover, it has been suggested that future state practice — shaped by concerns for stability and predictability in international relations — is likely to reconfirm this widely-accepted presumption of continuity of treaty rights and obligations. See Oscar Schachter, 'State Succession: The Once and Future Law' (1993) 33 *Virginia Journal of International Law* 253, 260.

that 'successor states were automatically bound by obligations under international human rights instruments [which applied previously to the respective territories].'[168] Indeed, the Committee further emphasized that no declaration of confirmation was required of the successor governments.[169]

Will acquired property rights be protected after 1997?
Would contracts, leases and agreements signed and ratified by the Hong Kong government be valid after 30 June 1997?

According to a well established principle of international law, 'private rights acquired under existing law do not cease on a change of sovereignty.'[170] The *droits acquis principle* has been applied in respect of a variety of rights in ownership and possession of assets, whether vested in natural or jurisdic person, claimed against other private person or against the state.[171] Under European Community law, moreover, acquired rights (*acquis communautire*) encompass *all* rights held by citizens (*qua* citizens) of the Community by virtue of EC legislation and regulation (including freedom of movement within the EC, freedom to establish business and the right to continued payment of national social welfare and medical benefits).[172]

Yet, the *perpetual* maintenance of these rights is not guaranteed and, following the transfer of sovereignty, a successor state is not prohibited from introducing new legislation which would modify or even expropriate private property rights.[173] To safeguard against such eventuality — and to achieve

---

[168] See UN ECOSOC, Commission on Human Rights, *Succession of States in Respect of International Human Rights Treaties, Report of the Secretary-General*, E/CN.4/1995/80 (28 November 1994), 4.

[169] Note that all former republics did confirm officially that they continued to be bound by obligations under the relevant international human rights treaties.

[170] Advisory Opinion, *Certain Questions Relating to Settlers of German Origin in the Territory Ceded by Germany to Poland* 1923 PCIJ (Ser. B) No 6, at 36 ('. . . It can hardly be maintained that, although the law survives, private rights acquired under it have perished'). The principle was also confirmed in *Certain German Interests in Polish Upper Silesia (Germany v Poland)* 1926 PCIJ (Ser. A) No 7. For a most comprehensive exposition of the doctrine of acquired rights and relevant practice see O'Connell, supra (note 152), vol. I, pp. 237–481.

[171] For references to cases regarding land leases, right to exploit forest resources and right to exercise a profession or established business see Michael John Volkovitch, 'Righting Wrongs: Towards a New Theory of State Succession to Responsibility for International Delicts' (1992) 92 *Columbia Law Review* 2162, 2204 (notes 227–9).

[172] See Volkovitch, ibid, at 2205 (citing the *Oxford Encyclopedia of European Law: Institutional Law*, pp. 9–10 to support the contention that the concept of *droits acauis* 'has become a fundamental tenet of European Community Law').

[173] See G. Kaeckelbeck, 'The Protection of Vested Rights in International Law' (1936) *British Yearbook of International Law* 1, 17.

smooth transition with a view to maintaining the economic prosperity and social stability of Hong Kong — the preservation of laws currently in force in Hong Kong (including common law, rules of equity, ordinances, subordinate legislation and customary law) beyond 1997 has been secured by an internationally binding agreement, namely the Sino-British Joint Declaration.[174] Thus, whether valid under the territory's common law or granted pursuant to existing ordinances,[175] legal rights acquired prior to the establishment of the HKSAR are to be recognized and protected after 1997. In particular, '[p]rivate property, ownership of enterprises . . . and foreign investment will be protected by law.'[176]

The obligation to honour pre-1997 acquired rights is entrenched in the SAR's Basic Law which — apart from providing in general that the HKSAR 'protect the right of private ownership of property in accordance with law'[177] as well as the 'right of individuals and legal persons to the acquisition, use disposal and inheritance of property and their right to compensation for lawful deprivation of their property'[178] — specifically states that 'documents, certificates, contracts and rights and obligations valid under laws previously in force in Hong Kong shall continue to be valid and be recognized and protected by the Hong Kong Special Administrative Region, provided they do not contravene the [Basic] Law.[179]

No distinction is drawn between rights arising out of private legal arrangements and contracts, leases and agreements signed and ratified by the Hong Kong government. Nor is the legality of any action to be determined by political considerations or approval,[180] if the Rule of Law is upheld. Hence, notwithstanding the termination of Britain's rule over Hong Kong on 30 June 1997, and regardless of any strain in the relationship between the Chinese and British governments, valid legal transactions — entered into by government of private individuals — should retain their validity beyond 1997 (if consistent with the Basic Law). Included are also employment contracts

---

[174] JD, Annex II, art II, para 1; see also BL, Art 8.

[175] For example, franchises granted under the Telecommunication Ordinance, the Ferry Service Ordinance, the Cross Harbour Tunnel Ordinance, the Peak Tram Ordinance, or the Television Ordinance.

[176] JD, Art 3(5); Annex I, art VI; BL, Arts 6, 105.

[177] BL, Art 6.

[178] BL, Art 105.

[179] BL, Art 160.

[180] According to a statement by the Hong Kong government, major government franchises and contracts straddling 1997 are discussed — 'as a matter of current practice' — with the Chinese side of the Joint Liaison Group. Reported in Fanny Fong, 'China Veto Threat' *South China Morning Post*, 1 December 1992, at 1.

of civil servants and members of the judiciary, which are in fact given added protection under the Joint Declaration and the Basic Law.[181]

In light of the 'important part which land plays in the development and economy of Hong Kong',[182] a special agreement has been reached under the Sino-British Joint Declaration with respect to land leases. Specifically, all existing leases which extend beyond June 30, 1997 and all rights in relation to such leases, 'shall continue to be recognized and protected under the law of the Hong Kong Special Administrative Region'.[183] Moreover, all long-term leases of land granted by the British Hong Kong government which expire before 30 June 1997 without a right of renewal may be extended until 30 June 2047, without payment of an additional premium.[184] Leases of land which expire after the establishment of the HKSAR would be dealt with under the laws and policies formulated by the Region on its own.[185] The Hong Kong government may also grant new leases from the date of entry into force of the Joint Declaration (for terms expiring no later than 30 June 2047),[186] although it is limited to an annual grant of fifty hectares and must share premium income from land transactions equally with the government of the SAR.[187] Particular consideration is given under the Joint Declaration to the maintenance of title to land held by indigenous villagers (those whose families resided in a Hong Kong village in 1898 and have remained on that property since that time), who will pay the same nominal rent as long as the property stays in the male line of the family.[188]

Are foreign investments in the territory safe?

Investors in Hong Kong have to assume a (not uncommon) risk that the territory might experience changes in its political and economic systems. Clearly, not all property rights affected or losses accruing as a result are protected or indemnifiable under general international law. Yet, the right of a state to nationalize, expropriate or transfer ownership of foreign property is subject to generally recognized (both in state practice and judicial decisions)

---

[181] JD, Annex I, art IV; BL, Art 100 (all public servants may remain in their employment and retain their conditions of service after 1997); JD, Annex I, arts I, II, III; BL, Arts 8, 19, 80 to 93 (preservation of the existing legal system, judicial system and independence of the judiciary).

[182] JD, 'Explanatory Notes', art 53.

[183] JD, Annex III, art 1.

[184] Ibid., art 2.

[185] Ibid.

[186] Ibid., art 3.

[187] Ibid., art 8.

[188] Ibid., art 2.

international legal restraints. In particular, such acts must not be arbitrary, discriminatory or motivated by considerations of political nature unrelated to the internal well-being of the state. Neither may changed political, economic or social circumstances be invoked to avoid liability for a deprivation of an alien's property that is attributed to the state.[189] Furthermore, the 'taking'[190] of property[191] is contingent upon the payment of appropriate compensation (although opinions diverge regarding the standard and measure of compensation). Foreign nationals must, in any event, be allowed access to the domestic courts to assert their rights and are entitled to due process of the law in respect of a legal dispute arising in the state.

Despite the protection afforded by international law, the Hong Kong government has sought to provide additional assurances in an attempt to stave off fears foreign investors may have over the future of the territory under Chinese rule. Accordingly, it has been negotiating Investment Promotion and Protection Agreements [IPPAs] with its major trading partners.[192] Under such internationally binding treaties (which, being approved by China, are to remain in force after 1997), the parties assume obligations to ensure equality of treatment between foreign and domestic investors; restrict the circumstances in which investments can be expropriated; pay prompt, adequate and effective compensation, should expropriation occur; guarantee that foreign investors are able to remove their investment without restriction in a convertible currency; and provide for the settlement of disputes between investors and local authorities in accordance with agreed procedures by an impartial body. The latter provision is particularly necessary given

---

[189] For a detailed discussion of the circumstances in which liability arises see: George H. Aldrich, 'What Constitutes a Compensable Taking of Property? The Decisions of the Iran-United States Claims Tribunal' (1994) 88 *American Journal of International Law* 585.

[190] Including 'constructive taking' [see Burns H. Weston, '"Constructive Takings" under International Law: A Modest Foray into the Problem of "Creeping Expropriation"' (1975) 16 *Virginia Journal of International Law* 103] and interference which renders property rights 'useless', regardless of whether the state has purported to expropriate these rights and whether legal title to the property formally remains with the original owner [see, e.g. *Starratt Housing Corporation v Iran* (1983-III) 4 Iran-USCTR 122, repr. in (1984) 23 *International Legal Materials* 1090].

[191] 'Property' is not limited to tangible assets but may include valuable intangible assets such as contractual rights, intellectual property and rights of management and control. See Martin Dixon, *Textbook on International Law*, 2nd ed. (London: Blackstone Press, 1993) 213 (and cases cited therein). It should be noted that certain contracts between an individual/ company and a state are regarded as 'internationalised' and hence subject to international law; breach of such contracts may give rise to international responsibility. See ibid., at 218–220.

[192] IPPAs have been concluded with Netherlands, Australia, Sweden, Denmark, Switzerland. See *List of Bilateral Treaties*, supra (note 46). Six more are expected to be signed with Canada, Italy, Germany, France, New Zealand, Belgium, and Austria.

that neither Hong Kong nor China are parties to the 1964 International Convention for the Settlement of Investment Disputes between States and Nationals of Other States. It should nonetheless be added that China is at present signatory to over 18 bilateral Agreements Concerning the Encouragement and Reciprocal Protection of Investment which contain *inter alia* some mutually agreed ad hoc dispute settlement schemes.

Capacity to bear international responsibility

Can Hong Kong be held internationally responsible for failing to perform international obligations?

With the state widely regarded as the fundamental unit of international relations and international law, questions of responsibility in international law are commonly expressed in the context of 'state responsibility'. Nonetheless, there are other bodies or entities which have been recognized or accepted as being capable of incurring international responsibility. Thus, for example, responsibility is borne by international organizations under the 1967 Treaty on Principles Governing the Activities of States in the Exploration and Use of Outer Space, Including the Moon and Other Celestial Bodies. The European Community has assumed responsibility under the various international treaties and conventions it has concluded, particularly in the areas of trade and international environmental law.

Of particular significance is the increasing tendency under international law to cast responsibility on individuals for international deliquencies: the commitment of 'piracy' as defined under international law engages the individual offender in a crime against the international society punishable by international tribunals or by any state; individual responsibility for crimes against peace, war crimes, and crimes against humanity is well established following the Nuremberg Trials and the Nuremberg Charter as confirmed by the General Assembly; the 1948 Genocide Convention emphasizes that ordinary persons guilty of offences connected with genocide could be tried either by national courts of the territory in which the acts were committed or by international penal tribunals; narcotics and hijacking offences have also been made triable and punishable universally by a series of international conventions; individuals are also bound directly by international criminal laws pertaining to espionage, counterfeiting currency, illicit traffic in dangerous drugs, slave trading, trading in women and children, pollution of the seas, damaging submarine cables, offences against persons protected by international law, unlawful despatch of explosives through post, pirate broadcasting, and theft of national and archaeological treasures.

This is not to suggest that the nature or scope of responsibility are identical in respect of all 'subjects' of international law. Most noticeably, while state responsibility ensues *ipso facto*, the responsibility of other international legal persons — as 'creatures of [international] law' — can be said to arise only *ipso jure*. Such entities are beholden to their international responsibilities according to their distinctive role and functions under international law and hence the variance in substance and degree of responsibility among them.

Despite a dearth of international legal rules directly governing the international responsibility of nonstate actors, it may be observed that current discussion surrounding 'state responsibility'[193] has not been oriented towards connecting international legal responsibility with state sovereignty or exclusivity.[194] Indeed, lack of sovereignty is not seen as an obstacle to the attribution of international responsibility: agreements concluded by component units of federal states acting within the limits of proper international personality are the responsibility of such units; similarly, an insurrectionist movement which does not become the new government of a state may, if vested with international personality, engage eventually its own responsibility.

Rather than sovereignty, international responsibility appear to be founded upon 'jurisdictional' competence, namely the competence to make and apply law, and effective control over territory. In this vein, a belligerent state, which exercises jurisdictional competence within the territory it occupies, may be held liable for consequences of activities over which it exercises jurisdiction; whereas in circumstances such as unlawful occupation, annexation, or intervention, responsibility may be based on control of *de facto* jurisdiction. In fact, responsibility for what possibly constitutes the major part of 'state responsibility' — failure to discharge international duties owed to aliens within its borders — is ascribed to the territorial controlling authority.

For its part, the Hong Kong government (and the HKSAR after 1997) is endowed with both jurisdictional competence and effective control over the territory. Consequently, it may be held liable for internationally injurious consequences of activities which originate in the territory and about which the government has knowledge or which fall under its regulatory capacity. Acting as an international juridical person within the limits of its personality,

---

[193] The most authoritative study of the topic has been undertaken by the International Law Commission (which has had the topic of state responsibility on its agenda since 1953).

[194] For a recent general analysis of the trend away from a sovereign-centred approach towards a 'functional' one which reflects a 'multi-layered reality consisting of a variety of authoritative structures', see: Christoph Schreuer, 'The Waning of the Sovereign State: Towards a Paradigm for International Law' (1993) 4 *European Journal of International Law* 447.

the Hong Kong government may engage its own responsibility, attributable neither to Britain nor to China. Indeed, it is arguable that the territory's admission as a party to international agreements or as a member of international organizations is impliedly contingent on both an authority (to enter international agreements and join international organizations) and an undertaking to assume responsibility for its own actions.

Accordingly, the local government may be internationally responsible for violating its obligations under treaties to which Hong Kong is a party. It may likewise bear responsibility for infringements of [customary] international law resulting from activities or events over which it has control or jurisdiction. Such infringements may arise, for example, in the context of its obligations pertaining to the treatment of aliens (including refugees), privileges and protection of diplomats, or protection of the environment.[195]

Capacity to bring international claims

Does Hong Kong possess the capacity to bring claims before international forums?

An inquiry into the substance of Hong Kong's international legal identity, its constellation of rights and obligations, is left incomplete without considering the territory's capacity to bring international claims. That the Hong Kong government has the capacity to contract, acquire and dispose of property as well as institute legal proceedings is readily substantiated. Moreover, the government's juridical personality, and that of its 'successor' the HKSAR government, are not confined to the sphere of private law. As explicitly enunciated in the Sino-British Joint Declaration,[196] and reaffirmed in the Basic Law,[197] the territory has been endowed with considerable power to conclude international treaties in its own name and assume overall responsibility for the conduct of its external affairs. Hong Kong's international juridical personality is further manifested in its extensive participation in the activities of international and intergovernmental organizations which invariably entails undertakings of international duties.

Concurrently with the liabilities it has accepted, the territory is bequeathed with international rights both under conventional-treaty law and general-customary international law. Thus, when entering into international

---

[195] For a discussion of applicable international obligations in the areas of international refugee law and international environmental law, see Chapter 3.

[196] See JD, Art 3(10); Annex I, art XI.

[197] See BL, Art 151.

agreements with other states, Hong Kong has the right to demand performance under the agreement in accordance with a fundamental rule of international law: *pacta sunt servanda* (treaties are binding on the parties and must be performed in good faith). The territory is similarly entitled to privileges and immunities afforded under general international law to entities discharging governmental functions,[198] including immunity from jurisdiction of foreign domestic courts without the express consent of the Hong Kong government as well as reciprocal privileges and immunities for its official representatives.[199]

It also follows that to vindicate the rights it is bestowed upon by international law, Hong Kong must be deemed to possess the capacity to claim the due benefits and enforce such claims through the appropriate international judicial channels. To enable it to seek reparations on the international plane, the territory should be allowed to gain access to international dispute-resolution forums. Given, however, traditionalist notions regarding *locus standi* before international tribunals, could Hong Kong bring a case on its own behalf to the International Court of Justice?

After conducting a thorough analysis of both the relevant United Nations Charter provisions and international practice, a renowned international lawyer has concluded[200] that '[t]here is a firm policy in favour of increasing the participation of territorial communities in that Statute of the International Court of Justice.' Furthermore, even a 'territorial community with minimum independence and minimum international activity [such as Liechtenstein][201] may elect to become a party to the Statute'. Indeed, 'the prescription of conditions set by the Security Council[202] aims [not at precluding an applicant but] at ensuring effective participation in the work of the Court and related United Nations activity'.

---

[198] Under modern doctrine and practice of international law, 'state function' has replaced 'sovereignty' as the rationale and standard of immunity.

[199] It should be noted, however, that there is no obligation under international law to grant immunity (*ratione personae*) to nonstate entities and practice is largely contingent on recognition.

[200] See W. Michael Reisman, *Puerto Rico and the International Process* (Washington: West Publishing, 1975) at 78.

[201] Liechtenstein was admitted as a party to the Statute of the ICJ notwithstanding the fact that it had delegated full authority to Switzerland to administer its foreign affairs. In fact, Liechtenstein was actually involved in proceedings before the ICJ during the time it had deprived itself of capacity to conduct its own foreign relations. See *Nottebhom Case* (Liechtenstein v Guatemala) [1955] ICJ Reports 4.

[202] Under UN Charter, Art 93(2): 'A State which is not a Member of the United Nations may become a party to the Statute of the International Court of Justice on condition to be determined in each case by the General Assembly upon the recommendation of the Security Council.'

As reflected in the UN's deliberations of Liechtenstein's application for membership in the ICJ Statute, emphasis has been placed on factors such as (1) whether the applicant 'would benefit by adherence to the Court, (2) [whether] other states with which it has relations would benefit by its adherence and (3) [whether] the general principle of universality of participation would be realized'.[203] In an analogous context, Hong Kong's status and capacity as an international actor, its extensive international relationships, and the obvious benefits all parties would derive from its adherence to the Statute of the International Court of Justice, should act to reinforce the territory's case for becoming a party to the Statute.

Potentially, Hong Kong may gain access to the International Court of Justice by virtue of its membership in a 'specialized UN agency'.[204] Thus, should the International Labour Organization, for example, be authorized by the General Assembly to request the ICJ's Advisory Opinion[205] on matters related to the territory, Hong Kong is likely[206] to be permitted to communicate relevant grievances. Similar 'procedural' allowances to present claims before the Court could possibly be secured by reference to comparable concessions made to individuals[207] and other legal persons,[208] in the light of a growing concern for human rights and a recognition of the imperative role of non-state actors in addressing global security challenges (e.g. environment, refugees, etc.).[209]

---

[203] See Reisman, supra (note 200) at 69–70.

[204] UN 'specialized agencies' include the: International Labour Organization, World Health Organization, the World Bank, International Monetary Fund, International Civil Aviation Organization, UN Educational, Scientific and Cultural Organization, Universal Postal Union, International Communication Union, Inter-Governmental Maritime Consultative Organization, World Trade Organization.

[205] In accordance with UN Charter, Art 96(2).

[206] Based on previous practice of the Court. Note, for example, the right granted by the ICJ to the International League for the Rights of Man to submit a written statement on legal issues in respect of the international status of South West Africa, [1950] ICJ Reports 128.

[207] See discussion in P.K. Menon, 'The International Personality of Individuals in International Law: A Broadening of the Traditional Doctrine' (1992) 1 *Florida State University Journal of Transnational Law and Policy* 151, 158–174. Note that individuals have *locus standi* before international tribunals such as the Iran-United States Claims Tribunal and the United Nations Compensation Commission established after the 1990–1991 Persian Gulf Crisis. Regionally, the European Court of Justice grants standing to individuals or other non-state actors for certain types of cases.

[208] For example, the International League for Human Rights was permitted to submit information in the *South-West Africa* proceedings.

[209] For a forceful argumentation in favour of allowing nongovernmental organizations active involvement in the international adjudicatory process see: Dianah Shelton, 'The Participation of Nongovernmental Organizations in International Judicial Proceedings' (1994) 88 *American Journal of International Law* 611.

Could the Hong Kong/HKSAR government offer 'diplomatic protection' to 'its people'?

Apart from the issues of Hong Kong's capability to bring international claims on its own behalf and the territory's *locus standi* before international tribunals, a related question may arise in respect of the right of the Hong Kong/HKSAR government to [diplomatically] protect or make specific representation involving claims to reparation and compensation arising from injuries to 'its nationals'. As currently understood, 'diplomatic protection' is the 'protection given by a subject of international law to individuals, i.e. natural or legal persons, against a violation of international law by another subject of international law'.[210] Hence, statehood is not a necessary condition of diplomatic protection, and the lack of statehood should not in itself preclude Hong Kong from extending protection to its inhabitants.

However, subjects of international law are entitled to protect only those individuals with whom they have a special relationship. This relationship is usually defined as nationality, although exceptions have been admitted. For instance, the UN may institute a claim on behalf of an injured UN employee.[211] Another example is the practice of extending a state's diplomatic protection to seamen of any nationality who are serving on a ship flying that state's flag.[212] The rule can, in any event, be waived with the consent of the respondent state.

Not only have deviations from the traditional 'nationality rule' been accepted but the doctrinal foundation of the rule itself has been questioned. Predicated as it is on the assumption that

> [i]n taking up the case of one of its nationals, by resorting to diplomatic action or international judicial proceedings on his behalf, a state is in reality asserting *its own right*, the right to ensure in the person of its nationals respect for the rules of international law . . .[213]

the rule is at clear variance with both international legal theory and practice which recognize individuals as 'subjects' of international law. Indeed, it is contended that the emphasis on human rights in current international law

---

[210] William K. Geck, 'Diplomatic Protection' in Rudolf Bernhardt, ed., *Encyclopedia of Public International Law* (Amsterdam, New York, Oxford: North Holland Publishing, 1981-), Instl. 10 (1987) 99, 100.

[211] See *Reparation for Injuries Suffered in the Service of the United Nations* [1949] ICJ Reports 174.

[212] See A.D. Watts, 'The Protection of Alien Seamen' (1958) *International and Comparative Law Quarterly* 691.

[213] *Panevezys-Saldutiskis Railway Case* (Estonia v Lithuenia) [1939] PCIJ Reports (ser. A/B, No. 76) 16. [emphasis added]

finds its corollary in the right of each state to take protective measures in favour of *all* (regardless of nationality) persons whose rights are immediately threatened.[214]

It may, therefore, be concluded that even if some sort of relationship is to remain a prerequisite for diplomatic protection, that relationship need not be nationality. In fact, the *Nottebhom Case*,[215] often cited as authority for the nationality rule, could be said to have replaced the nationality nexus with that of a 'genuine link'.[216] Such a 'link' is also emphasized in the context of international maritime law[217] pertaining to diplomatic protection to ships against which international wrongs have been committed. Applying these contemporary international legal perceptions to the Hong Kong predicament, it is evident that the territory's residents stand in a sufficiently 'close relationship' to the Hong Kong government to place on the latter a responsibility for their welfare and protection and to permit the espousal of a claim for damages suffered by them as a result of breach of an international obligation. The competence of the HKSAR government to attribute national character to its ships[218] and the authority granted to it to issue passports and conclude visa abolition agreements with foreign states or regions[219] serve to uphold the right of that government to represent the interests of its citizens in the sphere of international relations.

It is also clear that neither the British Nationality (Overseas) [BN(O)] nor the Chinese nationality to be conferred on the inhabitants of the HKSAR could be regarded as providing real and effective nationality,[220] thus reinforcing the case for the HKSAR to afford diplomatic — or equivalent — protection for its people. Furthermore, given that British consular protection (or for that matter protection of other foreign countries where 'HKSAR Chinese nationals' have established a right of abode)[221] would not

---

[214] See Geck, supra (note 210), at 115.

[215] [1955] ICJ Reports 4. The case involved proceedings instituted by the government of Liechtenstein against Guatemala for acting unlawfully towards the person and property of Friedrich Nottebhom, a citizen of Liechtenstein.

[216] The International Court of Justice found that Nottebhom had little real/genuine connection with Liechtenstein, whereas he had been settled in Guatemala for 34 years and had an intention to remain there. His connection with Guatemala was held far stronger than his 'nationality' connection with Liechtenstein and, consequently, Liechtenstein was not entitled to extend to Mr Nottebhom diplomatic protection.

[217] See, e.g. Art 91(1), 1982 UN Convention on the Law of the Sea; 1987 UN Convention on Conditions for Regulation of Ships.

[218] Through registration and documentation. See JD, Annex I, art VIII, para 2; BL, Art 125.

[219] See JD, Annex I, art XIV; BL, Arts 154 & 155.

[220] For further elaboration see discussion in Chapter 4.

[221] See Chapter 4.

be available in the HKSAR 'and other parts of the People's Republic of China',[222] the right of the HKSAR government to furnish diplomatic protection to Hong Kong people should extend to injuries caused by internationally wrongful acts committed within the PRC. A contention that HKSAR citizens would be 'seeking remedy in international forums against their own government'[223] may not be invoked since the PRC, although the sovereign power, is not the 'government of the Hong Kong people'.

---

[222] See JD, 'Chinese Memorandum', para 4.

[223] A doubtful contention in any event in the light of rights granted to individuals under international law against their own state. See, e.g. International Covenant on Civil and Political Rights, art 41; European Convention for the Protection of Human Rights and Fundamental Freedoms, arts 24 & 48.

Chapter 2

Issues of Jurisdiction

Hardly astonishing is the fact that international law, which contains few clearly defined rules regarding the jurisdictional competence of states,[1] also offers limited guidance in respect of the nature and extent of jurisdiction exercised by non-state entities such as Hong Kong. The argument may nonetheless be made that, given the territory's 'international legal personality' and prominence in the international arena, jurisdictional issues affecting Hong Kong are best examined in the context of international — as distinct from municipal — law.

TERRITORIAL JURISDICTION

To what extent is Hong Kong guaranteed a right to exercise jurisdiction over its territory free from interference?
Could Chinese criminal jurisdiction be extended to acts committed in Hong Kong?

It is reasonable to assert that Hong Kong's possession of the factual 'stately' attributes of defined territory and permanent population implies jurisdictional competence 'over all persons and things within its territorial limits and in

---

[1]   As stated by Sir Gerald Fitzmaurice: 'It is true that under present conditions international law does not impose hard and fast rules on states delimiting spheres of national jurisdiction in such matters . . . but leaves to states a wide discretion in the matter. It does, however, (a) postulate the existence of limits — though in any given case it may be for the tribunal to indicate what these are for the purposes of that case; and (b) involve for every state an obligation to exercise moderation and restraint as to the extent of the jurisdiction assumed by the courts in cases having a foreign element, and to avoid undue encroachment on a jurisdiction more properly appertaining to, or more appropriately exercisable by, another state.' *Barcelona Traction* Case [1970] ICJ Reports 3.

all cases, civil and criminal, arising within these limits'.[2] By virtue of what is known as the 'territorial principle' of jurisdiction, Hong Kong is entitled under international law[3] to subject to its legal system incidents occurring in, or persons within, its territory. Such competence is equally applicable to the HKSAR government which is 'vested with executive, legislative and independent judicial power'[4] over the SAR.

Geographical scope

For jurisdictional purposes, 'Hong Kong territory' is generally regarded as consisting of the land mass, internal waters (including ports) and their beds, territorial sea and its subsoil and the air space above all the former.[5] Under local law,[6] the term 'Hong Kong' (or alternatively the 'Colony'), when used in statutes or public documents, denotes 'the area of land and the area [waters] of Deep Bay and Mirs Bay lying within [the specified boundaries][7] and the territorial waters appertaining thereto'. No attempt is made to demarcate the HKSAR territory in the Sino-British Joint Declaration, which merely refers to the 'Hong Kong area (including Hong Kong Island, Kowloon and the New Territories)'.[8]

---

[2]   Lord Macmillan in *Compania Naviera Vascongado v SS Cristina* [1938] AC 485 at 496–7 (alluding to essential attributes of statehood).

[3]   Leaving aside constitutional or other constraints which may affect the prescriptive powers of the legislature in Hong Kong. See in this connection, Peter Wesley-Smith, 'Legal Limitations Upon the Legislative Competence of the Hong Kong Legislature' (1981) 11 *Hong Kong Law Journal* 3; William S. Clarke, 'The Constitution of Hong Kong and 1997' in Y.C. Jao et al., eds., *Hong Kong and 1997: Strategies for the Future* (Hong Kong: Centre of Asian Studies, University of Hong Kong, 1985) 215.

[4]   JD, Art 3(3).

[5]   See B.H. Oxman, 'Jurisdiction of States' in R. Bernhardt, ed., *Encyclopedia of Public International Law* (Amsterdam: North-Holland Publishing, 1981-), Instl.10 (1987) 277.

[6]   Sec. 3, Interpretation and General Clauses Ordinance (Chapter 1, Laws of Hong Kong 1989 ed.).

[7]   Ibid., Schedule 2.

[8]   JD, Art 1. Interestingly, a reference to the 'New Territories' (comprising the area north of Kowloon up to the Shumchun river, as well as 235 islands off the coast, all of which were included in the 99-year Lease of 1898 granted to Britain by China) is omitted from the territorial description of Hong Kong under the 'Decision of the National People's Congress on the Establishment of the Hong Kong Special Administrative Region' (adopted at the Third Session of the Seventh National People's Congress on 4 April 1990), which states: 'that the area of the Hong Kong Special Administrative Region covers the Hong Kong Island, the Kowloon Peninsula, and the islands and adjacent waters under its jurisdiction.' It has been suggested, however, that the area in question is subsumed under the 'Kowloon Peninsula' and that such omission is due to the reluctance of the Chinese government to use a term that had a strong colonial connotation. See Lorna Wong, 'Islands Dispute

The 'waters of Hong Kong' have been defined[9] as 'all inland waters,[10] territorial waters and tidal waters'.[11] 'Territorial waters', in turn, are to be interpreted to mean 'all such part of the sea adjacent to the coast of the Colony as is deemed by international law to constitute the territorial waters of Hong Kong.' Any reference, however, to that which is 'deemed by international law' is of a somewhat limited value in determining with precision the extent of Hong Kong's territorial waters, given the diversity of claims made by states regarding the breadth of their territorial sea.[12] Hong Kong's own 'state practice' is also rather ambiguous in this area, as exemplified by the *Huey Fong* incident.[13] The extension of the United Kingdom's territorial sea from three to twelve nautical miles in the Territorial Sea Act of 1987 has clearly removed the previous restriction of 'one marine league off the coast measured from low water mark' when in respect of criminal offences committed in 'Her Majesty's dominions'. The Act, however, does not shed any further light on the delimitation of Hong Kong's territorial waters'.[14]

Delays Decision on Post-1997 Boundary' *South China Morning Post*, 30 April 1992, at 3. No official map of the HKSAR has been issued by China's State Council, in accordance with the above Decision of the NPC.

9   See Sec. 2, Water Pollution Control Ordinance (Chapter 358, Laws of Hong Kong 1980 rev. ed.).

10 Defined as 'any river, stream, watercourse, lake, pool or pond, whether natural or artificial or above or below ground, and the bed or channel of any such river, stream, watercourse, lake, pool or pond which is for the time being dry, and includes ground water and the ground in which ground water is from time to time found.'

11 Defined as 'any part of the sea or of a river within the ebb and flow of the tide at ordinary spring tides': Sec. 2, Shipping and Port Control Ordinance (Chapter 313, Laws of Hong Kong 1986 rev. ed.).

12 According to Ian Brownlie, *Principles of Public International Law* (Oxford: Clarendon Press, 4th ed., 1990) 189–190 n. 53, currently nine states claim 3 miles; four – 6 miles; one hundred and seven – 12 miles; one – 20 miles; two – 30 miles; and eleven states claim 200 miles. It should be noted that under Art. 3 of the 1982 UN Convention on the Law of the Sea, every state has the right to establish the breadth of its territorial sea up to a limit not exceeding 12 nautical miles, measured from baselines determined in accordance with the Convention.

13 The *Huey Fong,* carrying refugees from Vietnam, was required to anchor at a point well within the territory's 3-mile limit (under the Interpretation and General Clauses Ordinance) yet was considered by the government to be 'outside the colony'.

14 It may be noted that while the UK has extended territorial seas around some of its overseas territories (South Georgia and the South Sandwich Islands, St Helena, Ascension Island, Tristan da Cunha and the Turks and Caicos Islands in the Caribbean as well as the Falkland Islands), it has not increased territorial limits around Hong Kong and the Channel Islands. Contentions have been made, however, that the British 'practice' regarding the application of the 3-mile rule to Hong Kong has not been consistent. See Lorna Wong, 'Fresh Talks Over SAR Boundaries' *South China Morning Post*, 9 July 1992, at 2 (citing local academics).

The Chinese position towards its own territorial sea — laid down in China's 1958 Declaration on the Territorial Sea — has been recently confirmed in its 1992 Law on the Territorial Sea and the Contiguous Zone. Accordingly, '[t]he breadth of the territorial sea of the People's Republic of China shall be twelve nautical miles.' Such a provision applies to 'all the territories of the PRC', namely 'the mainland and its offshore islands, Taiwan and the various affiliated islands including Diaoyu Island, Penghu Islands, Dongsha Islands, Xisha Islands, Nansha Islands and other islands that belong to the PRC' (Article 2). Were the 'straight baseline' method — which has been adopted by China for measuring its coastline (Article 3) — to apply without qualification,[15] the whole territory of Hong Kong would have been enclosed by a baseline drawn from the islands east, south and west of it. Yet, in practice, China appears to have accepted the notion of 'Hong Kong's territorial sea', and despite occasional claims of sovereignty over the territory, the PRC authorities have generally[16] respected Hong Kong's exercise of jurisdiction in these waters.

Although no express reference to airspace is made in the statutory definition of Hong Kong's territory, it may be assumed to be included therein. As noted above, 'territory' as understood in international law encompasses the surface, sub-surface, and a column of air (whose absolute height has not

---

[15] China has not published charts depicting the baselines for measuring the breadth of its territorial sea or the limits derived therefrom. The employment of a 'straight baseline' approach for the Chinese coastline has been subject to strong criticism, including the charge of inconsistency with the 1982 Law of the Sea Convention to which the PRC is a party. See Hyun-Soo Kim, 'The 1992 Chinese Territorial Sea Law in the Light of the UN Convention' (1994) *International and Comparative Law Quarterly* 894.

[16] Several incidents were reported involving 'infringements of Hong Kong waters by Chinese security vessels.' See S. Macklin, 'Sailing in Dangerous Waters' *South China Morning Post*, 12 May 1990, Review, at 3. See, however, Chinese acknowledgement of 'incorrect infringement of Hong Kong's territory' as reported in L. Tam, 'Hong Kong Receives Incursion Apology' *South China Morning Post*, 30 October 1992, at 1. Another incident was justified by some version of 'hot pursuit' (see Andy Gilbert, 'Border Forces Hijack Vessels' *South China Morning Post*, 24 March 1995, at 2). It may be added, however, that such a claim would not receive support under international law, given the fact that the pursuit was not 'contiguous or uninterrupted', and that any right of hot pursuit ceases as soon as the vessel pursued entered the maritime belt of its own [flag] country (the Chinese security armed forces seized the local tug and lighter in Hong Kong waters). By the same token, it may be said that the Hong Kong authorities have acquiesced in Chinese exercise of jurisdictional powers over that is formally 'Hong Kong waters'. Particular reference is made to Mirs Bay — or more specifically five kilometres from the Chinese coast where an unofficial border has been erected — over which PRC security forces have been allowed [under the guise of Smuggling into China (Control) Ordinance, Cap. 242] exclusive rights. See Andy Gilbert, 'HK Turns Blind Eye to China Incursions' *South China Morning Post*, 26 February 1996, at 5.

yet been determined) within a set of land and sea boundaries. The 1944 Chicago Convention on International Civil Aviation, which has been extended to Hong Kong, gives 'complete and exclusive sovereignty' to contracting states over the airspace above their territory. Evidently, the Hong Kong government considers the air above the territory as falling within its legislative jurisdiction, as reflected, for example, in the 1987 Air Pollution Control Ordinance which vests the Governor in Council with authority to 'declare any part of Hong Kong to be an air control zone' for the purpose of application of 'air quality objectives'.

Conceptual scope

Although the principle of territoriality — the right to exercise jurisdiction over persons and property, acts or events occurring within one's territory — is basically undisputed, its application has given rise to some controversy, particularly where parts of a single offence have taken place in several states or offences perpetrated outside a state have produced repercussions within that state. In the course of local jurisprudence, several theories have been considered. The prevailing approach appears to be modelled on the English version of the 'objective territorial principle',[17] namely that an offence is deemed to have been committed within the territory if it was completed, or intended to be completed, there. A Hong Kong Chief Justice, citing case law in Britain and other Commonwealth countries, held that:

> the Hong Kong courts have, and should assume jurisdiction to try those who are charged with a conspiracy formed out of the jurisdiction if any act has been committed within the jurisdiction in furtherance of the agreement. Such jurisdiction is not affected if: (a) the act is performed by an agent, innocent or guilty; (b) no conspirator had carried out any such act within Hong Kong; (c) no conspirator has entered the jurisdiction until the conspiracy is discharged.[18]

---

[17] Under such a principle jurisdiction may be assumed where the offence is consummated or the last constituent element occurs or effects are felt. The principle is of particular relevance regarding the exercise of jurisdiction with respect to multinational/transnational corporations. It may be noted that the approach taken by US courts is that the country in the territory of which *effects* or results are felt of action taken by head office (in another country) of the multinational corporation is entitled to exercise jurisdiction, e.g. against employees or assets of branches/subsidiaries locally situated. Needless to say, the head office's action may have concurrent affairs in a large number of countries, all of which would be entitled to exercise jurisdiction.

[18] *Attorney General v Yeung Sun-shun and Another* [1987] Hong Kong Law Reports 987, 997 (per Roberts CJ).

Indeed, as the Chief Justice observed,[19] even if no acts in furtherance of a conspiracy are committed within Hong Kong, the local courts should assume jurisdiction on the grounds that '(a) the conspiracy is aimed at Hong Kong and intended to bring about a breach of the peace here; (b) since the conspiracy is not directed at the residents of the country where it is entered into, the courts of that country could raise no reasonable objection to this course' (for reasons based on 'comity' — goodwill, civility, courtesy — among nations).

A similar approach was adopted by the Hong Kong Court of Appeal in 1990[20] and subsequently reaffirmed by the Judicial Committee of the Privy Council in an appeal from the Hong Kong decision.[21] The Law Lords further emphasized that 'unfortunately in this century crime has ceased to be largely local in origin and effect' but is 'now established on an international scale and the common law must face this new reality'. They could

> find nothing in precedent, comity or good sense that should inhibit the common law from regarding as justiciable in England inchoate crimes committed abroad which are intended to result in the commission of criminal offences in England. Accordingly a conspiracy entered into in Thailand with the intention of committing the criminal offence of trafficking in drugs in Hong Kong is justiciable in Hong Kong even if no overt act pursuant to the conspiracy has yet occurred in Hong Kong.

A like version of the 'objective territorial principle' also underlies the recent amendment to the Offences Against the Persons Ordinance.[22] Specifically,

> where — (a) an act takes place on the high seas or in any other place outside Hong Kong; (b) the person against or in relation to whom the act is committed or took place dies in Hong Kong as a result of the act; and (c) the act would, if taking place in Hong Kong constitute murder or manslaughter or being accessory to murder or manslaughter, whatever the citizenship or nationality of the person committing it or responsible for it, the act shall constitute the crime of, as may be appropriate, murder or manslaughter or so being accessory.

---

[19] Ibid., at 998.

[20] In *Somchai Liangsiriprasert v The Government of the United States of America and Another* [1990] 1 Hong Kong Law Reports 85.

[21] [1990] 2 Hong Kong Law Reports 612 (note that when sitting on appeal from a Hong Kong decision, the Privy Council constitutes part of the territory's judicial system).

[22] Sec. 8B (Chapter 212, Laws of Hong Kong 1990 ed.); note that the amendment in fact merely 'localises' (i.e. brings within the ambit of locally made laws) jurisdiction heretofore exercised under the Admiralty Offences (Colonial) Act 1849, section 3 of which deems the relevant offences taken place at sea or any place out of the Colony to have been 'wholly committed in [the] Colony'.

Such an assertion of jurisdiction — designed to apply mainly in circumstances where it may be difficult to locate the place of the actual offence, and confined to the general crimes of murder or manslaughter — appears to be consistent with international practices and expectations.

Freedom from interference

Like any 'subject' of international law vested with jurisdictional competence, Hong Kong may benefit from fundamental international principles designed to safeguard the exercise of its legitimate powers. Thus, by virtue of the principle of 'non-intervention',[23] Hong Kong should be guaranteed a right to exercise jurisdiction over its territory free from interference by any foreign state. Hong Kong's entitlement to self-determination and a 'high degree of autonomy' should equally prevent an assertion of jurisdiction by another state which would infringe its right freely to maintain its political, legal, economic, social or cultural system. Additionally, in line with the established principle of respect for territorial integrity, foreign states are enjoined from exercising enforcement powers (such as arrest or seizure of property to enforce a judgment) within the territory of Hong Kong, without the latter's consent.[24]

Extension of Chinese criminal jurisdiction to Hong Kong

In general, Chinese criminal jurisdiction reflects to a large extent recognized grounds of jurisdiction, such as the 'territorial principle', 'active personality principle',[25] 'protective principle',[26] 'passive personality

---

[23] Note that this principle forms one of the Five Principles of Peaceful Coexistence (EPPC) which are entrenched in the PRC Constitution. Its applicability in the context of different normative systems is aptly demonstrated by the 'one country, two systems' formula which has been said to provide a 'textbook model of creative and flexible application of the EPPC'. See S.S. Kim, 'The Development of International Law in Post-Mao China: Change and Continuity' (1987) 1 *Journal of Chinese Law* 117, 155.

[24] Such consent should not be lightly presumed, unless perhaps in circumstances entailing the commission of so-called 'universal crimes' (e.g. in order to seize terrorists or war criminals). Arguments of 'hot pursuit' (on land) may not be used in justification of arrests across the border in adjoining territory.

[25] Under this principle jurisdiction is assumed by the state of which the person, against whom proceedings are taken, is a national.

[26] Under the protective principle, a state can claim jurisdiction over offences committed outside its territory which are considered injurious to its security, integrity or vital economic interests. The principle is most often used in cases involving currency, immigration and economic offences but its application remains controversial in the light of potential for abuse (given that the state is presumed to be its own judge as to what endangers its security or essential interests).

principle',[27] and 'universality principle'.[28] Thus, for example, consistently with the territorial principle, the 1979 Criminal Law of the People's Republic of China[29] stipulates that '[t]he Law is applicable to all who commit crimes within the territory [including 'aboard a ship or airplane'] of the People's Republic of China except as specifically stipulated by law' [Article 3(1)(2)]. A version of the 'objective territorial principle' is embodied in another provision deeming a crime to have been committed within Chinese territory when 'either the act or consequence of a crime takes place within the territory of the People's Republic of China' [Article 3(3)].

Yet, notwithstanding apparent conformity with a common basis of jurisdiction, deviations from accepted international norms may occur if ideological considerations are allowed to enter the application of China's Criminal Law in respect of Hong Kong (which is ostensibly perceived, together with Taiwan, as part of 'one China'). Specifically, an assertion of Chinese criminal jurisdiction over acts committed in Hong Kong based on such construction of the territorial principle would transgress the proscription of non-intervention, which is grounded not only on respect for the sovereignty of other states but also in cognizance of the right of self-determination of national entities. It would equally encroach on the 'high degree of autonomy' pledged by China under the Sino-British Joint Declaration, echoed in official pronouncements and incorporated in formal constitutional documents (e.g. the Basic Law). Given, its implied recognition of the geographical 'separateness' of Hong Kong, as well as its intention, as signified in the Basic Law,[30] to confine the application of Chinese national laws to 'those relating to defence and foreign affairs' or 'other matters outside the limits of the autonomy of the Region', the Chinese government would arguably be 'stopped'[31] from extending jurisdiction to Hong Kong on territorial grounds.

---

[27] The most controversial of all grounds — jurisdiction is asserted over all crimes where the victim is a national, irrespective of the place where the crime was committed or the nationality of the offender.

[28] Under this principle, offences which are contrary to the interest of the international community as a whole — for example, piracy, war crimes, crimes against humanity — are regarded as *delicta jure gentium* and hence subject to the jurisdiction of *all* states irrespective of the nationality of the victim and perpetrator or the location of the offence.

[29] English translation in *The Criminal Law and the Criminal Procedure Law of China* (Beijing: Foreign Languages Press, 1984) 5–64.

[30] See Article 18 and Annex III (listing the 'National Laws to be Applied in Hong Kong Special Administrative Region').

[31] *Estoppel* is a general principle of international law, resting on the principles of good faith and consistency in state relations. It has 'played a significant role in territorial disputes' and 'may involve holding a government to a declaration which in fact does not correspond to its real intention'. See Brownlie, supra (note 12), at 161.

Finally, when exercising criminal jurisdiction by virtue of some form of the 'objective territorial principle', China, like any other member of the international community, is bound by the general rule of *nullum crimen nulla poena sine praevia lege* (the 'predictability' principle)[32] which mandates a precise legislative delimitation of the criminal law's scope of application.[33] Chinese legislative competence, when based on perceived 'effects' is further circumscribed by the widely-accepted doctrine of 'self-restraint'.[34]

Similar constraints should be imposed on Chinese claims of jurisdiction founded on the 'active personality principle'. Article 4 of the Criminal Law of the People's Republic provides for the Law to be applied to citizens who have committed the following crimes outside Chinese territory: counter-revolution, counterfeiting national currency and valuable securities, corruption,[35] accepting bribes, disclosing state secrets, posing as state personnel to deceive, and forging official documents, certificates and seals. Under Article 5, jurisdiction is also claimed in respect of crimes punishable by a 'minimum sentence of not less than a three-year fixed term of imprisonment' provided such crimes are also punishable according to the law of the place where committed.[36] Although generally within acceptable bounds, when combined with the Chinese broad criteria for ascribing nationality[37] and applied to ill-defined and politically charged

---

[32] The binding force of this rule under international law is grounded in the conventions relating to the protection of fundamental human rights.

[33] It may be noted that under the PRC Criminal Law, crimes not expressly stipulated may be 'determined and punished' according to the most closely 'analogous article', subject to approval of the Supreme People's Court (Article 79); needless to say, the use of analogy violates international law standards against *ex post facto* laws ('no one shall be held guilty of any criminal offence on account of any act or omission which did not constitute a criminal offence . . . at the time when it was committed' — International Covenant on Civil and Political Rights, Article 15).

[34] See Council of Europe, Select Committee of Experts on Extraterritorial Jurisdiction, *Report on Extraterritorial Criminal Jurisdiction* (Strasbourg, 1990).

[35] Citing Article 4, a member of China's Supreme People's Procuratorate has recently asserted the 'power to prosecute corrupt officials working for mainland enterprises in Hong Kong [and Macao]'. The claim has been countered by Hong Kong's Independent Commission Against Corruption, restating Hong Kong's jurisdiction over breaches of local law committed in the territory. See Connie Law, 'Mainland "Can Prosecute Chinese Officials in HK"'. *South China Morning Post*, 27 September 1994, at 6.

[36] Note that the 'double criminality' reflected hereby does not pertain to the crimes listed in Article 4.

[37] See the 1980 Nationality Law of the People's Republic of China (1980) 40 *Beijing Review* 17; see also the Chinese Memorandum, Sino-British Joint Declaration, which stipulates: 'Under the Nationality Law of the People's Republic of China, all Hong Kong Chinese compatriots, whether they are holders of the "British Dependent Territory citizen's passport" or not, are Chinese nationals.'

offences,[38] criminal jurisdiction thus based[39] could lead to objectionable consequences for the people of Hong Kong.

An unrestricted exercise of jurisdiction founded on the principle of 'protection' and 'passive personality'[40] would be similarly repudiated as contrary to the general objectives of international law.[41] The extension of Chinese criminal law to the broadly categorized 'crimes against the State of the PRC or against its citizens' committed by foreigners abroad, even if somewhat qualified by a 'double criminality' requirement,[42] lays wide open the possibility of abuse. Should excessive jurisdictional claims be nonetheless

---

[38] Of particular local concern is the malleable crime of 'counterrevolution', defined as 'all acts endangering the People's Republic of China committed with the goal of overthrowing the political power of the dictatorship of the proletariat and the socialist system' (Article 90); other provisions punish the use of 'counterrevolutionary slogans, leaflets or other means' to 'propagandise for and incite the overthrow of the dictatorship of the proletariat and the socialist system' (Article 102) and participation in a 'counterrevolutionary group' (Article 98).

[39] Note claims made in respect of residents of Taiwan as 'Chinese citizens': 'Operating on the premise that there is only one China, the PRC judiciary cannot treat cases involving people from Taiwan in the same manner as those involving foreigners from another country. Not only should the PRC's criminal laws be applied to crimes committed by Taiwan residents in the PRC, but they should also be applied to violations of PRC law in Taiwan. This will effectively protect the interests of citizens on both sides of the Strait': Zhao Bingzhi (Deputy Secretary General of the Criminal Law Institute of China), 'Issues in Criminal Law Across the Taiwan Strait' (1989) 3 *Journal of Chinese Law* 227, 229.

[40] Articles 6 and 7, the Criminal Law of the PRC.

[41] The rationale underlying the 'protective principle' is to enable jurisdiction over offences of utmost gravity and concern to the state against which they are directed, especially where in the absence of such jurisdiction offenders would escape punishment altogether because they did not contravene the law of the place where they were committed or because extradition would be refused by reason of political character of the offence. The assertion of jurisdiction on the basis of the 'passive personality principle' is considered both unnecessary (as the majority of criminal matters fall within the jurisdiction of at least one other state under the four recognized grounds) as well at variance with the 'well-settled principle that a person visiting a foreign country, far from radiating for his protection the jurisdiction of his own country, falls under the domination of the local law and, except so far as his government may diplomatically intervene in a case of a denial of justice, must look to that law for his protection'. *The Lotus Case* (France v Turkey) [1927] Permanent Court of International Justice Reports, Series A, No. 10 (*per* Judge Moore).

[42] Under Art 7 of the Criminal Law of the PRC, '[a]ny person who commits a crime outside the territory of the People's Republic of China and according to this Law should bear criminal responsibility may still be dealt with according to the Law even if he has been tried in a foreign country; however, a person who has already received criminal punishment *may* be exempted from punishment or given a mitigated punishment [emphasis added].'

asserted by China, Hong Kong is not inhibited[43] under international law from denying effect to such claims within its territory (by adopting 'blocking statutes' or invoking the *ordre public* defence). Yet, a more 'preventive' approach in the form of, for example, agreements concerning mutual assistance in criminal matters and extradition arrangements, would commend itself.

EXTRATERRITORIAL JURISDICTION

Is Hong Kong internationally barred from extending jurisdiction beyond its territorial boundaries?

Extraterritorial criminal jurisdiction

There is little doubt that Hong Kong's criminal law, like its common law counterparts, is essentially local in its effects, and that it does not concern itself with crimes committed abroad. The underlying rationale — to paraphrase the Privy Council's pronouncement in *Somchai Liangsiriprasert v Government of the United States of America and Another*[44] — is that the 'criminal law is developed to protect [the local society] and not that of other nations which must be left to make and enforce such laws as they see fit to protect their own societies . . . It was for this reason that the law of extradition was introduced between civilized nations so that fugitive offenders might be returned for trial in the country against whose laws they had offended.' Linking criminal jurisdiction with territory has also been justified on the grounds that state where the offending act is committed has the strongest interest in punishing it (i.e. to uphold law and order and deter criminal activities within its borders); that it is in this state that the offender is likely to be found; and that, generally, the state of the *locus delicti* is the most convenient forum for collection of evidence.[45]

In fact, according to the authors of the *Report on Extraterritorial Criminal Jurisdiction* (Strasbourg, 1990),[46] '[t]here seems to be no longer any major

---

[43] For the view that there exists in fact a rule of international law 'permitting' states not to recognize or give effect to extraterritorial norms adopted by other states see: P. Weil, 'International Law Limitations on State Jurisdiction' in C.J. Olmstead, *Extra-territorial Application of Laws and Responses Thereto* (Oxford: ESC Publishing Limited, 1984) 32, 36.

[44] See supra (note 20) at p. 619 (per Lord Griffiths).

[45] See G. Williams, 'Venue and Ambit of Criminal Law' (1965) 81 *Law Quarterly Review* 276, 276–7.

[46] Supra (note 34).

criminal law systems which do not base their rules on jurisdiction primarily on the principle of territoriality'. The 'territorial' approach, furthermore, is said[47] to be in harmony with contemporary international norms such as 'comity'[48] and 'non-intervention'[49], promoting distribution of competences among states based on reciprocity and tolerance. The paramountcy of the territoriality principle is clearly reflected in a domestic canon of statutory interpretation that a presumption exists according to which legislation does not apply extraterritorially unless the legislature has specifically indicated that it applies to acts or conduct abroad. In the words of Donalson LJ, 'every parliamentary draftsman writes on paper which bears the legend albeit in invisible ink, "this Act shall not have an extra-territorial effect, save to the extent that it expressly so provides"'.[50]

Be that as it may, while the primacy of the territorial principle of jurisdiction implies perhaps a need to justify the exercise of jurisdiction on the basis of other principles, public international law does not impose any limitations on the freedom of states to establish forms of extraterritorial criminal jurisdiction.[51] It appears that in general, if a state is able to identify a 'sufficient nexus between itself and the object of its assertion of jurisdiction',[52] no objections grounded in international law may be raised regarding legal competence, particularly where 'international solidarity' [in the fight against crime] is served.[53] By the same token, non-sovereign entities such as colonies or federal units are not internationally barred from extending

---

[47] Ibid.

[48] 'Comity is a notion which does not entail binding legal obligations, but presupposes —
(i) a reciprocal recognition of equality by the participants in international intercourse; and
(ii) mutual respect for the integrity of each of the participants in international intercourse.
The latter idea might also be expressed by stating that each participant in international intercourse is expected to observe an attitude of moderation and restraint *vis-a-vis* other participants in laying claims to exercise state authority outside its own national territory.'
Ibid.

[49] 'States must refrain from unjustified interference in the internal affairs of other states.'
Ibid.

[50] *R. v West Yorkshire Coroner, ex p. Smith* [1983] QB 335, 358; For a Hong Kong authority, see *Somchai Liangsiriprasert v The Government of the United States and Another,* supra (note 20) at p. 104 (*per* Fuad, V.-P.) [citing *Air India v Wiggins* (1980) 71 Cr App R 213, *per* Lord Diplock at p. 217]

[51] See the *Lotus* case, supra (note 41), at p. 214: 'Far from laying down a general prohibition to the effect that States may not extend the application of their laws and the jurisdiction of their courts to persons, property and acts outside their territory, [international law] leaves them in this respect a wide measure of discretion which is only limited in certain cases by prohibitive rules . . . '

[52] See Oxman, supra (note 5) at p. 278.

[53] See the Strasbourg Report, supra (note 34).

a [prescriptive] jurisdiction beyond their territorial boundaries.[54] Nor, for that matter, can a 'doctrine of colonial (criminal) extraterritorial incompetence' be said to exist under relevant constitutional theories, although the scope of power to legislate extraterritorially may differ between fully sovereign and subordinate legislatures.

As reaffirmed by the Hong Kong Court of Appeal in *The Queen v Lau Tung-sing*,[55] the 'issue is not whether the law has some extra-territorial application but whether it was enacted for the peace, order and good government of the colony. What the court must ask is whether, given the delegated legislative power of the colonial legislature, it is making a law with regard to matters that are properly its business'.[56] In fact, it was the Court's view that regardless of any extraterritorial application, a law which concerns itself with the peace, order and good government of Hong Kong is not the 'extraterritorial legislation' that may require special authorization or justification to rebut the presumption against extraterritoriality.

The formula 'for the peace, order and good government' is, in turn, to be interpreted 'liberally' and 'a court will not inquire whether any particular enactment of this character does in fact promote the peace, order or good government of the colony'.[57] In the event of ambiguity, the court will 'seek so to construe an Ordinance as to render its provisions consistent with the

---

54 See *Croft v Dunphy* [1933] AC 156 (PC) [*re* a 'Hovering Act' passed by the then Dominion Parliament of Canada — extraterritoriality itself does not invalidate the law as long as it is made in the valid exercise of a power conferred, whatever that power may be]; *Wallace Brothers & Co. Ltd. v Commissioner of Income Tax, Bombay City and Bombay Suburban District* (1948) LR 75 Ind App 86 (PC) ['There is no rule of law that the territorial limits of a subordinate legislature define the possible scope of its legislative enactments or mark the field open to its vision. The ambit of the powers possessed by a subordinate legislature depends on the proper construction of the statute conferring those powers. No doubt the enabling statute has to be read against the background that only a defined territory has been committed to the charge of the legislature. Concern by a subordinate legislature with affairs or persons outside its own territory may therefore suggest a query whether the legislature is in truth minding its own business. It does not compel the conclusion that it is not.']; *Robinson v Western Australia Museum* (Australia, HC) repr. in (1986) 70 *International Law Reports* 51 [federal units may operate extraterritorially as long as the extraterritorial operation is something which can be said to be for the peace, order and good of the government of the state].

55 [1989] 1 HKLR 490.

56 Ibid., at p. 500. The Court expressed reservations [ibid., at p. 496] with respect to the approach adopted in early Hong Kong decisions [e.g. *Re Iu Ki-shing* (1908) 3 HKLR 20; *Re Chan Yue-shan, ex p. King-po* (1909) 4 HKLR 128; *Wong Cheong-wai v S.S. Holstein* (1909) 4 HKLR 223] which sought to circumscribe a possible extraterritoriality fetter by deeming local ordinances that had been assented to or not disallowed by the Queen as the legislation of the British Crown and as such capable of having extraterritorial effect.

57 *Winfat Enterprises (H.K.) Co. Ltd. v Attorney General* [1983] HKLR 211, at 225.

comity of nations and the established rules of public international law'.[58] Thus, for example, the Court of Appeals rejected an argument put forward by the Appellant that the court had no jurisdiction to try him because the entire offence took place in China and that the law in question (Section 37J of the Immigration Ordinance) — which provides that any person in Hong Kong may be charged and convicted of offences which occur wholly or partly outside the territory — was extraterritorial and hence *ultra vires* to the powers of the Hong Kong legislature. The Court ruled that it was within the lawful power of the legislature to impose liabilities on a person who arranged for illegal immigrants to come to Hong Kong because the matter was sufficiently linked to the peace, order and good government of Hong Kong.[59] In a similar vein, '[t]he Hong Kong legislature could readily conclude that it was in the interests of "order and good government" that it should do everything in its power to meet [the threat posed to Hong Kong by the international drug trade] by legislating [with extraterritorial effects] against conduct in relation to dangerous drugs which was aimed or directed at Hong Kong.'[60]

Finally, a notice may be taken of recent authorizing statutes which should remove any persisting doubts concerning the competence of the Hong Kong legislature to enact laws which have extraterritorial effects. Thus, under the Hong Kong (Legislative Powers) Order 1986[61] (passed in pursuant to the Hong Kong Act 1985)[62], '[t]he Governor of Hong Kong, by and with the advice and consent of the Legislative Council of Hong Kong, may, in addition to any other power conferred on the legislature of Hong Kong . . . make laws having extra-territorial operation, being an enactment or laws relating to (i) civil aviation, (ii) merchant shipping, (iii) admiralty jurisdiction'. The Governor in Council is similarly empowered, by the Hong Kong (Legislative Powers) Order 1989,[63] to legislate extraterritorially 'to the extent required in order to give effect to an international agreement which applies to Hong Kong, and for connected purposes'.

It is indeed within the above contexts which have been selected for special authorization that assertions of extraterritorial jurisdiction by the Hong Kong government have manifested themselves. Thus, for example, Hong Kong's international responsibility in the area of marine pollution has given rise to

---

[58] Ibid.

[59] *Lau Tung-sing,* supra (note 55) at p. 500.

[60] *Somchai Liangsiriprasert v The Government of the United States of America and Another,* supra (note 20) at p. 105.

[61] LHK 1986 ed., App. III, W1.

[62] LHK 1985 ed., App. II, B1.

[63] LHK 1989 ed., App. III, T1.

legislation providing for extensive intervention powers (including the sinking and destruction of any ship) in relation to incidents on the high seas involving spillage of oil and other hazardous substances.[64] Similarly, the Dumping at Sea Act 1974 as applied to Hong Kong[65] imposes extraterritorial controls over 'British ships'[66] as well as [indirectly] regulating dumping activities of non-British ships outside Hong Kong territory by prohibiting their being loaded with material within Hong Kong, which is to be dumped either within or outside Hong Kong's territorial waters.[67]

Other illustrations of claims to extraterritorial jurisidiction arising out of implementation by Hong Kong of its international legal obligations pertain to offences committed on board aircrafts,[68] hijacking,[69] acts against the safety of civil aviation,[70] crimes against internationally protected persons,[71] hostage taking,[72] and genocide.[73] Yet, notwithstanding the general legitimacy accorded to jurisdiction (based on the 'universal principle'[74]) over these so-regarded

---

[64] See Merchant Shipping (Prevention and Control of Pollution) Ordinance No. 37 of 1990.

[65] See Dumping at Sea Act 1974 (Overseas Territories) Order 1975.

[66] Sec. 1, ibid. Note that the provisions against dumping at sea extend not only to ships but also to aircraft, hovercraft and marine structures — sec. 1(2).

[67] Sec. 1(1), ibid.

[68] See The Tokyo Convention Act 1967 (Overseas Territories) Order 1968 and the Extradition (Tokyo Convention) Order 1971 [extending to Hong Kong the 1963 Convention on Offences and Certain Other Acts Commited on Board Aircraft (1969) UKTS 126, Cmnd. 4230].

[69] See The Hijacking Act 1971 (Overseas Territories) Order 1971 and the Extradition (Hijacking) Order 1971 [extending to Hong Kong the 1970 Convention for the Suppression of Unlawful Seizure of Aircraft (1972) UKTS 39, Cmnd. 4956].

[70] See The Protection of Aircraft Act 1973 (Overseas Territories) Order 1973 and the Extradition (Protection of Aircraft) Order 1973 [extending to Hong Kong the 1971 Convention for the Suppression of Unlawful Acts Against the Safety of Civil Aviation (1974) UKTS 10, Cmnd. 5524].

[71] See Internationally Protected Persons Act 1078 (Overseas Territories) Order 1979 and the Extradition (Internationally Protected Persons) Order 1979 [extending to Hong Kong the 1973 Convention on the Prevention and Punishment of Crimes Against Internationally Protected Persons, Including Diplomatic Agents (1980) UKTS 3, Cmnd. 7765].

[72] See The Taking of Hostages Act 1982 (Overseas Territories) Order 1982 and Extradition (Taking of Hostages) Order 1985 [extending to Hong Kong the 1979 Convention Against the Taking of Hostages (1980) Misc. 12, Cmnd. 7893].

[73] See Extradition (Genocide) Order 1970 [extending the 1948 Convention on the Prevention and Punishment of the Crime of Genocide (1970) UKTS 58, Cmnd. 4421].

[74] The 'universal principle' of jurisdiction is premised on the recognition that certain offences are so heinous and so widely condemned that 'any state if it captures the offender may prosecute and punish that person on behalf of the world community regardless of the nationality of the offender or victim or where the crime was committed.' See M. Bassiouni (ed.), *International Criminal Law,* Vol. II (Dobbs Ferry, N.Y.: Transnational Publishers, 1986) p. 298.

'international crimes',[75] it is doubtful that the Hong Kong authorities will assume jurisdiction unless the offender is found to be present in the territory and extradition is not available.

Nor for that matter is another recognized basis for jurisdiction, namely the 'protective principle',[76] likely to be extensively utilized in the absence of other factors tying the accused to the forum. The local law, however, contains several examples of jurisdictional assertions which are justifiable on such a principle.[77] It is also arguable that the formula of 'peace, order and good government' resorted to by Hong Kong judges[78] combines the 'protective' and 'effects' approaches in establishing the courts' jurisdiction.

Extraterritorial civil jurisdiction

Local assertions of jurisdiction over civil wrongdoings have been largely confined to claims exhibiting some form of 'territorial' link. In fact, even where Hong Kong law[79] has conferred on the courts discretionary power to allow 'service outside the jurisdiction', the plaintiff must establish the existence of one of the territorial connecting factors[80] enumerated in the

---

[75] See *United States of America v Unis (No. 2)*, US District Ct, Dist. of Columbia, repr. in (1990) 82 *International Law Reports* 343, 348–9, for the ruling that offences of aircraft piracy and hostage taking, which had been widely condemned by a majority of states in a series of international agreements, were recognized as universal crimes over which all states could exercise jurisdiction; In *Regina v Finta*, repr. in (1990) 82 *International Law Reports* 425, 443–7, Canada's High Court of Justice held that '[i]t was generally recognized that war crimes and crimes against humanity fell within the category of international crimes over which any state could exercise jurisdiction over an individual found within its territory irrespective of the place where the alleged offences of that individual were committed'; In *DPP v Doot* 1973 AC 807, Lord Wilberforce was of the opinion that drugs-related offences were crimes of universal jurisdiction.

[76] Under this principle a state may exercise jurisdiction over acts committed abroad which are prejudicial to its security and national interests — see Harvard Research in International Law, 'Draft Convention on Jurisdiction With Respect to Crime' (1935) 29 *American Journal of International Law* Supp. 435, 445.

[77] See, e.g. provisions pertaining to treason, offences against the Crown such as incitement to mutiny, incitement to disaffection, seditious intentions, forgery of public documents, coinage offences — Crimes Ordinance (Cap. 200, 1984 ed.) and bribery [Prevention of Bribery Ordinance (Cap. 201, 1987 ed.).

[78] See supra (notes 55, 57, 60 and the respective text).

[79] See Rules of the Supreme Court, Order 11.

[80] The various heads of jurisdiction include territorially-related subject-matters, e.g. torts committed in Hong Kong, contracts or trusts governed by the Hong Kong law, land or property situate in Hong Kong. Note that jurisdiction founded on subject-matter is regarded as acceptable under contemporary international law. See Akehurst, supra (note 1) at p. 175.

relevant statute (apart from satisfying the court that there is a 'good arguable' case on the merits and that the case is a proper one for service out of the jurisdiction). Similarly, where a foreign defendant is summoned before a Hong Kong court, a determination of jurisdiction would generally involve an assessment of the defendant's contacts with the territory and consideration of whether the local court is the 'appropriate forum'.[81]

At the same time, in line with the wide admiralty powers devolved on Hong Kong[82] (as part of an expanded British admiralty jurisdiction) and consistent with an international convention extended to the territory by the United Kingdom, the Hong Kong authorities are empowered to exercise jurisdiction[83] in actions arising out of the collision of ships, whether the collision occurred on the high seas or in the waters of a foreign state. Yet, notwithstanding the admiralty jurisdiction vested in them, the local courts, as 'masters of their own procedure', retain the power, inherent or statutory, to stay proceedings. In exercising their procedural jurisdiction, they engage in a three-stage process to determine a) whether it has been shown that Hong Kong was not the appropriate forum and that another forum was more appropriate; b) whether the plaintiff has demonstrated the existence of any personal or juridical advantages which would not be available in the foreign forum; and c) whether it was just to allow the plaintiff to exploit the Hong Kong advantages or unjust to confine the plaintiff to the remedies obtainable in the foreign court.[84]

The apparent reluctance of Hong Kong judges to surrender jurisdiction to foreign courts aside, no clear 'homeward trend' (i.e. the 'tendency to arrive if possible at the application of domestic law')[85] may be discerned. Normal choice of law rules are complied with and the *lex fori* is not generally applied

---

[81] See *The Owners of Cargo lately laden on board the Ship or Vessel 'Adhiguna Meranti' v The Owners of the Ships or Vessels 'Adhiguna Harapan' and Others* [1987] HKLR 904; *Deak Perera Far East Limited (in Liquidation) v R Leslie Deak,* Civ. App. No. 116 of 1990, 18 December 1990 (CA); *The Owners of Cargo Lately Laden on Board the Ship or Vessel 'Lanka Muditha' v The Owners of the Ship or Vessel 'Lanka Athula',* Civ. App. No. 101 of 1990, 7 March 1991 (CA); *First National Bank of Chicago v Carroway Enterprises Ltd.* [1990] 2 HKLR 10 (HC); *Louvet v Louvet* [1990] 1 HKLR 670 (CA).

[82] See Admiralty Jurisdiction (Hong Kong) Order in Council 1962, S.I. No. 1547.

[83] Jurisdiction is established through the arrest of the defendant ship or a sister ship under the provisions of Secs. 1 & 3(iv) of the Administration of Justice Act 1956, applied to Hong Kong by the Admiralty Jurisdiction (Hong Kong) Order in Council 1962, ibid.

[84] See *The Adhiguna Meranti,* supra (note 81).

[85] See Michael Akehurst, 'Jurisdiction in International Law' (1972–73) 46 *British Yearbook of International Law* 145, 185. It is Akehurst's view that although a systematic application of the *lex fori* in all cases may not be in accordance with public international law, the prevalence of such a practice casts doubts on the existence of a general rule to this effect. Ibid., at p. 187.

to facts which have little or no connection with Hong Kong. The local courts, however, will follow their UK counterparts in excluding the application of penal,[86] revenue[87] or other public laws[88] as well as expropriatory laws[89] of a foreign state. In fact, the courts have been content to merely reaffirm the application in Hong Kong of the 'well-settled conflict of laws principle which is set out as Rule 3 in 1 *Dicey and Morris on Conflict of Law*',[90] and have not attempted to explore any underlying international norms which may mandate a refusal to recognize foreign public laws.[91] Nor, for that matter, have the Hong Kong courts relied upon notions of judicial restraint or domestic public policy to support decisions to reject or accept foreign public laws.[92]

The unwillingness of the Hong Kong judges to embrace a more 'doctrinal' approach also means that no firm observations may be made regarding their response to excessive jurisdiction claims on behalf of other states. It is thus not clear to what extent the local courts would resist the prevalent attempts by some states to impose their economic laws and regulations upon, or exercise procedural authority over, conduct of foreign persons or corporations or acts and property outside their territories, if these could not be readily categorized as 'penal, revenue or other public law'. The

---

[86] Including all breaches of public law subject to monetary punishment at the instance of government.

[87] e.g. laws imposing income tax, profits levy, succession duty, municipal rates, customs duty.

[88] e.g. import and export regulations, price control regulations, anti-trust legislation.

[89] i.e. laws which deprive those to whom it apply of property or interests in property.

[90] See *Nanus Asia co. Inc. v Standard Chartered Bank* [1990] 1 HKLR 396 at 406. 'Rule 3. English courts have no jurisdiction to entertain an action: (1) for the enforcement, either directly or indirectly, of a penal, revenue or other public law of a foreign state.' Applying this rule, the court held that US civil treble penalty provisions as well as disgorgement proceedings under the Securities Exchange Act to recover money generated as a result of insider tradings are 'penal' laws and could not be enforced (hence, orders made under these two fold provisions cannot be invoked by way of defence to the plaintiff originating summonses).

[91] The modern view is that there is 'no general rule of public international law prohibiting the transnational recognition or enforcement of foreign public laws'. See *Report of the International Committee on Transnational Recognition and Enforcement of Foreign Public Laws* in ILA Warsaw Conference 1988. Evidently, 'if a rule of foreign law is intrinsically repugnant to public international law, or if its application would in the circumstances of a case clearly involve contravention of some established rules of public international law, that rule of foreign law, be it public or private law, should not be applied in any Forum'. Ibid.

[92] Presumably to avoid problems of comity and international relations implicated by a rejection of foreign judgments on the basis of domestic policy.

Hong Kong legislature, it may be added, has not followed its British,[93] Canadian[94] or Australian[95] counterparts in reacting legislatively to what are perceived to be exorbitant assertions of extraterritorial jurisdiction.

PERSONAL JURISDICTION

Over whom can Hong Kong's jurisdiction extend by virtue of the 'personal' ('national') link?

Personal criminal jurisdiction

Given the ambiguities surrounding the 'Hong Kong nationality', it is not surprising that the 'personality principle' of jurisdiction is infrequently invoked by the local authorities as a basis for jurisdiction over offences or civil wrongs committed outside the territory. Recent legislation,[96] however, has confirmed local jurisdiction over acts of any 'British national' — defined as including a [Hong Kong] British Dependent Territories Citizen, a British Overseas Citizen and British National (Overseas)[97] — which take place 'on board a Hong Kong ship in any port or harbour outside Hong Kong' or 'on board a ship which is neither a Hong Kong ship nor a ship to which the person belongs'.[98] As a 'flag state', Hong Kong would also exercise jurisdiction over '[a]ny act of any person which . . . takes place on board a Hong Kong ship on the high seas' (which would constitute an offence under the law of Hong Kong, were it to take place here).[99]

---

[93] See The Protection of Trading Interests Act, Stats. UK 1980, C. 11.

[94] See Foreign Extraterritorial Measures Act, S.C. 1984, C. 49; The Combines Investigation Act, R.S.C. 1970, C. c-23.

[95] See Foreign Antitrust Judgments (Restriction of Enforcement) Act 1979, repr. in (1979) 18 *International Legal Materials* 869.

[96] See Criminal Law (Amendment) Ordinance No. 89 of 1990.

[97] Ibid., sec. 2 (amending Part III of the Crimes Ordinance by adding after section 23 — '23A. Interpretation . . .')

[98] Ibid., sec. 2 (amending Part III of the Crimes Ordinance by adding section 23B(3)). In fact, the new section merely 'localizes' part of section 686 of the Merchant Shipping Act 1894 extended to Hong Kong thus far.

[99] Ibid. [making criminal acts now triable in Hong Kong by virtue of jurisdiction conferred by UK enactments (sec. 1 of the Offences at Sea Act 1799, sec. 1 of the Admiralty Offences (Colonial) Act 1849 and part of sec. 686 of the Merchant Shipping Act 1894) offences under the law of Hong Kong itself].

The 'nationality' nexus in respect of ships has been determined under the law[100] to be the mere registration or licensing of the ship in Hong Kong, rather than a more 'genuine link' which is currently expected under general international law.[101]For the purpose of jurisdiction (in respect of offences against the person or against property committed either ashore or afloat, in any place outside Hong Kong) the personal link is even further extended to 'any master, seaman or apprentice who at the time when the offence is committed is, or *at any time within the previous 3 months* was, employed in any Hong Kong ship'.[102]

In accordance with the Chicago Convention on International Civil Aviation, which is applicable in Hong Kong,[103] registration of aircraft in the territory would render the government 'competent to exercise jurisdiction over offences and acts committed on board' [Article 3(1)]; indeed, would require it to take 'such measures as may be necessary to establish its jurisdiction as the state of registration over offences committed on board' [Article 3(2)].[104] The establishment of a local aircraft register, as laid down by the Sino-British Joint Declaration,[105] would clearly provide additional scope for the application of Hong Kong's criminal law.

---

[100] See supra (note 82).

[101] See Art. 5, 1958 Convention on the High Seas (extended to Hong Kong by the UK, (1963) UKTS 5, Cmnd. 1929); Art. 91, 1982 UN Convention on the Law of the Sea, repr. in (1982) 21 *International Legal Materials* 1261; UN Convention on Conditions for Registration of Ships, repr. in (1987) 26 *International Legal Materials* 1229. The latter two conventions are not yet in force but the Law of the Sea Convention on this point is generally regarded as expressing existing customary international law. It may be interesting to note that, while offering favourable tax rates, the proposed new shipping register for the Hong Kong Special Administrative Region [HKSAR] seeks to avoid the possibility of Hong Kong being branded a 'flag of convenience' by introducing a 'genuine link' clause. Under such a clause, although the ship need not be owned by Hong Kong concerns to fly the flag, representatives of owning companies must be physically based in Hong Kong.

[102] See supra (note 82) ['localizing' sec. 687 of the Merchant Shipping Act 1894] [emphasis added].

[103] By virtue of the Civil Aviation Act 1949 (Overseas Territories) Order 1969 and the Air Navigation (Overseas Territories) Order 1977.

[104] Note, however, that the Convention provides remarkably wide bases for concurrent jurisdiction by states other than the state of registration over events happening on board an aircraft — see Art. 4.

[105] Sec. IX, Annex I, Joint Declaration of the Government of the United Kingdom of Great Britain and Northern Ireland and the Government of the People's Republic of China on the Question of Hong Kong (1985) UKTS 26, Cmnd. 9543.

Personal civil jurisdiction

Like in other common law systems, civil jurisdiction in Hong Kong is seldom founded on the nationality of the parties.[106] Under local law,[107] the 'personal' link — generally presumed to underlie the assertion of jurisdiction in actions involving matters of personal status — is to be determined primarily by reference to the notion of 'domicile' (i.e. place of permanent home). As remarked above, the problematic nature of the Hong Kong nationality lends some support to the adoption locally of domicile as a major 'connecting factor'. However, certain conditions mandated by the concept — for instance, residence free from contemplation of certain events which will cause a termination of the residence — render 'domicile' unsuitable in circumstances such as in Hong Kong of people beset by an uncertain future.

It is not surprising therefore that the less complex[108] concept of 'ordinary residence' has been incorporated into the domestic law. Thus, for example, it forms a basis of jurisdiction in proceedings by a wife for divorce[109] and nullity,[110] in an action for judicial separation,[111] in a petition by a wife for presumption of death and dissolution of marriage[112] as well as in bankruptcy proceedings.[113] A defendant's ordinary residence provides a plaintiff with a ground on which to support an application to the court to exercise jurisdiction 'extraterritorially'.[114] Such a residence in relation to corporations has been held to be the place of 'central management and control' (i.e. where policy and commercial decisions are made).[115] It may also be noted that ordinary residence is a significant *nexus* with respect to both immigration issues in

---

[106] Note that for some conflict of laws purposes (and to avoid potential conflicts with other legal systems), nationality has been admitted as a relevant connecting factor. See, e.g. Wills Ordinance (Cap. 30, 1970 ed.) sec. 24 [formal validity of wills]; Matrimonial Causes Ordinance (Cap. 179, LHK 1983 ed.) sec. 56 [recognition of the validity of an overseas divorce or legal separation].

[107] See, e.g. Matrimonial Causes Ordinance, ibid., secs. 3, 4, 5, 6, 49(4).

[108] Although not devoid of difficulties, e.g. in relation to prolonged absences or illegality of stay.

[109] Matrimonial Causes Ordinance, ibid., sec. 3(b)(i).

[110] Ibid., sec. 4(b)(i).

[111] Ibid., sec. 5(b).

[112] Ibid., sec. 6(1)(b).

[113] See Bankruptcy Ordinance (Cap. 6, LHK 1986 rev. ed.) sec. 3(2)(b) [a 'debtor' is defined as including any person, whether British subject or not, who at the time when any act of bankruptcy was done or suffered by him was ordinarily resident in Hong Kong].

[114] RSC, Order 11, rule (1)(a).

[115] See *The Owners of Cargo Lately Laden on Board the Ship Artemis v Artemis Transportation Corp. and Barber Ship Management Ltd.*, [1983] HKLR 364.

Hong Kong[116] and abode rights in the Hong Kong Special Administrative Region.[117] On the other hand, neither residence nor nationality are the determined persons' amenability to Hong Kong's tax law. Rather, '[a]s a colonial territory Hong Kong adopted the Model Colonial Ordinance and, with it, the source-based system of taxation'.[118] Thus, '[t]he basic principle of the Inland Revenue Ordinance is that only income arising in or derived from a source in Hong Kong is subject to tax'.[119]

EXCEPTIONS FROM JURISDICTION

Who is immune from Hong Kong's jurisdiction?

Consistent with its international legal obligations, as contained in the relevant international conventions which have been extended to the territory,[120] as well as the pertinent customary international law, immunity from Hong Kong's jurisdiction is granted to foreign states, their Heads and public ships, diplomatic and consular representatives of foreign states, international organizations, and visiting armed forces.

---

[116] See Immigration Ordinance (Cap. 115, LHK 1989 rev. ed.), sec. 2 and First Schedule [defining a permanent resident of Hong Kong as 'any person who is wholly or partly of Chinese race and has at any time been ordinary resident in Hong Kong for a continuous period of not less than 7 years . . .']

[117] See BL, Art. 24 (permanent residents of the HKSAR).

[118] See A. Halkyard and M. Olesnicky, 'Revenue Law' in R. Wacks (ed.), *The Law in Hong Kong 1969–1989* (Hong Kong: Oxford University Press, 1989) 233 at p. 234.

[119] Loc.cit.

[120] See 1946 Convention on Privileges and Immunities of the United Nations, (1950) UKTS 10, Cmnd. 7891; 1947 Convention with annexes on the Privileges and Immunities of the Specialized Agencies of the United Nations, (1959) UKTS 69, Cmnd. 855; 1961 Convention on Diplomatic Relations, (1965) UKTS 19, Cmnd. 2565 [applied in Hong Kong by the International Organizations and Diplomatic Privileges Ordinance (Cap. 190); Diplomatic Privileges Act 1964]; 1963 Convention on consular Relations, (1973) UKTS 14, Cmnd. 5219 [applied in Hong Kong by the Consular Relations Ordinance (Cap. 259); Consular Relations Act 1968; Consular conventions Ordinance (Cap. 267)]; 1972 European Convention on State Immunity, (1979) UKTS 74, Cmnd. 7742 [applied in Hong Kong by the State Immunity (Overseas Territories) Order 1979, S.I. 1979, No. 458]; see also 1926 Convention and 1934 Protocol for the Unification of Certain Rules concerning the Immunity of State-Owned Vessels, (1980) UKTS 15, Cmnd. 7800 [applied in Hong Kong by the State Immunity (Overseas Territories) Order 1979, S.I. 1979, No. 111].

Sovereign (state) immunity

The position adopted by the local courts with respect to sovereign (state) immunity largely reflects the prevailing 'doctrine of restrictive immunity', whereby a foreign state is allowed immunity for 'sovereign' (*jure imperii*) acts only. Indeed, as early as 1956, it was held 'necessary for the foreign sovereign, if he wishes to discharge the onus of satisfying the court that he is entitled to sovereign immunity [in a case concerning alleged seizure of property], to produce satisfactory evidence that the property seized is dedicated or destined to *public use*'.[121] In a similar vein, no claims of immunity from jurisdiction would be entertained in proceedings related to acts *jure gestionis* (commercial acts).[122] Thus, '[s]eagoing vessels owned or operated by states, cargoes owned by them, and cargoes and passengers carried on Government vessels, and the states owning or operating such vessels, or owning such cargoes' are subject to the jurisdiction of Hong Kong courts and to the 'same rules of liability and the same obligations as those applicable to private vessels, cargoes and equipments.'[123] On the other hand, excepted from any judicial process are 'ships of war, Government yachts, patrol vessels, hospital ships, auxiliary vessels, supply ships, and other craft owned or operated by a State, and used at the time a cause of action arises exclusively on Governmental and non-commercial service'.[124] Comparable exemptions are granted under the Merchant shipping (Liability and Compensation for Oil Pollution) Ordinance[125] to 'any warship or any ship for the time being used by the government of any state for a purpose other than a commercial purpose'.

---

[121] [Emphasis added] *Midland Investment Co. Ltd. v The Bank of Communications* [1956] HKLR 42, 48 [dismissing an application by the defendant to set aside the proceedings on the ground that the court had no jurisdiction to entertain the action as it impleads the sovereign state of China]. Such an approach was later affirmed by the Full Court which ruled that immunity should be granted only where it was established that the vessel in respect of which it was claimed was 'destined for public use'. *Wallem Shipping (Hong Kong) Ltd and Another v The Owners of 'Philippine Admiral'* [1974] HKLR 111, 145; The court further observed that not every use which is for the public benefit may be regarded as 'public use' and that an element of immediate control by the foreign government is required. Ibid., at 146.

[122] As identified and listed, for example, under the 1972 European Convention on State Immunity.

[123] See the Brussels Convention for the Unification of Certain Rules Concerning the Immunity of State-owned Vessels.

[124] Ibid., Art. 3.

[125] No. 37 of 1990 (implementing in Hong Kong the 1969 Convention on civil Liability for Oil Pollution Damage).

It may be assumed that HKSAR judges will continue to follow the 'restrictive approach' to state immunity as incorporated in the common law, although this may give rise to some doctrinal conflicts with their Mainland counterparts. China's practice relating to sovereign immunity, while not always consistent,[126] reflects a determined adherence to the doctrine of absolute immunity. Chinese authorities have repeatedly asserted the incompatibility of compulsory jurisdiction over a foreign state with the principle of sovereign equality.[127] They have also rejected the restrictive doctrine as practically unworkable and noted the 'arbitrary and varied practice' involved in distinguishing between sovereign and non-sovereign acts.[128] Chinese officials have further contended that allowing foreign states to be sued in domestic courts would result in international tension and disruption to intergovernmental trading arrangements.[129] At the same time, the PRC, consistently with its pragmatic attitude to foreign relations, has not found it objectionable to conclude treaties with other states which provide for the waiver of immunity.[130] It has also acceded to some multilateral conventions which embody 'restrictive' elements of state immunity.[131]

A potential for a rift in the context of sovereign immunity may nonetheless be anchored in China's generally blurred boundaries between

---

[126] See R. O'Brien, 'Sovereign Immunity and the People's Republic of China' (1983) 13 *Hong Kong Law Journal* 202.

[127] See *Aide Memoire* submitted by the Chinese Minister of Foreign Affairs, Wu Xueqian to the US Secretary of State, George Shultz during the latter's visit to China, 10 February 1983, repr. in (1983) 22 *International Legal Materials* 81: 'Sovereign immunity is an important principle of international law. It is based on the principle of sovereign equality of all states as affirmed by the Charter of the United Nations. As a sovereign state, China incontestably enjoys judicial immunity. It is in utter violation of the principle of international law of sovereign equality of all states and the UN Charter that a district court of the United States should exercise jurisdiction over a suit against a sovereign state as a defendant, make a judgment by default and even threaten to execute the judgment. The Chinese Government firmly rejects this practice of imposing US domestic law on China to the detriment of China's sovereignty and national dignity. Should the US side, in defiance of international law, execute the above-mentioned judgment [*Huguang Railway Bonds case*] and attach China's property in the United States, the Chinese Government reserves the right to take measures accordingly.' See also Wang Houli (Director of the Department of Treaties and Law of the Chinese Ministry of Foreign Affairs), 'Sovereign Immunity: Chinese Views and Practices' (1987) 1 *Journal of Chinese Law* 23.

[128] See Houli, ibid., at p. 29.

[129] See ibid., at p. 30.

[130] See Huang Jin and Ma Jingsheng, 'Immunities of States and Their Property: The Practice of the People's Republic of China' (1989) *Hague Year Book of International Law* 163, 165–6.

[131] e.g. 1969 International Convention on Civil Liability for Oil Pollution Damage; 1944 Chicago Convention on Civil Aviation. See Huang & Ma, ibid., at 166–7.

the state and 'state-owned' corporations, enterprises or property (e.g. vessels). Although it has been suggested that recent legislation gives expression to a Chinese recognition of the separate personalities of certain economic entities,[132] some difficulties may still be anticipated given the degree to which state and commercial activities are inextricably tied in the PRC. Such difficulties could possibly be obviated if the more contemporary 'functional' test[133] — as distinct from 'status' or 'legal personality' tests — is adopted. Accordingly, whether an entity qualifies for 'state immunity' will be determined not by the separateness of its legal personality or its place in the government machinery but in reference to the governmental or public nature of the transactions or acts which give rise to the claim.[134]

Apart from doctrinal concerns, skeptics have also questioned the competence of courts in the Hong Kong Special Administrative Region to rule on questions of sovereign immunity, given the exclusion of foreign and defence affairs from the jurisdiction of the local courts. Yet, such an inhibited perception is manifestly inconsistent with the 'independent judicial power' vested in the HKSAR under both the Sino-British Joint Declaration[135] and the Basic Law[136] (as well as incompatible with the Region's generally wide responsibility for external affairs).[137] To preserve also congruity with the constitutional doctrines hitherto affecting the decision-making process by local judges,[138] no wholesale ousting of the courts' jurisdiction should be envisaged. Rather, while the conduct of foreign affairs may not attract judicial

---

[132] See Huang & Ma, supra (note 130) at 174–6 [citing the 1982 Regulations of the People's Republic of china on the Exploitation of Offshore Petroleum Resources in Co-operation with Foreign Enterprises, Art. 5(2) — according judicial personality to the China National Offshore Oil Company; 1983 Interim Regulations on State-Owned Industrial Enterprises, Art. 8 — providing state enterprises with legal personality; 1986 General Principles of the Civil Code of the People's Republic of China, Arts. 36(1), 41(1), 48 — status of state-owned enterprises as legal persons].

[133] See, e.g. Art. 3 of the International Law Commission Draft Articles on Jurisdictional Immunities of States and their Property, repr. in (1987) 26 *International Legal Materials* 625.

[134] Thus, e.g. state-owned ships, if employed in commercial service, would not constitute state instrumentalities for the purpose of state immunity.

[135] JD, Annex III, Sec. III.

[136] BL, Art. 19.

[137] See JD, Annex I, Sec. XI; BL, Chap. VII; specifically, the reference to the SAR's authority 'on its own, using the name "Hong Kong, China" [to] maintain and develop relations and conclude and implement agreements with states, regions and relevant international organizations in the appropriate fields . . .'

[138] Note that under the Basic Law, ibid., '[t]he courts of the Hong Kong special Administrative Region shall have jurisdiction over all cases in the Region, except that the restrictions on their jurisdiction imposed by the *legal system and principles previously in force in Hong Kong* shall be maintained' [emphasis added].

review,[139] the courts are not prevented from adjudicating upon other aspects of the cases before them. Thus, where certain questions arise in the course of proceedings concerning facts, circumstances, or events which are 'peculiarly within the cognisance of the Executive'[140] (e.g. extent of territory, existence of a state of war, belligerency or neutrality, or recognition of a state or government), Hong Kong judges would be expected (by virtue of the principle that the courts should in such matters 'speak with the same voice as the Executive')[141] to seek the executive's statement or certification.[142] Once granted, such a statement or certificate would be binding and conclusive, although the legal effects of the certified 'facts of state' (as well as the interpretation of the certificate itself) is a matter that falls solely within the province of the judiciary.[143]

It is, of course, conceivable that the SAR courts would find it inexpedient to investigate the actions of a foreign state even though they fall within their formal jurisdiction.[144] Clearly, given their customary conservative attitude and the 'judicial restraint and abstention' which is 'inherent in the very nature of the judicial process',[145] the local judges may be trusted not to 'embarrass or interfere with the Executive'[146] or prejudice the PRC government in the conduct of its foreign policy.

Diplomatic/consular immunities

State representatives enjoy in Hong Kong jurisdictional immunities with respect to their person, property and servants, in accordance with local legislation which complies generally with relevant international standards.

---

[139] Note however that the so-called Act of State doctrine as a bar to judicial investigation of the validity of acts of foreign governments is not a rule of general international law. In fact, as observed by an expert, there is 'no trace' of such a doctrine outside Anglo-American law and there is on the other hand 'much authority of the greatest weight for its rejection in Europe.' See F.A. Mann, *Foreign Affairs in English Courts* (Oxford: Clarendon Press, 1986) pp. 175–6.

[140] Mann, ibid., at p. 23.

[141] *Re Westinghouse Uranium Contract* [1978] AC 547, 617.

[142] Such a notion is incorporated in Art. 19 of the Basic Law which stipulates: 'The courts of the Region shall obtain a certificate from the Chief Executive on questions of fact concerning acts of state such as defence and foreign affairs whenever such questions arise in the adjudication of cases . . . Before issuing such a certificate, the Chief Executive shall obtain a certifying document from the Central People's Government.'

[143] See Mann, supra (note 139) at p. 52.

[144] Following authorities such as *Luther v Sagor* [1921] 3 KB 532; *Buttes Gas & Oil Co. v Hammer (Nos. 2 & 3)* [1982] AC 888; and *Fayed v Al-Tajir* [1987] ALL E R 396.

[145] *Buttes Gas v Hammer,* ibid., at 932 (per Lord Wilberforce).

[146] The rationale underlying the 'Act of State' doctrine: see the leading American decision in *Baker v Carr* 369 US 186 (1962).

Similar immunities and privileges are conferred on international organizations and the persons connected with such organizations;[147] on judges and registrars of the International Court of Justice as well as suitors to that court, their agents, counsel and advocates;[148] and on senior officers of the Commonwealth Secretariat.[149] Special ordinances have been enacted to grant privileges and immunities in Hong Kong to the local Visa Office of the Ministry of Foreign Affairs of the PRC, its officers and their dependents as well as to the Chinese members of the Joint Liaison Group, to the Chinese members of the Land Commission and to certain other persons' (including 'experts' and 'supporting staff' and their dependents).[150]

The Consular Relations Ordinance[151] — which as its (long) title proclaims, is designed '[t]o give effect in Hong Kong to the Vienna convention on Consular Relations' and 'to enable effect to be given in Hong Kong to other agreements entered into by Her Majesty's Government in the United Kingdom concerning consular relations' — grants consular officers and consular employees immunity from the jurisdiction of the local judicial and administrative authorities regarding acts performed in the exercise of consular functions.[152] Under the same Ordinance, the Governor is also

---

[147] Sec. 2, International Organizations and Diplomatic Privileges Act (Cap. 190, LHK 1977 ed.). Notifications of application have been made with respect to FAO, IMCO, IAEA, ICAO, ILO, ITU, UN, UNESCO, UPU, WHO, WMO, ADB, APTN (Asia-Pacific Telecommunity Notification). See also Privileges and Immunities (International Committee of the Red Cross) (Cap. 402, LHK 1984 ed.) [granting immunity from suit and legal process to the Committee and its delegates].

[148] Sec. 4, Cap. 190 ibid.

[149] Sec. 7, ibid.

[150] See Chinese Visa Office (Privileges and Immunities) Ordinance (Cap. 224, LHK 1984 ed.) and Privileges and Immunities (Joint Liaison Group and Land Commission) Ordinance (Cap. 36, LHK 1985 ed.) respectively.

[151] Cap. 259, LHK 1970 ed.

[152] Note, however, that consistently with the Vienna Convention on Consular Relations (Art. 41), the Ordinance permits the arrest or detention of consular officers in the case of a 'grave crime' [defined as 'any offence punishable (on a first conviction) with a term that may extend to five years or with a more severe sentence'] and pursuant to a decision by the competent judicial authority. The application of this provision provoked some controversy in Hong Kong when the Venezuelan Consul-General was arrested by the Independent Commission Against Corruption [ICAC] in connection with offences under the Prevention of Bribery Ordinance. Questions were raised, for example, with regards to (a) the differing perceptions of the countries involved as to what is a 'grave crime'; (b) the meaning of 'pursuant to a decision by the competent judicial authority' (the decision in question was said to have been taken by the Governor, after a provisional warrant was issued by a magistrate and following consultation with London). Another issue brought up on that occasion pertained to a more general claim of consul-generals in Hong Kong for assimilation of their status to that of diplomatic representatives given the 'political importance of Hong Kong'. See R. Vines, 'Diplomats Call for Governor to Resign' *South China Morning Post*, 15 March 1990 at p. 1.

authorized to make by order 'provision for securing that, where an offence is alleged to have been committed on board any ship [or aircraft] by the master or a member of the crew and the ship [or aircraft] belongs to a State specified in the order, proceedings for the offence instituted otherwise than at the request or with the consent of a consular officer of that State are not entertained by any court in Hong Kong'.[153] Similar orders may be issued by the Governor for 'excluding or limiting the jurisdiction of any court in Hong Kong to entertain proceedings relating to the remuneration or any contract of service of the master or commander or a member of the crew of any ship or aircraft belonging to a State specified in the order, except where a consular officer of that State has been notified of the intention to invoke the jurisdiction of that court and has not objected within such time as may be specified by or under the order'.

Finally, by virtue of the Visiting Forces Act (Application to the Colonies) Orders 1954 to 1967,[154] Hong Kong courts reserve the right to exercise jurisdiction in respect of acts or omissions constituting an offence against any local laws committed by a member of a visiting force or a dependant. Yet, as provided under the Orders, the service authorities and the service courts of a visiting force may exercise within Hong Kong in relation to members of the force and their dependants jurisdictional powers conferred upon them by the sending state. In particular, they are afforded absolute jurisdiction with respect to alleged offences concerning the property or security of the sending state, the person or property of another member of the visiting force or dependant, or an act done or an omission in the performance of official duty. If tried by the service courts, no member of the visiting force or his dependents may be brought to trial in the local courts for the same offence.

The jurisdictional restrictions currently imposed in the territory by virtue of the relevant provisions relating to diplomatic/consular immunities are unlikely to differ substantially in post-1997 Hong Kong. Although the 1986 Regulations of the People's Republic of China on Diplomatic Privileges and Immunities[155] — and, presumably, the recently promulgated Consular

---

[153] The courts, however, retain jurisdiction where '(a) the offence is alleged to have been committed by or against a person who is British citizen, a British Dependent Territories citizen or a British Overseas citizen; or (b) the offence is one involving the tranquillity or safety of a port, or the law relating to safety of life at sea, public health, oil pollution, wireless telegraphy, immigration or customs or is of any other description specified in the order; or (c) the offence is one comprised in the definition of "grave crime".'

[154] App. III, LHK 1968 ed.

[155] See *The Laws of the People's Republic of China 1983–1986* (Beijing: Foreign Languages Press, 1987) p. 283.

Privileges and Immunities Regulations[156] — are to apply in the Hong Kong Special Administrative Region,[157]they basically mirror respective stipulations in the 1961 Vienna Convention on Diplomatic Relations and the 1963 Vienna Convention on Consular Relations to which the PRC is a party. Indeed, under Article 27 of the 1986 Regulations, '[w]here there are other provisions in international treaties to which China is a contracting or acceding party, the provisions of those treaties shall prevail.'[158]

Yet, while the traditional notions and the generally accepted diplomatic/consular immunities may persist after 1997, the enforcement of certain common restraints pertaining for example, to non-interference in the internal affairs of the host country, may assume a more stringent form, given Chinese sensitivity in this regard. It is also reasonable to assume that political pressures would be brought to bear on the local administration with respect to foreign representation from countries having no diplomatic relations with the PRC but which have established consular offices in the territories or from countries which have currently no official presence in Hong Kong but maintain diplomatic ties with China. Some changes may naturally be anticipated in the HK-PRC 'diplomatic' interrelationship. Thus, the 'one-country' predicament is likely to mean the repeal of the ordinance providing for immunities and privileges in Hong Kong for Chinese officials.[159] Nor are such immunities and privileges granted under the Basic Law, which stipulates that '[a]ll offices set up in the Hong Kong Special Administrative Region by departments of the Central Government, or by provinces, autonomous regions, or municipalities directly under the Central Government, and the personnel of such offices, shall abide by the laws of the Region.'[160] On the other hand, the PRC might nonetheless wish to secure to its officials involved in the 'monitoring' of the working of the SAR certain immunities from the local legal system. A similar desire may be expressed by the HKSAR government in relation to any offices it might establish in Beijing.[161] In conformity with common international practice, it is expected that a Chinese martial court will be set up in the territory after 1997 to try servicemen in the People's Liberation Army stationed in Hong Kong. In order to minimize potential conflicts of jurisdiction, such a tribunal will apply a British-modelled military law.

---

[156] For the text and English interpretation of the Regulations which are effective from 30 October 1990, see (1991) V 4 *China Law and Practice* 59.

[157] As per list in Appendix III of the Basic Law.

[158] A similar provision is also contained in the 1990 Regulations (Article 27).

[159] See supra (note 150).

[160] BL, Art. 22.

[161] As authorized under Article 22, ibid.

EXTRADITION

How would the change of sovereignty in 1997 affect Hong Kong's extradition relations?

The current position

While no general duty to extradite common criminals is imposed by customary international law on Hong Kong (nor is it obliged to prosecute or punish fugitive offenders when extradition fails), as an autonomous legal entity with its distinct criminal system, the territory's exercise of jurisdiction is invariably affected by its extensive[162] extradition relations. Deriving its extradition powers constitutionally from United Kingdom statutes,[163] Hong Kong is not only bound by the prescribed procedures and substantive requirements but is also naturally guided by the principles and perceptions underlying the English legislation. Accordingly, although recent changes in English extradition laws might be slow to impact on local attitudes, the latter may still be influenced by the overall direction towards a more relaxed and simplified process which allows foreign states an easier means of securing the surrender of fugitives from Hong Kong.

Of significance in this connection is the 'no list' or 'eliminative' method introduced under the 1989 Extradition Act. The new system — which has replaced the mode of specifically listing offences that are extraditable under

---

[162] According to one writer, Hong Kong presently enjoys extradition relations with at least seventy-five states, their colonies and dependent territories. See J.M. Brabyn, 'Extradition and the Hong Kong Special Administrative Region' (1988) 20 *Case Western Reserve Journal of International Law* 169, 170.

[163] Basically, the municipal authority and machinery for extradition between Hong Kong and non-Commonwealth countries have been created under the 1870 Extradition Act (which has been followed by other Acts in *pari materia* which are cited collectively as the Extradition Acts 1870–1935). Under sec. 17, the 1870 Act 'when applied by Order in Council, shall, unless it is otherwise provided by such order, extend to every British possession in the same manner as if throughout the Act the British possession were substituted for the United Kingdom or England.' By Order in Council of 1877, Her Majesty directed that the Extradition (Hong Kong) Ordinance 1875 (Cap. 236, LHK 1964 ed.) is to have an effect in Hong Kong as if it were part of the 1870 Extradition Act. The 1870 Act has now been repealed by the Extradition Act 1989, which entered into force on, and is applicable in Hong Kong, as from 27 September of the same year. Note, however, that the system provided by the Extradition Act 1870, as amended, will continue to govern proceedings with foreign states with which the United Kingdom enjoys extradition treaties until such time as new agreements are concluded with them. Note also that the law in respect of extradition from Hong Kong to China is formally to be found in the Chinese Extradition Ordinance 1889 (Cap. 235). The Ordinance, however, has not been used since 1935.

English law — defines extradition offences in terms of severity of punishment. Thus, apart from providing a simpler procedure, the Act expands considerably the scope of offences that may attract extradition (including all common law offences as well as additional statutory offences). In addition, by contrast to the 1870 Extradition Act that was predicated on the assumption of a strong territorial link between the offence alleged and the requesting state, the 1989 Act reflects the government's recognition that in the interests of justice the United Kingdom ought to be able to surrender fugitives in respect of the growing range of extraterritorial offences.[164] To this end the nationality *nexus* has been accepted for the purpose of extradition and provisions are made under the new Act for surrender of a fugitive for extraterritorial offence where the requesting state bases its jurisdiction on the nationality of the offender.[165]

In fact, even prior to the entry into force of the 1989 Act, Hong Kong judges have displayed a fair measure of flexibility in determining whether the fugitive's conduct amounted to an 'extradition crime'. For example, pursuant to a request by the Attorney General for a declaration on a true construction of the relevant legislation, the High Court ruled[166] that amendments or modifications to the original Extradition Act of 1870 *as made from time to time* (including additions to the list of extradition crimes contained in the First Schedule to the Act) apply directly to Hong Kong without the need for special enabling legislation. Consequently, offences under the Misuse of Drugs Act 1971 or the Drug Trafficking Offences Act 1986, which amended the 1870 Act to provide for extradition for such offences, are potentially extradition crimes in Hong Kong regardless of the absence of local legislation expressly extending the acts to the territory.[167]

---

[164] See *Green Paper on Extradition,* Cmnd. No. 9421 (1985) at 21.

[165] Two other conditions must be met, namely that the conduct occurred outside the United Kingdom and that, if it occurred in the United Kingdom, it would constitute an offence under the law of the United Kingdom. See 1989 Act, sec. 2.

[166] See *In re an Application by the Attorney General for Judicial Review by way of Declaration* [1985] HKLR 381.

[167] Ibid. Needless to say, the list of extradition crimes may be, and has been, supplemented by special Orders extended to the territory. See, e.g. The Extradition (Genocide) Order 1970; The Extradition (Hijacking) Order 1971; The Extradition (Tokyo Convention) Order 1971; The Extradition (Protection of Aircraft) Order 1973; The Extradition (Internationally Protected Persons) Order 1979; The Extradition (Taking of Hostages) Order 1985 [deeming as 'extradition crimes' offences established under the following respective conventions: 1948 Convention on the Prevention and Punishment of the Crime of Genocide; 1970 Convention for the Suppression of Unlawful Seizure of Aircraft; 1963 Convention on Offences and Certain Other Acts Committed on Board Aircrafts; 1971 Convention for the Suppression of Unlawful Acts Against the Safety of Civil Aviation; 1973 Convention for the Prevention and Punishment of Crimes Against Internationally Protected Persons, Including Diplomatic Agents; 1979 Convention Against the Taking of Hostages.

In a similar vein, Hong Kong courts have followed their British counterparts in relinquishing a stringent 'double criminality test' in favour of a more relaxed 'conduct test'. According to this yardstick, 'the test whether a person in respect of whom a warrant for his arrest had been issued in a foreign state for an offence alleged to have been committed in that state was liable to be surrendered as a fugitive criminal was *not*: whether the offence specified in the foreign warrant of arrest as that for which it had been issued was substantially similar to a crime under English law falling within the list of offences described in Schedule 1 to the Extradition Act 1870, as currently amended (i.e. the so-called 'double criminality' test). The right test, as stated by the Division Court in the *Nielsen* case was: whether the *conduct* of the accused, if it has been committed in England would have constituted a crime falling within one or more of the descriptions included in that list.[168] Such a flexible approach has enabled the local courts to accommodate requests for the surrender of fugitives engaged in the commitment of new and 'more sophisticated' crimes[169] (e.g. 'continuing criminal enterprise'; 'insider's trading').

Also to be relaxed in accordance with the 1989 Extradition Act is the 'speciality rule'.[170] Specifically, it need no longer be demanded that the surrendered fugitive 'be tried in [the] foreign state for any offence committed prior to his surrender other than the extradition crime proved on the facts on which the surrender is grounded'.[171] Rather, the position has been aligned with the requirement in respect of extradition between British Commonwealth

---

[168] *Government of U.S.A. v McCaffery* [1984] 1 WLR 867, 869 (per Lord Diplock), cited with approval and followed in *Lawrence Louis Levy (alias John William Dearman) v Attorney General* [1987] HKLR 777, 780 (CA).

[169] For an evaluation of the effectiveness of the present Hong Kong system in dealing with the increased sophistication of crimes (as well as the 'modus operandi of criminals and the arguments of their lawyers') see: J.M. Brabyn, 'An Analysis of Hong Kong's Extradition Procedure with Specific Reference to United States' Requests' (1990) 20 *Hong Kong Law Journal* 31.

[170] Under the 'speciality rule' — which is incorporated in almost every treaty and statute and may be regarded as a rule of general international law — a fugitive should not be detained, tried or in any way punished in the requesting state for any offence committed prior to his surrender other than the one for which extradition was granted, unless by consent of the surrendering state. A requested state, which is called upon to renounce its jurisdiction over and protection of a fugitive, has now come to expect (and indeed it has become the consistent practice of states) express assurances from the requesting state that it will respect the speciality rule. Note, however, that the principle of speciality does not impose any limitation on the particulars of the charge so long as it encompasses only the offence for which extradition was granted [see *Demjanjuk v Petrovsky* (US CA, Sixth Circuit) 776F 2d 571 (1985)].

[171] Extradition Act 1870, sec. 3(2).

countries[172] whereby the returned fugitive may be dealt with for any lesser offence proved by the facts or for any other relevant offence to which the Secretary of State[173]consents.

Notwithstanding the above changes, which have been said to be 'influenced more by the cooperative aspect of extradition than by the protective understanding of the process',[174] Hong Kong's extradition law (like the English law) has retained other elements whose purpose is to ensure that the fugitive is not surrendered in circumstances where this would be manifestly unjust or oppressive.[175] Thus, a state requesting extradition of an accused (not yet convicted) person still needs to produce sufficient evidence under the local law 'to justify the committal for trial of the prisoner if the crime for which he is accused had been committed in Hong Kong' (the *prima facie* case requirement').[176] What constitutes 'sufficient evidence' has been construed by the local courts with reference to Section 85 of the Magistrates Ordinance (which sets out the circumstances in which a magistrate court may properly commit for trial a person accused of an offence within the jurisdiction of Hong Kong). Two different standards of proof are stipulated therein and, as affirmed most recently by the Privy Council,[177] a magistrate

---

[172] A similar prescription is contained in the 1957 European Convention on Extradition [359 UNTS 274] which the United Kingdom intends to ratify [see 489 Par. Deb. H.L. (5th ser.) No. 20, col. 27 (20 Oct. 1987) (The Earl of Caithness)].

[173] To be substituted by 'the Governor' in relation to dependencies. See Schedule 1 of the Fugitive Offenders (Hong Kong) Order 1967 which provides: 'A person returned to Hong Kong shall not be dealt with in Hong Kong for or in respect of any offence committed before he was returned to Hong Kong other than (a) the offence in respect of which he was returned; (b) any lesser offence proved by the facts proved for the purposes of securing his return; or (c) any other offence in respect of which the Government of the country, or the Governor of the dependency from which he was returned may consent to his being dealt with.'

[174] C.J. Warbrick, 'The Criminal Justice Act 1988: (1) The New Law on Extradition' (1989) *Criminal Law Review* 4, 14.

[175] Note that protection is also afforded the fugitive under the relevant human rights conventions which extend to the territory as well as by the Hong Kong Bill of Rights Ordinance 1991. See further discussion infra in relation to circumstances precluding extradition.

[176] Extradition Act 1870, sec. 10. For the application of this requirement in Hong Kong, see *Somchai Liangsiriprasert v The Government of the United States of America and Another*, supra (note 20) and *Lawrence Louis Levy v Attorney General*, supra (note 168). The courts emphasized that the magistrate must be satisfied that the conduct alleged would amount to an offence according to the law of Hong Kong if it took place within Hong Kong (i.e. the magistrate must assume that the act constituting the offence took place within Hong Kong in order to determine whether it would constitute an offence against the law of Hong Kong and must then assume that the offence was committed in Hong Kong in order to determine whether the evidence would be sufficient to warrant his trial for the offence in Hong Kong).

[177] See *Cheung Ying-lun v Government of Australia and Another* [1990] 2 HKLR 731, 735.

is justified in committing a fugitive to custody to await extradition if a lower standard (i.e. evidence which is sufficient to put the accused upon his trial for an indictable offence, as distinct from a higher standard of evidence which raises a strong or probable presumption of guilt of the accused) is met.

The ability of the local authorities to surrender a fugitive offender is also circumscribed by other constraints, some of which may be held to be mandated by binding international legal norms. Thus, under Hong Kong law, in tandem with legislation in most democratic countries,[178] extradition is enjoined if the offence in respect of which the request has been made is of a 'political character' or if the fugitive proves to the satisfaction of the courts or the Governor that his return has in fact been requested in order to try or punish him for an offence of a political character.[179] No statutory definition is provided of what is to be regarded as 'of political character' and Hong Kong judges, following in the main English authorities, may vacillate between a rigid application of the traditional Anglo-American test of 'incidental to and forming part of a political disturbance[180] and a broader perception of political crimes as those committed in association with a political object.[181] At the same time, by virtue of an English statute[182] and international conventions[183] which have been extended to Hong Kong, certain offences have expressly been removed from the category of offences of a political character for the purposes of extradition. Included are common law offences

---

[178] See T. Stein, 'Extradition' in Bernhardt, op.cit., supra (note 5), Instl. 8 (1985), p. 222 at p. 226. Note, however, the author's observation that notwithstanding the prevalence of the 'political offence exception clause' in statutes and treaties, 'its character as a binding rule of customary law is at least debateable'.

[179] See sec. 3(1) Extradition Act 1870 as applied to Hong Kong; see also sec. 4, Fugitive Offenders (Hong Kong) Order 1967.

[180] See, e.g. *In re Castioni* [1891] 1 QB 149; *Schtraks v Government of Israel* [1964] AC 556.

[181] See, e.g. *R. v Governor of Brixton Prison, ex parte Koczynski* [1955] 1 QB 540.

[182] See The Prevention and suppression of Terrorism Act 1978 (giving effect to the 1977 European convention for the Suppression of Terrorism) which applies to Hong Kong by The Suppression of Terrorism Act 1978 (Hong Kong) Order 1987. It may be noted that should extradition fails, the 1987 Order confers jurisdiction upon the local authorities with respect to the offences listed therein even where committed outside the territory by a non-national (sec. 4).

[183] See supra (notes 68–73); see also the 1985 Supplementary Treaty Concerning the Extradition Treaty Between the Government of the United Kingdom of Great Britain and Northern Ireland and the Government of the United States of America, signed at London on 8 June 1972 (1985) 24 *International Legal Materials* 1105; applied to Hong Kong by United States (Extradition) Order 1986 and 1987] — which denies fugitives accused or convicted of serious offences of violence (mirroring the offences listed in the Suppression of Terrorism Act 1978) the ability to avoid extradition on the grounds that their offences were political.

such as murder, manslaughter or culpable homicide, rape, kidnapping, abduction or plagium, false imprisonment, assault occasioning actual bodily harm or causing injury and wilful fire-raising; offences against the person, abduction, taking of hostages, crimes related to explosives and firearms, criminal damage to property, offences in relation to aircraft, and genocide.

Closely linked with the 'political offence exception' is the so-called 'discrimination clause' which is incorporated in Hong Kong's extradition law[184] and restrains the grant of extradition where the requisition for a fugitive's return has in fact been made 'with a view to try or punish him on account of his race, religion, nationality, or political opinions, or that he might, if surrendered, be prejudiced at his trial or punished, detained or restricted in his personal liberty by reason of his race, religion, nationality, or political opinions'. While not specifically stipulated under the local law of extradition, surrender should also be denied if the fugitive may be subjected to torture or to inhuman or degrading treatment or punishment. As held by the European Court of Human Rights in its unanimous judgment in the celebrated *Soering* case,[185] the prohibition of torture or inhuman treatment contains an inherent obligation not to surrender a fugitive to another state in circumstances where there were substantial grounds for believing that he would be in danger of being subjected to, or face the risk of exposure to, torture or to inhuman or degrading treatment or punishment in the requesting country.[186]

---

[184] See 1870 Extradition Act, sec. 3(1), as amended by sec. 2 of the Prevention and Suppression of Terrorism Act 1978 (Hong Kong) Order; Fugitive Offenders (Hong Kong) Order 1967, sec. 4.

[185] *Soering v United Kingdom,* (1989) 161 Eur. Ct. H.R. (ser. A), repr. in (1989) 28 *International Legal Materials* 1063. Note that although the case involved an alleged violation of Article 3 of the European Convention for the Protection of Human Rights and Fundamental Freedoms, the relevant prohibition is reproduced in analogous terms in Art. 7 of the International Covenant on Civil and Political Rights (which is applicable in Hong Kong) and in Hong Kong's own Bill of Rights Ordinance 1991 (Art. 3). One may also argue that Article 3 reflects customary international law [see the Restatement (Third) of the Foreign Relations Law of the United States ß702(d) (1987) which lists 'torture or other cruel, inhuman or degrading treatment or punishment' as a violation of the customary international law of human rights] and hence forming part of the law of the land. It is, of course, not clear to what extent the local courts or executive decision makers would be persuaded by the European Court's interpretation of Article 3, if faced with a similar case.

[186] The European Court concluded that the UK's extradition of the applicant to the US to stand trial for capital murder would expose him to the 'death row phenomenon' and to a real risk of treatment going beyond the threshold set by Article 3. Accordingly, the Secretary of State's decision to extradite the applicant, if implemented, would violate the prohibition against 'inhuman or degrading treatment or punishment' in the European Convention on Human Rights.

No restriction, however, is imposed under Hong Kong law on the surrender of fugitive for offences carrying the death penalty,[187] although the Governor may exercise his discretion[188] to 'make no order' for the return of a person accused or convicted of an offence not punishable with death in Hong Kong if that person could be or has been sentenced to death for that offence in the country by which the request for his return is made. Alternatively, in accordance with the clause inserted, for example, in the 1972 United Kingdom-United States of America Extradition Treaty,[189] extradition may be refused unless the requesting Party gives assurances satisfactory to the requested Party that the death penalty will not be carried out.

It may finally be observed that, apart from the general constraints discussed above, the authorities' powers of extradition may be challenged under other local vehicles designed to ensure due process of the law. Thus, *habeas corpus* proceedings are available to check the magistrate's jurisdiction to hear the case and the existence of sufficient evidence to justify the committal (as well as to ensure that there are no bars — on grounds such as the 'political offence exception') to surrender. Furthermore, the Governor enjoys a discretion not to sign the surrender warrant, which may override a decision of the courts that a fugitive should be surrendered, and it is open to every prisoner who has exhausted his remedies by way of application for *habeas corpus* to petition the Governor for that purpose. In considering whether to order the fugitive's surrender, the Governor is bound to take account of fresh evidence which had not been before the magistrate. Upon rejection of his petition by the Governor and the latter's decision to sign the warrant, the prisoner may also resort to judicial review proceedings in accordance with general administrative law. In such proceedings the court may review the exercise of the Governor's discretion on the basis that it is tainted with illegality, irrationality or procedural impropriety.

Needless to say a 'disguised extradition' (e.g. a deportation order used to mask what is in effect extradition) or an 'irregular rendition' would constitute an improper exercise of administrative discretion and held illegal as a violation of the principle underlying the law of extradition, namely that no fugitive criminal may be surrendered to another country at the latter's request except in accordance with the applicable statutes. As affirmed by the Hong Kong Court of appeal in *Meng Ching Hai v The Attorney*

---

[187] Note that in the *Soering* case, the Court stopped short of interpreting Article 3 of the European Convention as generally prohibiting the death penalty, and concluded that it did not preclude extradition simply because it might subject the fugitive to the death penalty.

[188] Vested under sec. 12(2)(b) of the Extradition Act 1989 as applied to Hong Kong.

[189] Art. IV, (1977) UKTS No. 16 (Cmnd. 6723); incorporated into the domestic law by United States (Extradition) Order 1976.

General,[190] if it is established by the applicant [for a judicial review] that the appropriate authority [the Director of Immigration] made an order for deportation with the 'true and dominant purpose' of bringing about an unlawful extradition rather than properly setting in motion a 'genuine deportation' in accordance with the duty and power granted to him under the relevant law [Immigration Ordinance], the court would squash such an order. A 'disguised extradition', moreover, would amount to an infringement of human rights.[191] Specifically, a deprivation of liberty for grounds not established by law or not in accordance with the procedure prescribed by law is incompatible with the right to liberty and security of the person guaranteed under Hong Kong law.[192]

It appears, however, that when considered necessary in the interests of repressing 'international crime' the local courts would not be inclined to entertain submissions concerning 'procedural irregularities'. Support for such a stance would be found in a recent ruling by the Privy Council[193] to the effect that enticing an alleged criminal into Hong Kong from a country from which extradition is not possible, with the apparent cooperation of the authorities in that country, does not render extradition from Hong Kong an abuse of process. Their Lordships were unwavering in their holding that 'international crime has to be fought by international cooperation between law enforcement agencies' and that '[i]f the courts were to regard the penetration of a drug dealing organization by the agents of a law enforcement agency and a plan to tempt criminals into a jurisdiction from which they could be extradited as an abuse of process it would indeed by a red letter day for the drug barons'.[194]

Extradition post-1997

Since the main legal source of Hong Kong's extradition powers and the basis of its extradition relations (i.e. British extradition law) is to be extinguished upon the transfer of sovereignty in 1997, the issue of extradition could only be appropriately assessed when the relevant arrangements are

---

[190] Civ. App. Nos. 150 and 151 of 1990, 23 and 30 November 1990.

[191] See *Bozano v France* (1987) 9 EHRR 297 (concluding that the applicant's deprivation of liberty was neither 'lawful' within the meaning of Art. 5ß1 of the European Convention on Human Rights nor compatible with the purpose of this article, namely to protect individuals from arbitrariness, and hence a violation of the right to security of person).

[192] See Art. 5, Hong Kong Bill of Rights, incorporating Art. 9 of the International Covenant on Civil and Political Rights.

[193] See *Somchai Liangsiriprasert v The Government of the United States of America and Another,* supra (note 20).

[194] Ibid., at p. 618.

finalized. It appears, however, that the necessary mechanisms are being constructed[195] in accordance with the Sino-British Joint Declaration[196] and the Basic Law[197] to enable Hong Kong to negotiate and conclude the relevant accords with third countries for the return of fugitive offenders. The enactment of a local extradition ordinance is also contemplated to facilitate implementation of any agreements obtained, and ensure the continued applicability to the territory of generally accepted restrictions regarding double criminality, political offences, discrimination on account of race, and imposition of a death penalty.

Several concerns have nonetheless been voiced regarding extradition matters in post-1997 Hong Kong. As summarized by one writer, '[b]efore extradition to Hong Kong SAR is acceptable to most foreign jurisdictions it will be necessary to demonstrate that persons returned to the Region will be physically secure from removal to other parts of the People's Republic of China,[198] that the judicial and executive organs of the Region will be solely responsible for and able to control the manner and circumstances of such a person's trial and/or punishment and that the government of the Region will be able to ensure a genuine opportunity for surrendered persons to leave the Region in the manner speciality and non-resurrender safeguards require'.[199] The same writer proceeds to argue that potential extradition partners may find reassurance in several provisions contained in the Basic Law ('assuming acceptance of good faith on all sides') as well as in the proposed domestic legislation on extradition which is likely to include a 'speciality' clause and possibly a restriction on resurrender.[200] Consistent with international practice

---

[195] As part of a new network of extradition schemes which would operate after 1997, Hong Kong has signed/ratified five extradition agreements with the Netherlands, Canada, Australia, Malaysia and the Philippines; 13 additional agreements are expected to be in place before 1997.

[196] Annex I, Sec. XI (empowering the HKSAR to 'maintain and develop relations and conclude and implement agreements with states, regions and relevant international organisations in the appropriate fields'). Note that under this section international agreements which are implemented in Hong Kong may continue to be implemented in the HKSAR. See also Annex I, Sec. III (providing for the HKSAR's reciprocal arrangements of juridical assistance with other states).

[197] See Arts. 13, 151, 153 & 96 which replicate the Joint Declaration provisions ibid.

[198] Under agreements currently implemented in Hong Kong persons extradited to Hong Kong are prohibited from being transferred to 'another country'. Doubts are provoked, however, in relation to the preclusion of surrender to the PRC as 'another country' in the light of the 'one country' segment of the 'one country-two systems' formula.

[199] J.M. Brabyn, 'Extradition Between Hong Kong and Canada: Post-1997' in William H. Angus, *Canada-Hong Kong: Some Legal Considerations* (Toronto: Joint Centre for Asian Pacific Studies, 1992) p. 85, at p. 96.

[200] Loc.cit.

similar guarantees are expected to be incorporated in the respective bilateral agreements.

Concerns pertaining to the specific issue of extradition relations between the HKSAR and the PRC are derived largely from the general distrust of the quality of Chinese law and the system of administering justice. Particular anxiety has been generated by the prescription of the death penalty (which is virtually mandatory for more than forty crimes under the PRC's criminal code) and China's widespread use of this mode of punishment. To allay these fears, relevant arrangements between the territory and the Mainland[201] should contain adequate safeguards against extradition of fugitives who may face the death penalty.

Yet, notwithstanding the concerns and fears in respect of post-1997 extradition matters, and regardless of the absence of arrangements about extradition or the treatment of persons serving sentences in prison after extradition from other countries in July 1997, it was held by the Court of Appeal[202] that no additional restrictions may be imposed on current proceedings for the surrender of fugitives to Hong Kong. In the Court's view 'it would be quite wrong, and a wholly improper incursion by the court into matters which lie in the political and diplomatic sphere if [it] were to hold that no fugitive offender may now be surrendered [to Hong Kong] unless and until new arrangements are made with the Government of the People's Republic of China, if his sentence or conviction might extend beyond July 1997.'[203] The Court further found as 'wholly offensive and totally unacceptably' the assumption reflected in the appellant's submission that future legislation will not pay proper regard to the position of persons who have been brought back to Hong Kong under the existing legislation or that the legislature would ignore any obligations that the territory may owe such persons.[204] Similar sentiments were echoed by the Queen's Bench Divisional Court[205] which declined to 'speculate' on the effect a future change of

---

[201] No agreement has been reached yet concerning legal transfer of criminals between China and the HKSAR.

[202] In *Re an Application by Lorraine Osman for Leave to Apply for Judicial Review* [1988] 2 HKLR 378.

[203] Ibid., at 386.

[204] Ibid., 387–8.

[205] In *Regina v Governor of Brixton Prison, Ex parte Osman* (No. 2), *The Times Law Report*, 29 May 1991. See also *Tang Yee-Chun v Romolo J Immundi*, US District Ct., Southern District of NY, 87 Civ 8652 (ELP) (rejecting as remote and speculative the petitioner argument that extradition to HK after 1997 is effectively an extradition to the PRC); *Yin Choy v Robinson*, US Ct of App for the 9th Circuit, No 87–15055, at 12555 (1988) (holding that even if the appellant became subject to Chinese authority pursuant to the reversion of sovereignty in 1997, he will not have been extradited to China).

sovereignty would have on an undertaking given prior to that time by the Governor of Hong Kong to meet requirements [under section 6(4) of the Extradition Act 1989][206] designed to protect a person extradited to another country.

Prospective surrendered fugitives may find an added reassurance in the prohibition on re-surrender to 'another jurisdiction', contained in the newly concluded extradition agreements[207] which have been approved by the PRC. Jurisdictional separation, in turn, is further guaranteed under the Basic Law which stipulates the HKSAR's independent administration of criminal justice through its own separate police force, prosecution authorities and courts system, as well as its control over entry and departure from the Region.

JURISDICTION IN CIVIL MATTERS

How are jurisdictional conflicts between the PRC and Hong Kong over civil matters to be resolved?

There is little doubt that regardless of the general delineation of powers laid down in the relevant official documents, the potential for jurisdictional conflicts over civil matters would be increased as both the PRC and the HKSAR proceed to carve out their respective domains. While no private international law rules can be said to have received firm universal acceptance, certain principles have emerged which should inform prospective decision-making. To a large degree, Hong Kong judges when adjudicating cases have been guided by such norms in their selection of choice of law rules, determination of *forum conveniens* questions and the identification of the applicable law by reference to relevant 'connecting factors'. Yet, in order to ensure a desired measure of certainty, predictability and uniformity of results as well as attempting to eschew discord with the PRC, statutory directives may need to be formulated, outlining the germane values and objectives.[208]

---

[206] Section 6(4) requires a 'speciality protection' of a requesting state. As held by the Divisional Court, '[n]o state can give an undertaking beyond its sovereign powers nor can the United Kingdom require a state to give an undertaking to bind a different state.' See *R v Governor of Brixton, ex parte Osman* (No 3) [1992] 1 WLR 36 (*per* Russel LJ).

[207] See supra (note 195).

[208] See, e.g. *Restatement of the Law, Second, Conflict of Laws 2d,* ß6, (1971) Vol. 1, Introduction at viii: 'Choice-of-Law Principles,
(1) A court, subject to constitutional restrictions, will follow a statutory directive of its own state on choice of law. (2) When there is no such directive, the factors relevant to the

Chinese authorities, on their part, appear to have utilized *all* common jurisdictional bases (territorial, nationality, and protective) to avail themselves of pervasive (at times, rather remote) 'connecting elements'.[209] Neither do PRC tribunals readily enforce forum selection clauses agreed upon by the parties or concede to concurrent jurisdiction exercised by foreign courts.[210] Although some optimistic observers foresee a more curtailed approach 'as the PRC's courts gain more experience with international cases',[211] an attempt should be made to forge a reciprocal arrangement between the HKSAR and China, incorporating international guiding principles applicable to conflicts of prescriptive jurisdiction.

Of particular importance in this respect is the doctrine of comity which 'has become an international standard to be used as a moderating influence or as a restraint on the assertion of jurisdiction by a state over events and

---

choice of the applicable rule of law include (a) the needs of the interstate and international systems, (b) the relevant policies of the forum, (c) the relevant policies of other interested states and the relative interests of those states in the determination of the particular issue, (d) the protection of justified expectations, (e) the basic policies underlying the particular field of law, (f) certainty, predictability and uniformity of results, and (g) ease in the determination and application of the law to be applied . . . this mode of treatment leaves the answer to specific problems very much at large. There is, therefore, wherever possible, a secondary statement in black letter setting forth the choice of law the courts will "usually" make in given situations. These formulations are cast as empirical appraisals rather than purported rules to indicate how far the statements may be subject to revaluation in a concrete instance in light of the more general and open-ended norms.'

[209] Under, e.g. the Specific Rules Governing Jurisdiction Over Maritime Lawsuits Involving Foreign Interests (1986) 1 *Supreme People's Court Bulletin* 13, maritime courts may assume jurisdiction over maritime cases involving foreign interests when: the defendant resides in the PRC; the tort was committed or caused consequences in the PRC; the contract was signed or performed in the PRC; a vessel arrived in the PRC under certain circumstances; the subject matter of the action or other property subject to attachment is located in the PRC; the defendant fails to make a timely jurisdictional objection; the case involves disputes arising from harbour operations in the PRC; the vessel is arrested in the PRC; there is an agreement providing for PRC jurisdiction; or PRC citizens, vessels, or other properties are injured, damaged, or otherwise involved in certain disputes.

[210] According to 1992 Supreme People's Court Opinion on Issues Regarding Application of PRC Law of Civil Procedure, where a PRC court and foreign court have concurrent jurisdiction over a dispute and one party brings an action in the foreign court, but the other party brings an action before a PRC court, the PRC court may hear the case. A judgment or a ruling rendered by the foreign court under such circumstances will not be recognized or enforced by a PRC court, unless otherwise provided in an applicable international treaty. Cited in Zhengyu Tang, 'Maritime Jurisdiction of the People's Republic of China: Legal Framework, Recent Developments, and Future Prospects' (1994) 25 *Journal of Maritime Law and Commerce* 251, 277.

[211] Zhengyu Tang, ibid., at 276.

persons within or without its territory'.[212] A recourse to comity in the context of private law matters should arguably be acceptable to the Chinese authorities given that competing sovereign interests rarely arise. Comity should clearly underpin questions related to the mutual recognition and enforcement of judgments between Hong Kong and the PRC, although this need not take the form of a 'full enforcement model'.[213] Hong Kong may continue to apply its common law scheme of enforcement or amend its statutory registration system[214] to include PRC judgments. The PRC may opt to extend to Hong Kong provisions applicable in its relationships with some other jurisdictions.[215] Alternatively, arrangements may be laid down in a special bilateral agreement on mutual enforcement and recognition of judgments or as part of the general accord on private international law alluded to above. The application of an internationally binding treaty to govern other aspects of 'judicial assistance' between Hong Kong and the PRC (such as the service of documents or the taking of evidence) should also induce cooperation and decrease the probability of conflict. The parties are therefore urged[216] to take appropriate steps to ensure the implementation in their respective domestic laws of the 1965 Hague Convention on the Service Abroad of Judicial and Extrajudicial Documents in Civil or Commercial Matters.[217]

---

[212] J-G Castel, *Extraterritoriality in International Trade* (Toronto: Butterworths, 1988) pp. 233–4.

[213] For an analysis of this model — which is regarded as suitable in relations between components of a non-unified legal system — and other models, see Tai Yiu Ting, 'Mutual Recognition and Enforcement of Judgments between Hong Kong and the PRC', a paper presented at a Symposium on Legal Interaction between Hong Kong and China organized by The Chinese Law Research Group Faculty of Law University of Hong Kong, 29 June 1991.

[214] See Foreign Judgments (Reciprocal Enforcement) Ordinance (Cap. 319); Foreign Judgments (Restriction on Recognition and Enforcement) Ordinance (Cap. 46); At present the PRC is not included in the list [per schedule to the Foreign Judgments (Reciprocal Enforcement) Order] of states to which these statutes apply.

[215] The PRC has concluded bilateral agreements on mutual recognition and enforcement of judgments with France, Poland, Belgium, Germany and Mongolia. See Tai, supra (note 213).

[216] See the discussion in E.J. Epstein, 'Judicial Assistance between Hong Kong and China: Service of Documents', a paper presented at the Symposium on Legal Interaction, supra (note 213) (emphasizing that the Hague Convention on Service of Process is particularly designed 'to interface jurisdictions with just such instances of inconsistency and incompatibility' as Hong Kong and the PRC).

[217] The Convention has been in effect in Hong Kong since 19 July 1970 by virtue of a UK extension (1969) UKTS 50 (Cmnd. 3986); The PRC has acceded to the Convention on 2 March 1991 (see (1991) V 3 *China Law and Practice* 10]; the convention came into force for China on 30 April 1991.

Chapter 3

Hong Kong's International Legal Obligations

As a party to many international agreements and by virtue of treaties extended to the territory, Hong Kong has assumed international legal obligations in a wide range of fields, including civil aviation, communications, conservation, customs, drugs, economics and finance, health, human rights, intellectual property, international crime, labour, marine pollution, merchant shipping, nationality and refugees, politics and diplomacy, private international law, and science and technology.[1] International obligations are also imposed on Hong Kong under rules of customary or general international law, which apply to all members of the international community regardless of participation in specific conventions.[2] The territory may incur further obligations in accordance with other, 'softer' sources of international law.[3]

TREATMENT OF ALIENS

While Hong Kong is required to comply with international standards of treatment of aliens in general, particular attention is paid here to international obligations pertaining to asylum-seekers, given the momentous challenges confronted by the territory in this regard, especially in the last two decades.

---

[1] See *Revised List of Multilateral Treaties Applying to Hong Kong As of January 1990* (Hong Kong: Attorney General's Chambers, 1990).

[2] As will be elaborated in the last chapter of this book, in accordance with established British judicial practice, customary international law forms part of the common law of England and hence is applicable as part of the law of Hong Kong.

[3] For· a general discussion of the concept of 'soft law' see: Christine M. Chinkin, 'The Challenge of Soft Law: Development and Change in International Law' (1989) 38 *International & Comparative Law Quarterly* 850.

Admission of asylum seekers

The principle governing the admission of asylum seekers is laid down in Article 33(1) of the 1951 Convention Relating to the Status of Refugees,[4] which states that '[n]o Contracting State shall expel or return (*"refouler"*) a refugee in any manner whatsoever to the frontier of territories where his life or freedom would be threatened on account of race, religion, nationality, membership of a particular social group or political opinion.' The strictest interpretation of this principle, that refugees should face 'no return, no expulsion', has been broadened to include 'no rejection at the frontiers' where the effect on the refugee — namely, compulsory return to the country where the refugee risked persecution — would be the same as repatriation or expulsion.[5] It is further considered that as a 'logical and necessary corollary' of an otherwise incomplete regime of *non-refoulement*, a duty to provide temporary refuge is also implied.[6] *Non-refoulement* is moreover a peremptory rule, derogation from which is restricted to cases involving a refugee 'whom there are reasonable grounds for regarding as a danger to the security of the country in which he is, or who, having been convicted by a final judgment of a particularly serious crime, constitutes a danger to the community of that country'.[7]

The universal recognition this principle has received — in various international legal instruments, numerous declarations in different international fora, successive resolutions of the UN General Assembly resolutions and the Executive Committee of the UNHCR, as well as in the laws and practices of states — has reinforced the view that *non-refoulement* has matured into a norm of customary international law binding on all

---

4   189 UNTS 137; hereafter the Refugee Convention.

5   Note commentary by Atle Grahl-Madsen, *Territorial Asylum* (Stockholm: Almquist & Siksell, 1980) at p. 74 that the rule of *non-refoulement* as ordinarily formulated in Art. 33 *did* incorporate such a prohibition, in particular with regard to states sharing a common frontier with the country from which the refugees have fled. In Grahl-Madsen's opinion subsequent developments have simply served the function of clarifying the provision in question.

6   See Guy S. Goodwin-Gill, 'Entry and Exclusion of Refugees' (1982) *Michigan Yearbook of International Legal Studies* 306. See also International Institute of Humanitarian Law, *Report of the Round Table on the Problems Arising from Large Numbers of Asylum Seekers* (San Remo, 1981) para. 9: 'The first act of protection which the asylum seeker needed was admission in the territory of the state of arrival, in accordance with the generally recognised principle of *non-refoulement* and, therefore, of non-rejection at the border.'

7   Art. 33(2), Refugee Convention. Hence, claims of 'exhaustion' or 'resources drainage' often raised by Legislative Councillors do not amount to legitimate justifications for derogating from the rule.

members of the international community, whether or not they are party to the Refugee Convention.[8] Accordingly, Hong Kong, which is not a party to the Refugee Convention,[9] is bound by customary international law to observe *non-refoulement* and provide temporary refuge to asylum seekers, if refusal would involve their return to a country where their life or freedom would be threatened or would otherwise expose them to serious danger (e.g. on the high seas).

The territory's international obligations regarding the treatment of asylum seeker have also assumed a conventional/treaty force by virtue of pledges — to maintain Hong Kong as a 'country of first asylum', allow the safe arrival of and continue providing temporary refuges for asylum seekers from Vietnam and Laos — given at international conferences.[10] In accordance with a generally accepted rule of international law,[11] Hong Kong's unilateral declarations in 1979 and 1989 — made publicly, in respect of legal/factual situation and with intent to be bound — have had the effect of creating a legal obligation for the government to follow a course of conduct consistent with such declarations, independent of any *quid pro quo* (i.e. unconditional on reciprocal commitments of resettlement or other burden-sharing arrangements). Furthermore, the norms of *non-refoulement* and temporary refuge are grounded in the acceptance by the international community that the basic principles of humanity, protection of life and dignity must be granted to persons who have lost their national protection. These humanitarian-inspired duties are imposed regardless of the sovereign or otherwise status

---

8   For an analysis of the status of *non-refoulement* as a principle of customary international law see Guy S. Goodwin-Gill, *The Refugee in International Law* (Oxford: Clarendon Press, 1983) pp. 97–100; Patricia Hyndman, 'An Appraisal of the Development of the Protection Afforded to Refugees Under International Law' (1981) 1 *Lawasia* 229; Patricia Hyndman, 'Asylum and *Non-Refoulement* — Are These Obligations Owed to Refugees Under International Law?' (1982) 55 *Philippine Law Review* 43; Roda Mushkat, 'Human Rights Under Temporary Refuge' (1984) 62 *Revue de Droit International* 169.

9   The Convention, signed and ratified by the UK, has not been extended to the territory because of constraints inherent in the UK-China relationship regarding Hong Kong. See also House of Lords Debates, Vol. 460, Col. 968 (27 February 1985) for remarks by the Parliamentary Under-Secretary of State for the Armed Forces, Lord Trefgarne, that 'it was decided not to extend the Convention to Hong Kong because of the territory's small size and geographical vulnerability to mass illegal immigrants'. He added that '[t]he 1967 Protocol was applied only to those territories to which the 1951 was extended' and that '[t]he Hong Kong Government nevertheless co-operated fully with the Office of the UNHCR'.

10 UN Meeting on Refugees and Displaced Persons in South East Asia (Geneva, 20–21 July 1979); International Conference on Indochinese Refugees (Geneva, 13–14 June 1989).

11 See *Nuclear Tests Case* (Australia v France) [1974] ICJ Rep. 253, at pp. 267–70.

of the territory where asylum is sought.[12] Thus, Hong Kong's transition from British to Chinese rule in 1997 should not affect its compliance with these international obligations.[13] Nor, for that matter, could the territory's status as a 'country of first asylum' — which is firmly established under both customary and conventional international law — be 'withdrawn' (as 'warned' by the PRC authorities)[14] arbitrarily.

In fact, Hong Kong has so far displayed a remarkable level of observance of its 'admission' duties. The territory takes pride in the fact that for the past 154 years of its existence it has provided either temporary or permanent shelter to those who for a variety of reasons have entered its confined area. The policies adopted vis-a-vis arrivals from China — which until the 1970s constituted the largest group of asylum seekers into the territory — have reflected the government's typical pragmatic approach to managing such problems.[15] Its response to the massive influx of asylum seekers from Indo-

---

[12] That the respective obligations are viewed as Hong Kong's own responsibility is further evidenced by the Administration's stand that the collection of debts owed by the UNHCR for the maintenance of asylum seekers in the territory merits no involvement of the British government. The territory's responsibility in this regard was also implied in a statement by the British Minister for Foreign Affairs (Rifkind) to the effect that as Hong Kong's sovereign power, Britain is [merely] responsible for foreign relations relevant to Hong Kong [as reported in Kwai-Yan No, 'China Demands Britain Deal with Boat People' *South China Morning Post*, 9 January 1996, at 1.

[13] Indeed, the territory's responsibility may derive an additional legal force, should the PRC extend to the HKSAR the Refugee Convention to which it is a party.

[14] See Scott McKenzie, 'HK to Lose Status as Port of First Asylum' *South China Morning Post*, 22 February 1995, at p. 2.

[15] Thus, between 1949 and 1961 a relatively relaxed posture at the border was taken to accommodate on humanitarian grounds the refugee influx prompted by the civil war in China and the new Communist regime. Declaring the wave of new arrivals in 1962 to be 'motivated principally by economic and not political pressures' the Hong Kong government (in order to avoid the creation of a large 'underground' population of unregistered illegal immigrants and to meet the requirements of the local labour market) nevertheless introduced in 1974 a 'touch base' policy whereby illegal immigrants (IIs) who managed to reach the urban areas were not repatriated but permitted to register with the Immigration Department for identity cards. In 1980, however, following an official report on the severe strain imposed by illegal immigration on government services as well as demands expressed by opinion leaders, the government moved to abolish the 'touch base' policy. Under legislation passed on 23 October 1980, illegal immigrants entering the territory after that date, and regardless of where they are found or whether they have family ties in the territory, are to be arrested and returned to China. While Mainland arrivals are either 'legal' or 'illegal' immigrants, both the British and Hong Kong governments have from time to time acknowledged that they would protect 'genuine' refugees fleeing from China if the case could be demonstrated. It appears, though, that rather than allow any asylum seekers from China residence in Hong Kong, the government facilitates their departure to another country or enable them to submit requests to relevant consulates.

China since 1975, although not underpinned by strong legal convictions or undiluted compassion — largely accords with Hong Kong's international obligations as a 'first port of call'.[16]

Determination of refugee status

The screening process

The 1951 Refugee Convention and its 1967 Protocol do not contain provisions regarding the method for determining who is a refugee entitled to protection. 'It is therefore left to each Contracting Party to establish the procedure that it considers most appropriate, having regard to its particular constitutional and administrative structure.'[17] At the same time, by virtue of the basic norm of international law, *pacta sunt servanda* (treaties must be observed), 'states ratifying the 1951 Convention and the 1967 Protocol necessarily undertake to implement these instruments effective and [in] good faith'.[18] Thus, '[w]hile the choice of means may be left to states, some such procedure [for identifying those who are to benefit] would seem essential for effective implementation and fulfilment of convention obligations.'[19] It is equally clear that observance of the fundamental principle of *non-refoulement* (and its 'temporary refuge' corollary) hinges on the institution of appropriate determination procedures. In the words of one expert, if any meaning is to be attached to *non-refoulement*, it must be assumed that 'a person claiming to be a refugee has a right to have his claim examined'.[20]

The pivotal aspect of the refugee status determination process was also recognized in the Comprehensive Plan of Action (CPA) of the 1989 International Conference on Indochines Refugees, which required that such a process be established and 'take place in accordance with national legislation and internationally accepted practice' (Section D6). Specifically,

---

[16] Consistently with what may be said to be a 'widespread usage', asylum seekers who have 'settled' elsewhere prior to arrival in Hong Kong are classified as 'illegal immigrants' and repatriated, subject to the relevant government's agreement to take them back. More recently, however, allegations have been made that a stay as short as two days (coupled with a lack of knowledge of Vietnam's current affairs) were regarded as a sufficient basis for repatriation. See Scott McKenzie, 'Asylum Seekers to be Deported' *South China Morning Post*, 13 April 1995, at 3.

[17] Office of the UNHCR, *Handbook on Procedures and Criteria for Determining Refugee Status* (Geneva, 1979) [hereafter UNHCR Handbook], para. 189.

[18] Goodwin-Gill, supra (note 8), at p. 147.

[19] Ibid., p. 148.

[20] Atle Grahl-Madsen, 'Refugees and Refugee Law in a World of Transition' (1981) 19 *AWR Bulletin* 95.

'the procedures to be followed will be in accordance with those endorsed by the Executive Committee of the Programme of the UNHCR in this area'.[21] More detailed requirements are set out in a 1990 UNHCR 'Note on Fair and Efficient Procedures'.[22] Assuming in this regard a leading role in the region, the Hong Kong government established a 'screening' machinery, designed to determine the status of arrivals from Vietnam, in accordance with commitments made under a Statement of Understanding concluded with the UNHCR on 20 September 1988. In particular, a Refugee Status Review Board (RSRB) was set up to act on behalf of the Governor in Council in considering applications for review of negative determination decisions. The process is further enhanced by a measure of monitoring provided by the UNHCR as well as by the assistance of AVS (Agency of Voluntary Services) Appeals Councillors, employed under contract with the UNHCR to ensure that persons denied refugee status were visited and advised as to the merits of their claims and how to submit appeals to the RSRB. The UNHCR, in any event, retains a discretionary power to request the government that an asylum seeker be 'mandated in' as a refugee despite rejection by the RSRB.

While recourse to the local courts to challenge refugee status determination procedures is also available, the readiness to 'intervene', demonstrated by some judges,[23] has not been echoed in the territory's Court

---

[21] Such procedures will include: (i) the provision of information to asylum seekers about procedures, criteria and the presentation of their cases; (ii) prompt advice of the decision in writing within a prescribed period; (iii) a right of appeal against negative decisions and proper appeals procedures for this purpose, based upon existing laws and procedures of the individual place of asylum, with the asylum seekers entitled to advice, if required, to be provided under UNHCR auspices. As noted by one commentator, the Conclusions of the Executive Committee of the UNHCR Programme (which consists of government and meets annually in Geneva to oversee the work of the UNHCR) are regarded as 'soft law' sources that provide interpretative and informing principles on issues of international refugee protection. See Arthur C. Helton, 'Judicial Review of the Refugee Status in Hong Kong: the Case of Do Giau' (1991) 17 *Brooklyn Journal of International Law* 263, 287n. On the general standing of Executive Committee Conclusions, see J. Sztucki, 'The Conclusions on the International Protection of Refugees Adopted by the Executive Committee of the UNHCR Programme' (1989) 1 *International Journal of Refugee Law* 285.

[22] Cited in Helton, ibid.

[23] See, e.g. Mortimer, J. in *R v The Director of Immigration and the Refugee Status Review Board, Ex parte Do Giau and Others* [1992] HKLR 287 (especially, the ruling that RSRB's decisions may be reviewed despite a broad exclusion clause in the Immigration (Refugee Status Review Boards) (Procedure) Regulations, purporting to insulate the Board's decisions from 'review or appeal in any court'); Liu, J. in *In the Matter of an Application for Leave for Judicial Review and of Le Tu Phuong and Others,* M.P. No. 2368 of 1992 (reaffirming that 'if for any reasons the [RSRB] failed, in effect, to exercise its power to review (e.g. applying the wrong test by paying attention to irrelevant considerations or paying no regard to relevant considerations . . .), or to conduct a full or balanced review . . . its determination may be then reviewable').

of Appeal.[24] Yet, as reflected in the applications for judicial review and in criticisms voiced by several bodies,[25] the screening process, even if 'not contrary to law',[26] exhibits various 'flaws' and falls short of the 'highest standards of fairness'[27] required in asylum cases. As a final note, it may be added that no formal procedure has been instituted to determine refugee status of applicants for asylum who are not previous residents of Vietnam.

Substantive criteria

The key criterion in establishing refugee status under the Refugee Convention is a well-founded fear of being persecuted. Persecution, however, has not been defined in any of the major international instruments concerning refugees, including the 1951 Convention, with the result that states have displayed considerable divergencies in approaches. Although a threat to life or freedom based on one's race, religion, nationality, membership in a particular social group or political opinion — the five categories listed in the Convention — will always constitute persecution, extending the concept beyond these parameters is a policy exercise, the outcome of which hinges on whether one takes a conservative or liberal approach.

Pursuing a more liberal approach towards refugee determination is arguably more consistent with both the spirit and practice of international refugee law. In keeping with its humanitarian objective and spirit, the 1951 Convention attempts to place the refugee within a greater human rights framework from the first paragraph of its Preamble by emphasizing the basic principle affirmed in the 1948 Universal Declaration of Human Rights:[28] that human beings shall enjoy fundamental rights and freedom without discrimination. A definition of 'persecution' that includes serious violations

---

[24] See, e.g. *Le Tu Phuong, Dinh Thi Bich Chinh v Director of Immigration and Refugee Status Review Board,* (1994) 4 HKPLR 337 (adopting a rather narrow, 'legalistic' approach in respect of the reviewability of the screening process).

[25] See, e.g. Lawyers Committee of Human Rights, *Hong Kong Refugee Status Review Board: Problems in Status Determination for Vietnamese Asylum Seekers* (New York: Lawyers Committee for Human Rights, 1992).

[26] The strict 'test' which appears to have been imposed by the Court of Appeal in *Le Tu Phuong,* ibid.

[27] See *Le Tu Phuong* (High Court, *per* Liu, J., citing with approval a host of English cases).

[28] The 1989 CPA also refers to the 1948 Universal Declaration on Human Rights, stipulating that '[t]he criteria will be those recognized in the 1951 Convention Relating to the Status of Refugees and its 1967 Protocol, bearing in mind, to the extent appropriate, the 1948 Universal Declaration of Human Rights and other relevant international instruments concerning refugees, and will be applied in a humanitarian spirit taking into account the special situation of the asylum-seekers concerned and the need to respect the family unit' [Sec. D6(b)].

of human rights or discrimination for cognizable grounds is certainly in accord with such a principle. A human rights orientation is also implied in the 'letter' of the Refugee Convention. Where reference is made to 'threats to life and freedom' of individuals, the text invites an interpretation of the concept of 'persecution' that surpasses deprivation of life or attacks on physical integrity to include violation of fundamental human rights. That a humanitarian rather than strictly legalistic attitude should be taken in defining persecution is also evinced in a recommendation by the drafters, who urged states to apply the Refugee Convention beyond its narrow contractual scope to other refugees within their territory.[29]

For its part, the UNHCR — as the principal institution charged with international protection of refugees — has not confined itself to following the legal or statutory definition of a refugee and its criterion of 'well-founded fear of persecution'. Instead, its mandate has expanded to cover 'displaced persons' and it has adopted much looser working categories which encompass persons who are unable to meet the technical requirements stipulated under the Convention. Indeed, to the extent that the UNHCR represents collective state practice and *opinio juris* — and as further borne out in regional[30] and individual state policies regarding asylum and resettlement — it may be argued that reference to a threshold based on a more 'liberal' interpretation of persecution has evolved into customary international law. Agreement on a liberal interpretation of 'persecution' will not, however, eliminate other uncertainties in the criteria for determining refugee status, such as the standard for evaluating the fear of persecution, the scope of recognized grounds of persecution, and the persons or organizations responsible for persecution ('agents of persecution'). Guiding notes incorporated in the *UNHCR Handbook*[31] may nonetheless be said to reflect the true letter and spirit of the Refugee Convention, and ought to be adhered to.

Regarding the standard of fear, for example, the UNHCR calls for an approach that assesses the applicants' subjective fear — which in turn involves an examination of the applicants' past experiences and background as well as their future prospects if required to return to their country of origin — and supporting objective evidence. Unless there are 'good reasons to the contrary', applicants should be given the 'benefit of the doubt' if their accounts appear credible. In respect of the five grounds for persecution

---

[29] Conference of Plenipotentiaries, Final Act, Recommendation E: UNHCR, *Collection of International Instruments Concerning Refugees* (Geneva, 1979) p. 38.

[30] Especially by African and Latin American countries operating under the more liberal regimes of, respectively, the 1969 OAU Convention Governing the Specific Aspects of Refugee Problems in Africa and the 1984 Cartagena Declaration.

[31] Supra (note 17).

specified in the Refugee Convention, the *Handbook* notes, *inter alia*, that 'race' is to be understood in its widest sense, to include ethnic groups; 'nationality' is also to be interpreted broadly to cover citizenship as well as membership of specific ethnic or linguistic groups; 'political opinion' is not limited to active participation in groups, unions, demonstration, protests or to the persecuted victim's conscious expression of conventional political belief; and that 'membership of a social group' frequently overlaps with other categories since it can refer to persons sharing similar background, habits, economic activity or social status as well as ethnic, cultural or linguistic origins. On the issue of 'agents of persecution' — which are often confined to the authorities of the country of origin — the *Handbook* advises that '[w]here serious discriminatory or other offensive acts are committed by the local populace, they can be considered as persecution if they are knowingly tolerated by the authorities, or if the authorities refuse, or prove unable to offer effective protection'.

Whether Hong Kong has complied with the above guidelines is somewhat difficult to assess, since neither the immigration authorities involved in the first stage of the determination process, nor the Refugee Status Review Boards charged with reviewing negative determination decisions, have ever disclosed the criteria actually deployed or the burden of proof required to be discharged by the applicants for refugee status. In general, however, in its 1988 Statement of Understanding with the UNHCR, the Hong Kong government has confirmed that 'appropriate humanitarian criteria for determining refugee status will be applied', and that '[t]hese criteria, based on the UNHCR *Handbook on Procedures and Criteria for Determining Refugee Status* under the 1951 Convention and the 1967 Protocol, take into account the special situation of asylum seekers from Vietnam'. The government has further declared[32] that — in accordance with its objective of identifying genuine refugees, and a commitment to 'granting refugee status to all Vietnamese migrants arriving in Hong Kong with a reasonable claim' — 'a large measure of the benefit of the doubt' is given to Vietnamese claiming refugee status 'with the result that there are probably a great many more successful claims than would be warranted by a strict application of the UNHCR criteria'.

Some evidence has nonetheless been adduced[33] to show that, whether due to a lack of familiarity with relevant international standards and/or human rights situation in Vietnam, or because of attitudinal, cultural or other reasons,

---

[32] See Hong Kong Government, *Status Determination Procedures* (Hong Kong, March 1995), sec. 3.

[33] For detail see Roda Mushkat, 'Implementation of the CPA in Hong Kong: Does it Measure up to International Standards?' (1993) 5 *International Journal of Refugee Law* 559, 567–8.

a restrictive approach, not consistent with a 'humanitarian spirit', is adopted. Several cases have been cited of asylum seekers who fell squarely within the Convention definition yet were 'screened out' in the determination process. Certain misconceptions also appear to prevail among determination officials, including the assumptions that only persecution for political opinion (narrowly construed) counts as persecution (although four other grounds are recognized in the 1951 Convention; that 'mere' harassment, discrimination or severe economic deprivation (e.g. of the right to earn a livelihood) do not constitute 'persecution' and that in the absence of singling out for special treatment (as distinct from general policy directed against 'the enemies of the Communist regime') or actual infliction of suffering (thus, no fear of persecution is said to be established if 'only' family members have been persecuted or deprived of economic or social rights).

Standards of treatment of asylum seekers

While it is undoubted that a large influx of asylum seekers may present receiving states with considerable strategic challenges and management problems, host governments remain at all times bound by a fundamental international legal obligation to respect the right to liberty and security of all persons within their territory, regardless of distinctions such as alienage. In particular, such a right — which is proclaimed in all major international human rights conventions, been reaffirmed by international and domestic tribunals and generally acknowledged as a core human right — guarantees protection from arbitrary arrest or detention. In recognition of the distinctive predicament of asylum seekers/refugees, special provisions have been incorporated in international instruments, enjoining states to refrain from imposing penalties, detention measures or unwarranted restrictions on movement solely on ground of 'illegality' of entry.

Although exceptions to the prescribed rules are acknowledged and derogation from standards permitted under certain circumstances, the basic principle is that detention of refugees and asylum seekers should only be resorted to when a genuine necessity exists and, if applied, should not be unduly prolonged (i.e. only as long as the exigencies of the situation demand). Thus, in individual cases some initial period of deprivation or limitation of freedom of movement may be necessary for administrative purposes in connection with determination of status. Detention beyond the initial period ought to be based only on the most serious reasons, such as criminal associations or intent, or the fact that the person is likely to abscond. In situations of mass influx (which inevitably bring into play a more complex set of factors), the grounds for detention may include also considerations of national security or public order, subject however to the requirements of 'necessity' and 'proportionality'. Apart from the substantive restrictions imposed on resort to the exceptional measure of detention, authorities in the receiving states are also constrained by requirements of procedural justice such as availability of review and appeal avenues, access to legal counsel as well as opportunity for the grant of provisional liberty on suitable conditions.

Should detention be found 'necessary' or justified, applicable international rules must be adhered to. Of overriding importance is the duty — codified in the comprehensive 1988 UN Body of Principles for the Protection of All Persons under Any Form of Detention or Imprisonment — to treat all detainees with humanity and with respect for the inherent dignity of the human person, and in particular not to subject them to torture or to cruel, inhuman or degrading treatment or punishment. Needless to say, humane treatment is mandated under international rules pertaining to asylum seekers and refugees, 'whose tragic plight requires special understanding and sympathy'. Conditions of detention should in no case fall below the 'basic human standards' laid down in the relevant international documents, including provision of basic necessities of life and a respect for family unity.

That Hong Kong's policy of confining asylum seekers in detention centres for prolonged periods of time deviates from the international rules outlined above is discussed in detail elsewhere.[34] A formal submission to this effect was made to the UN Commission on Human Rights Working Group on Arbitrary Detention by the Lawyers Committee for Human Rights. A decision is yet to be adopted by the Commission, having considered a British response, justifying the territory's detention policy as 'necessary to protect the territory and its lawful citizens'. It is nonetheless questionable whether condemnation could be withheld in respect of detention based solely on the need to deter new arrivals and the unpopularity of allowing Vietnamese migrants to live and work freely in Hong Kong, while repatriating illegal immigrants from China. Especially doubtful is the validity of such grounds given diminishing arrivals and in the absence of evidence to support the authorities' fear of 'serious social unrest and a breakdown of public order'.

Of more recent concern is the continued detention of asylum seekers who are unable to 'release themselves' by entering the voluntary repatriation scheme because of classification as 'non-nationals' by Vietnam (and recognized as nationals by no other country). Indeed, the illegality of detention in the absence of 'reasonable prospects of removal' was duly

---

[34] See Roda Mushkat, 'Balancing Western Legal Concepts, Asian Attitudes and Practical Difficulties — A Critical Examination of Hong Kong's Response to the Refugee Problem' (1993) *Asian Yearbook of International Law* 45, 81–87.

acknowledged by Hong Kong's High Court.[35] The Court's decision, however, was overturned by the Court of Appeal which considered that '[n]o court can declare with confidence that the purpose of detention is spent when, factually, dialogue and negotiations are still under way'.[36] Nonetheless, in an appeal/ *habeas corpus* proceedings from Hong Kong,[37] the Judicial Committee of the Privy Council has reaffirmed that the 'burden lay on the executive to prove to the court on the balance of probabilities the facts necessary to justify the conclusion that the applicants were being detained "pending removal", and that, failing such proof (e.g. in the face of evidence that the policy of the Vietnamese government is not to accept repatriation of non-Vietnamese nationals),[38] continuing detention for that purpose was unreasonable.

Yet, the 'circumscribed'[39] release from detention of asylum seekers in a similar predicament (sparked by the Privy Council judgment) falls short of full compliance with Hong Kong's international legal obligations. Specifically, under the 1954 Convention Relating to the Status of Stateless Persons and the 1961 Convention on the Reduction of Statelessness — which have been extended to the territory, it is incumbent on the government to regularize the status of such persons (some of whom, in fact, qualify to become permanent residents in the territory by virtue of their Chinese ethnic origin and length of stay).[40]

Criticisms have also been directed at the harsh conditions of detention[41]

---

[35] *In the Matter of Chung Tu Quan and Others and in the Matter of an application for writs of habeas corpus and subjiciendum,* 1994 MP No. 3417 (Keith, J.).

[36] (1995) Civil Appeals Nos. 31 & 65 (per Litton, V.-P).

[37] *Tan Te Lam and Others v Superintendent of Tai A Chau Detention Centre and Another,* Privy Council Appeal No. 55 of 1995 (judgment delivered on 27 March 1996).

[38] Note, however, that under legislation passed subsequent to the Privy Council decision, a mere proof that the applicant is a non-national of Vietnam may not suffice. Rather, where a request has been made to the government of Vietnam for approval to remove the person to Vietnam, 'pending removal' includes 'awaiting a response to the request from the Government of Vietnam'. See Immigration (Amendment) Ordinance 33 of 1996 (30 May 1996). On the other hand, the provision emphasizes that it does not limit the ability of the courts to determine that a person is being detained otherwise than 'pending removal' or specifically that he has been detained for an unreasonable period.

[39] Subject to redetention and repatriation without notice as well as required to report to the Immigration Department every three months.

[40] Note, however, the position expressed by PRC officials that allowing such asylum seekers to stay in the territory and become permanent residents would be a breach of the Basic Law since they do not 'ordinarily reside in the territory'.

[41] 'Prison-like detention centres surrounded by barbed wire. The Government provided the detainees little protection from Vietnamese gangs that terrorised their fellow inmates. Extortion, rape, theft and wife and child abuse were rampant. Mental health problems were also prevalent.' Annual Review, US Committee for Refugees, cited in Simon Beck & Scott McKenzie, 'Wide Abuse of Viets Claimed' *South China Morning Post,* 1 June 1995, p. 2.

as well as the subjection of detained asylum seekers to 'unprecedented levels of violence by the Hong Kong authorities'[42] including 'gross breaches of human rights'.[43] Echoing 'deep concern' at an international official level, the UN Committee on Economic, Social and Cultural Rights,[44] has urged the government, inter alia, 'to take immediate steps to ensure that children in refugee camps and those released from them, are accorded full enjoyment of the economic, social and cultural rights guaranteed to them under [the UN Covenant on Economic, Social and Cultural Rights]'.

Repatriation

The principle of *non refoulement*, underlying the duty of admission of asylum seekers, is also the fundamental rule applicable (with emphasis on its 'no expulsion/no return' aspect) to the issue of repatriation. The binding force of *non refoulement* in Hong Kong, notwithstanding the lack of statutory codification, has been highlighted earlier. The principle is also incorporated in the 1984 Convention Against Torture and Other Cruel, Inhuman or Degrading Treatment or Punishment as well as in the 1954 Convention Relating to the Status of Stateless Persons, both of which have been ratified by the UK and extended to the territory. The local authorities are, therefore, under the respective obligations not to 'expel or return ("*refouler*") a refugee in any manner whatsoever to the frontier of territories where his life or freedom would be threatened on account of his race, religion, nationality, membership of a particular social group or political opinion'; not to 'expel, return ("*refouler*") or extradite a person to another state where there are substantial grounds for believing that he would be in danger of being subjected to torture'; and not to expel a stateless person lawfully staying in the territory, except on grounds of national security or public order.

Evidently, should the cause of fear or danger generating the departure and request for asylum be eliminated or at least substantially reduced — and subject to the country of origin's undertaking to readmit its nationals and to cooperate with the country of asylum in arranging for their safe return — 'voluntary repatriation' may be considered a legitimate option. Yet,

---

[42] Loc.cit. Reference is made, for example, to the forced removal of detainees for repatriation in April 1994 which resulted in hundreds of injuries and controversy over the use of tear gas.

[43] Especially condemned were the tear-gassing of Vietnamese children during an operation on 20–21 May 1995 to transfer detainees to another camp with a view to forced repatriation to Vietnam.

[44] At its 53rd meeting (eleventh session), held on 7 December 1994.

fundamental to this option (which is firmly grounded in human rights law) is the respect of the right of persons to return *voluntarily under conditions of safety and dignity*. 'Voluntariness', in turn, denotes 'uninduced' (e.g. by a decrease in level of assistance in the country of refuge) free expression of the returnee's wishes, having been fully informed of the situation in the country of origin (including information concerning the extent of assistance and protection available to repatriates). Furthermore, repatriation must be carried out in accordance with 'accepted international practice', ruling out the deployment of force. On the other hand, 'mandatory repatriation' of non-refugees must be premised on a fair and reliable status determination process, and, like its 'voluntary' counterpart, may not be implemented unless there are sufficient assurances in place that no returnees would be subjected to punitive or discriminatory treatment.

Regarded by the Administration as 'consistent with the Comprehensive Plan of Action [CPA]' — as well as geared towards meeting targets for the closure of the region's refugee camps set by the Steering Committee of the International Conference on Indochinese Refugees[45] — three repatriation schemes operate in Hong Kong: a Voluntary Repatriation Programme (organized by the UNHCR since March 1989); a Non-Objectors Scheme (introduced by the UNHCR in September 1990); and an Orderly Return Programme (run by the government as of 29 October 1991). While such schemes, being supported by respective agreements and statements of understanding,[46] are generally within the contours of 'legitimacy', the territory's full compliance with relevant international obligations may nonetheless be questioned. Particularly vulnerable to criticism — apart from the fairness and reliability of the screening process — is repatriation in the absence of adequate guarantees for safe return, including the failure of Vietnam to repeal its laws against unauthorized departure or to formally undertake to withhold punishment from involuntary (as distinct from

---

[45] As resolved in a meeting in Kuala Lumpur on 21 February 1995 — and reaffirmed in Geneva on 16 March 1995 — all camps in the region were to be cleared by the end of 1995 except for Hong Kong which, in view of its 'special circumstances', was allowed to continue the return programme into 1996.

[46] The Voluntary Repatriation Programme is based on the agreement between the UK government and the Socialist Republic of Vietnam (SRV) concluded on 12 October 1988 and a Memorandum of Understanding between UNHCR and SRV of 16 December 1988; the Orderly Return Programme was instituted following a Statement of Understanding signed by the governments of UK, HK, and SRV on 29 October 1991. More recently, at a CPA conference in Geneva, Vietnam has agreed to take back 3600 asylum seekers from detention centres throughout Southeast Asia under new streamlined procedures.

voluntary) returnees[47] as well as restricted access to monitors of legal proceedings against returnees who are arrested. Concerns will linger as long as human rights continue to be abused in Vietnam, dissent is suppressed, and people caught trying to leave are harshly treated (facing detention without trial in re-education camps from between six months to two years). It may be added that whether or not the Hong Kong government is strictly liable under international law for breach of *non-refoulement*, the repatriation of asylum seekers — who have languished for several years in refugee camps — to a country which they fled at a great risk to their lives, is incompatible with 'elementary considerations of humanity', regarded by the International Court of Justice as part of 'general and well recognised principles' on which international obligations may be founded.[48]

PROTECTION OF THE ENVIRONMENT

Obligations under international treaty law

Hong Kong's obligations in the area of environmental protection emanate largely from international treaties applicable to the territory,[49] including agreements pertaining to the prevention and control of marine pollution,[50] curtailment of ozone-depleting substances,[51] protection of endangered plant and animal species,[52] and the preservation of natural habitats,[53] as well as

---

[47] Of further apprehension are prosecutions for slander of the state — a crime that carries the death penalty — based on statements made by returnees in the course of actions for judicial review in Hong Kong courts.

[48] See *Corfu Channel case* [1949] IC Reports 4, 22.

[49] Note that these treaties will continue to apply in Hong Kong after 30 June 1997, in accordance with agreements reached in the Sino-British Joint Liaison Group.

[50] The 1969 Convention on Civil Liability for Oil Pollution Damage (and its 1976 Protocol); 1969 Convention Relating to Intervention on the High Seas in Cases of Oil Pollution Casualties (and its 1973 Protocol); add 1972 Convention on the Prevention of Marine Pollution by Dumping of Wastes and Other Matters (and 1978 Amendments & 1980 Protocol Amending the 1972 Convention); 1973 Convention for the Prevention of Pollution from Ships (and its 1978 Protocol).

[51] The 1985 Convention for the Protection of the Ozone Layer; 1987 Protocol on Substances that deplete the Ozone Layer (and 1990 Amendments).

[52] The 1956 Plant Protection Agreement for the South East Asia & Pacific Region (and 1967 Amendment); 1973 Convention on International Trade in Endangered Species of Wild Fauna and Flora (and 1979 Amendment); 1979 Convention on the Conservation of Migratory Species of Wild Animals; 1946 International Convention for the Regulation of Whaling (and its 1956 Protocol).

regulation of activities in outer space[54] and liability in the field of nuclear energy.[55] For the most part, appropriate steps have been taken by the authorities to implement the respective duties, by incorporating the relevant conventions into domestic law.[56] Hong Kong, nonetheless, has lagged behind in discharging its global responsibilities with regard, for example, to movement and disposal of hazardous waste[57] or the conservation of tropical forests and their indigenous genetic resources.[58]

The government's tentative approach to its international environmental obligations — particularly when economic or commercial interests are involved — has come into focus recently in connection with the adoption of two new and significant multilateral conventions on environmental protection. Thus, in 1992, when more than 150 states became signatories to the

---

[53] 1971 [Ramsar] Convention on Wetlands of International Importance Especially as Waterfowl Habitat; 1972 Convention for the Protection of the World Cultural and Natural Heritage; 1988 Convention on the Regulation of Antarctic Mineral Resources Activities.

[54] 1967 Treaty on the Principles Government Activities of States in the Exploration and Use of Outer Space, Including the Moon and Other Celestial Bodies; 1968 Agreement on the Rescue of Astronauts, the Return of Astronauts and the Return of Objects Launched into Outer Space; 1972 Convention on International Liability for Damage Caused by Space Objects; 1974 Convention on Registration of Objects Launched into Outer Space.

[55] 1960 Convention on Third Party Liability in the Field of Nuclear Energy (and its 1964 Protocol).

[56] Re marine pollution see: Merchant Shipping (Prevention and Control of Pollution) Ordinance 1989; Merchant Shipping (Liability and Compensation for Oil Pollution) Ordinance 1990; Dumping at Sea Act (Overseas Territories) Order 1975; re restriction of ozone-depleting substances see: Ozone Layer Protection Ordinance 1989 (and 1992 Amendment); re protection of endangered species see: Animals and Plants (Protection of Endangered Species) Ordinance 1976 (and Amendments); Re preservation of habitats see: Country Parks Ordinance 1976; the Executive Council has given its approval on 1 March 1995 for the designation of Mai Po Marches and Inner Deep Bay (Hong Kong's last remaining wetland and a vital migratory resting ground for up to 53 000 birds at a time, including some of Asia's rarest birds) as a 'wetland of International Importance' under the 1971 Ramsar Convention (note, however, that the listing — which is still pending ratification by the British government — would provide no legal protection, although it might subject to international scrutiny current [judicially-sanctioned] encroachments by developers on the marchland borders).

[57] Hong Kong has not become a party to the 1989 Basel convention on the Control of Transboundary Movements of Hazardous Wastes and their Disposal. Hong Kong law currently allows the import, export and trans-shipment of radioactive and other toxic substances if a licence is obtained. It may also be noted that the territory is a major transhipment point for waste which is not necessarily destined for an internationally recognized specialist plant with adequate disposal facilities.

[58] Hong Kong has not acceded to the 1983 International Tropical Timber Agreement, although the Administration has taken action to reduce the consumption of tropical hardwood by banning their use in government construction sites.

Framework Convention on Climate Change and the Convention on Biological Diversity, Hong Kong officials have returned to the issues of 'designation problems' (should the territory be considered as developing or developed economy) and the territory's lack of sovereign status as reasons which may prevent Hong Kong from formally adopting these conventions, even though the government claims to generally endorse their objectives.

None of the arguments advanced seem convincing, however, in light of the territory's role as an international legal entity capable of extensive and autonomous participation in international agreements. Clearly, as acknowledged by the authorities, it may be 'possible for Her Majesty's Government to ratify the [Rio] Conventions on behalf of Hong Kong, as in the case of the Montreal Convention dealing with substances that deplete the ozone layer', subject to a proviso that the territory be appropriately designated as 'developed' or 'developing' in accordance with the accepted criteria.

In fact, to a certain degree, some requirements stipulated under the Global Change and Biodiversity conventions have been met. Of relevance, for instance, are the preparation of a greenhouse gas inventory by the Environmental Protection Department, the establishment of a Coordinating Group on Global Climate Change under the Director of the Royal Observatory, and the formation of an Energy Efficiency Advisory Committee chaired by the Secretary for planning, Environment and Lands. Yet, no legally enforceable measures have been introduced designed to reduce the emissions of carbon dioxide and other greenhouse gases. The protection of biological diversity is said to be pursued through the provision of country parks, conservation zoning under the Town Planning Ordinance and the designation of areas of outstanding nature value as 'Sites of Special Scientific Interest'. However, no clear rules are available for evaluating the application of the respective policies or monitoring their enforcement. Neither has any attempt been made to devise a national conservation strategy, enact appropriate regulations to protect diversity inside and outside the habitat of species or draw binding guidelines for assessment of projects that pose great dangers to species. Needless to say, in the absence of formal accession and incorporation into the domestic law, the government's response falls considerably short of effective implementation of the Rio treaties.

Obligations under customary international law

Attempting to identify customs that have been crystallized into international law in a novel, rapidly developing and indeterminate field as international environmental law is, unquestionably, a daunting task. From the outset, certain basic difficulties present themselves germane to a process of establishing general state practice (among over 170 states with diverse ideologies, cultures, interests, policies and legal systems), coupled with the need to verify an accompanying sense of legal obligation (*opinio juris*) distinct from mere comity, fairness or morality. Clearly, even more onerous is substantiating the claim that the obligation to protect the global environment is a peremptory norm of international law (*jus cogens*) accepted by the international community as a whole.

Yet, it may be argued with some force that certain principles of environmental protection and conservation possess the necessary 'material' and 'psychological' elements to found a status of customary international law and as such are binding on all nations. Regarded in this vein is, for example, the rule pertaining to the responsibility of states 'to ensure that activities within their jurisdiction or control do not cause damage to the environment of other states or of areas beyond the limits of national jurisdiction'.[59] Encompassed under such responsibility are the duties to control, prevent, reduce, and eliminate adverse environmental effects resulting from activities conducted in all spheres, cooperate in the abatement of transboundary environmental interferences, and assist in emergencies.

A customary status may also be ascribed to the general principle of 'sustainable development' — defined as 'development that meets the needs of the present without compromising the ability of future generations to meet their own needs' — first proclaimed by the World Commission on Environment and Development in 1986 and since reaffirmed in numerous resolutions and statements by various international bodies, most notably at the UN Conference on Environment and Development held in Rio in 1992. In particular, ample evidence may be marshalled in support of the normative nature of several decision-making principles that are imperative to achieving sustainable development. Included are: the 'precautionary principle', which aims at ensuring that activities posing a threat to the environment will be prevented, even if there is no conclusive scientific proof linking them to environmental damage; the 'polluter-pays principle' [PPP], whereby those who burden or harm the environment are required to bear the costs of avoiding, eliminating or compensating for these injuries; and the undertaking of environmental impact assessments [EIAs] for proposed activities that are likely to have a significant adverse impact on the environment and are subject to a decision of a competent national authority.

---

[59] For an analysis of the customary status of the rule and its application in the Hong Kong context, see: Roda Mushkat, 'The Daya Bay Nuclear Plant Project in the Light of International Environmental Law' (1990) 7 *UCLA Pacific Basic Law Journal* 87.

A move towards a growing recognition of the exigencies of sustainable development is clearly discernable in Hong Kong,[60] which has responded by enacting a large volume of pollution control laws. Inadequate effect, however, has been given to the pertinent international obligations. The territory has not incorporated the concept of sustainable development into its constitutional framework or legal system. Nor has it formally adopted a national, comprehensive[61] executive policy — aimed at preserving and improving the quality of life of present and future generations — which features a defined mandate for the integration of environment and development. Many local policy debates continue to be conducted within a conceptual framework depicting economic growth and environmental protection as mutually exclusive, and often result in the subordination of environmental imperatives to economic objectives.[62] In the absence of necessary legal constraints, such misperception is occasionally reflected in judicial decisions as well.[63]

Nor are the imbalances guaranteed to be redressed in post-1997 Hong Kong, given the status envisaged for the environment in the Administration's policy matrix. Of particular concern is the loose appending in the Basic Law of the HKSAR,[64] of a perfunctory statement — that the government 'pay regard to the protection of the environment' — to an explicit directive to the government of the SAR to 'formulate appropriate policies to promote and

---

[60] See in particular *The Hong Kong Environment: A Green Challenge for the Community. Second Review of the 1989 White Paper Pollution in Hong Kong — A Time to Act* (Planning, Environment and Lands Branch, Government Secretariat, November 1993) p. 21 ('Our objective should be not only to protect the environment for ourselves, for all flora and fauna, but also for our children and future generations so that they can also live healthy and active lives. This is because our children have a right to inherit from us an environment from which they can meet their needs as we have met ours, and because we have a duty — a duty of stewardship — to hand on to them an environment in good repair'). The Review further lays down ten 'foundation stones' for achieving the objective (pp. 33–35): stewardship, sustainable development, community responsibility, public information, realistic approach, precautionary principle, regulation, polluter pays principle, international cooperation, and private sector involvement.

[61] As distinct from the ad hoc, piecemeal efforts and the sectorial view of environmental issues which currently characterize policy thinking and programme development.

[62] Cases in point include the Lantao port and Chek Lap Kok airport developments and harbour reclamation. It may be added that, generally, given the lack of clear priorities for the allocation of government resources, implementation of policies and programmes hinges on the vagaries of whichever forces are ascendant when budget allocations are made.

[63] See most recently a High Court ruling (28 April 1995) to reject an application for judicial review of a decision by the Town Planning Appeals Board allowing developers to destroy vital ponds around the Mai Po marshes to build a golf course and luxury housing complex.

[64] See Article 119 which is located at the end of a detailed chapter on the 'Economy'.

coordinate the development of various trades such as manufacturing, commerce, tourism, real estate, transport, public utilities, services, agriculture and fisheries.' It is also evident that few limits are imposed on economic growth under the Territorial Development Strategy, Hong Kong's blueprint for infrastructural development up to 2011.

The current emphasis, clearly, is on 'cleanup'[65] operations rather than a 'precautionary'[66] planning of sound and sustainable environment. The government is yet to pass the necessary legislation requiring major project proponents, both public and private, to complete an EIA (environmental impact assessment) process before commencement of works and to implement all the ensuing recommendations.[67] Further legislative attempts are also required to integrate all aspects of land development with the environment.

Some 'statutory' bolstering has nonetheless been given to the implementation of the 'polluter-pays principle' (PPP) under the Sewage Services Ordinance 1995 (and subsidiary legislation),[68] with a view to encouraging a more careful use of resources. By and large, however, the Administration has preferred a 'permit system' as a means of pollution control (so as to avoid imposing an undue burden on the manufacturing sector) and has not adopted the more contemporary favoured economic and fiscal mechanisms (e.g. emission charges, CFC or other 'green' taxes). It may be added that notwithstanding significant increases in the level of penalties prescribed for infringements of environmental laws, enforcement remains less than strict.[69]

---

65 See the Governor's 1994 'Policy Commitments' referring to government's goal to 'restore the environment to a satisfactory condition.'

66 Critics point, for example, to the government's 'Strategic Sewage Disposal Scheme' which involves (in its second stage) the discharge of sewage into the South China, threatening to cause environmental pollution on a large scale.

67 Note, however, that an Environmental Impact Assessment Bill was gazetted in January 1996. Criticisms have nonetheless been levelled at the Bill's failure to require input from sources other than the government's Environmental Protection Department.

68 The introduction of charging schemes for the privately collected solid waste delivered to landfalls and for the disposal of chemical waste at the assigned treatment centre has been held up by disagreements within government regarding appropriate modes of levy, based on arguments such as harm to the economy. Note also claims from the private sector that imposition of such charges will result in thousands of small businesses being compelled to leave Hong Kong.' See Elizabeth Tracey, 'Polluter-Pays Rule "May Force Firms Out of HK" ' *South China Morning Post*, 4 February 1995, p. 2.

69 Both officials and judges are reluctant, respectively, to request and impose maximum penalties. According to a survey of prosecutions of environmental offenders in 1993, conducted by the Hong Kong Environmental Law Association, it is 'cheaper for companies to pollute than to clean up their operations.' Cited in Kathy Griffin, 'Survey Shock Over Low Pollution Fines' *South China Morning Post*, 9 June 1994, p. 4.

Obligations under 'soft' international environmental law

International environmental law has developed a plethora of standards and practices which — although outside the traditional categories of treaties and customary international law, and hence designated 'soft law' — do not lack authority, and are normatively expected to be adhered to. Probably the most important 'soft law' instruments in contemporary international environmental law are the three major documents adopted unanimously at the 1992 'Earth Summit'[70] namely, the Rio Declaration on Environment and Development, Agenda 21 (An Action Programme Extending into the Twenty-First Century and Covering All Areas Affecting the Relationship Between the Environment and the Economy), and the Non-Legally Binding Authoritative Statement of Principles for a Global Consensus in the Management, Conservation and Sustainable Development of All Types of Forests.

To a large extent, the Rio Declaration represents a codification of the general principles which should govern the economic and environmental conduct of nations and individuals in the pursuit of global sustainability. Some of the principles contained in the Declaration have in fact 'hardened' into customary international law, including the 'precautionary principle' (principle 15), the 'polluter-pays principle' (principle 16) and the requirement for environmental impact assessment (principle 17). Also affirmed are the fundamental democratic principles of access to information ['including information on hazardous materials and activities in their communities'],[71] public participation in decision-making processes and effective judicial/administrative redress (principle 10). The Declaration, additionally, restates accepted principles of transnational relations such as the avoidance of harm to other nations and to the global environment (principle 2), information and prior consultation on transnational environmental risk (principle 19), notification and assistance in environmental emergencies (principle 18), peaceful settlement of environmental disputes (principle 26) and, generally, cooperation in good faith in the fulfilment of the principles embodied in the Declaration (principle 27).

The obligations arising under the Rio Declaration are elaborated further in the 600-page Agenda 21 which identifies a set of priority action programmes and stipulates the activities and measures to be undertaken by governments for the accomplishment of internationally agreed-upon goals. While not assuming the form of a legally enforceable accord, because of the unique circumstances of its construction (a rigorously negotiated consensual

---

[70] Later endorsed in General Assembly Resolution 47/190 of 22 December 1992.
[71] Note in this connection particular local concerns in respect of the Daya Bay nuclear power plant.

product of most diversely composed political colloquium of the highest level), Agenda 21 constitutes a highly authoritative code of conduct to be followed by decision-makers at international, regional and national levels. In a similar vein, the 'non-legally binding' nature of the Statement of Principles on Forests does not detract from its status as a powerful soft law instrument in respect of the management, conservation and sustainable development of all types of forests, and more generally, for the 'greening of the world'.

In order to comply with the Rio prescriptions, the Hong Kong government must endow with legal force its proclaimed commitment to environmentally sound and sustainable development. Short of a constitutionally entrenched pledge to protect, preserve and enhance the environment for both present and future generations, it is incumbent on the authorities to draw a coherent 'national' policy, placing a prime duty on all government decision-makers to apply legislated criteria designed to foster sustainability. To implement directives contained in Agenda 21, laws and regulations pertaining to sustainable development, as well as the related institutional/administrative machinery, should be regularly assessed with a view to rendering them effective in practice. In addition, the government should develop integrated strategies to maximize compliance with the relevant legislation, including mechanisms for appropriate involvement of individuals and groups in the enforcement process. Indeed, to provide for a meaningful public participation, the Administration should guarantee free access to information, capable of being enforced judicially by any individual or collectivity (including a formal/ statutory recognition of NGO's special role and their right to protect the public interest through legal action). Firm legal expression should also be given to principles of redress for environmental injury which alleviate current hardships related to standing, causes of action, burden of proof and costs as well as extend the range of available judicial remedies.

Obligations under regional environmental law

Generally, no additional or distinctly different norms regarding environmental protection and conservation could be said to have emerged in the region. By the same token, the key concept of 'sustainable development' is enshrined in all recent pronouncements made by Asian Pacific governments, including *Ecomission 2020 — a Regional Strategy for Environmentally Sound and Sustainable Development.*[72] Moreover, the adoption and endorsement of all the Rio documents by virtually all countries in the region lends further weight

---

[72] Adopted at a Ministerial Meeting in Bangkok on 16 October 1990.

to international environmental obligations incurred by Hong Kong under other sources as outlined above.

It is also evident the international legal duty of cooperation assumes a special significance in a region confronted by environmental problems and degradation of the greatest magnitude. As a member of key regional economic and development institutions — such as ESCAP, ADB, APDC and APEC — Hong Kong is well positioned to contribute to an effective implementation of global environmental norms. At a bilateral level, of particular urgency are cooperative efforts with the PRC to prevent, manage and abate cross-border environmental harm (related, for example, to the Daya Bay nuclear plant, infrastructure developments in the Pearl River Delta, and the massive Three Gorges dam on the Yangtze River), as well as attempts at 'harmonization' of both environmental standards and enforcement measures with a view to discouraging relocation of polluting industries.

Chapter 4

Hong Kong and Human Rights

NATIONALITY

Few issues pertaining to the transfer of sovereignty over Hong Kong have engendered as much anxiety in the territory as those related to nationality and its perceived offshoots (citizenship, right of abode, permanent residence, passports). Such concern is easily comprehended, given the important attributes of nationality under international law — including the entitlement to diplomatic protection abroad and the right to enter or leave one's country[1] — as well as the significant political and social ramifications of nationality in post-1997 Hong Kong.[2] This topic, therefore, has been selected for particular attention within the broader context of human rights protection in Hong Kong. Discussion will focus on questions regarding the existence of an applicable international legal right to nationality and the extent of compliance with correlative duties by the respective authorities.

A 'right to nationality' for Hong Kong people?

While the conferment of nationality is deemed largely a matter 'for each state to determine under its own law',[3] the severe hardships and lack of

---

[1] Other incidents of nationality at international law pertain to jurisdiction (states frequently exercise criminal or other jurisdiction on the basis of nationality); extraditability (a state has the right to refuse to extradite its own nationals to another state requesting surrender); enemy status in time of war (which may be determined by the nationality of the person concerned); allegiance (e.g. a duty to perform military service for the state of nationality).

[2] Regarding, for example, the appointment of senior government officials (see Basic Law, Articles 44, 55, 61, 71, 90), the voting and standing for election to the Legislative Council (BL, Art. 67), unrestricted residence and appertaining rights (BL, Arts. 24, 25–40), entitlement to passport/travel document (BL, Art. 153).

[3] 1930 Hague Convention on Certain Questions Relating to the Conflict of Nationality Laws, Article 1.

security suffered by individuals who are not recognized as nationals by any country has long been acknowledged as a subject of international concern and action aimed at the elimination or reduction of this condition known as 'statelessness'.[4] Indeed, given the crucial role played by nationality in the life of individuals and the exercise of their basic civil and political rights, it was evident that rules pertaining to nationality ought to be ensconced in the realm of international human rights law. Thus, impelled by the wholesale denationalization of people during the Second World War, the international community proclaimed in the 1948 Universal Declaration of Human Rights that '[e]veryone has the right to a nationality' and '[n]o one shall be arbitrarily deprived of his nationality nor denied the right to change his nationality' (Article 15).

Although a 'right to nationality' is not expressly provided for under the International Covenant on Civil and Political Rights, Article 24(3) stipulates the right of every child to acquire nationality.[5] A right to nationality is, arguably, also implied in Article 12 which states that '[n]o one shall be arbitrarily deprived of the right to enter his own country'. At a regional level, the right to nationality is explicitly guaranteed in the 1948 American Declaration of the Rights and Duties of Man[6] and the 1969 American Convention on Human Rights,[7] whereas Protocol No. 4 to the 1950 European Convention for the Protection of Human Rights and Fundamental Freedoms prohibits the denial of an individual right to enter his/her country [Article 3(2)].

Whether or not a general right to nationality has crystallized into customary international law, by virtue of applicability to the territory of the relevant international instruments,[8] the people of Hong Kong are entitled

---

[4] See, in particular, 1930 Protocol on a Certain Case of Statelessness; 1930 Special Protocol with Regard to Statelessness; 1954 Convention Relating to the Status of Stateless Persons; 1961 Convention on the Reduction of Statelessness.

[5] This right has been reaffirmed recently in the 1989 Convention on the Rights of the Child, Article 7.

[6] Article XIX: 'Every person has the right to the nationality to which he is entitled by law and to change it, if he so wishes, for the nationality of any other country that is willing to grant it to him.'

[7] Article 20: '1. Every person has the right to a nationality. 2. Every person has the right to the nationality of the state in whose territory he was born if he does not have the right to any other nationality. 3. No one shall be arbitrarily deprived of his nationality or of the right to change it.'

[8] Including the 1948 Universal Declaration on Human Rights, 1966 International Covenant on Civil and Political Rights, 1989 Convention on the Rights of the Child, 1930 Convention on Certain Questions Relating to the Conflict of Nationality Law, 1930 Protocol on a Certain Case of Statelessness, 1930 Special Protocol Concerning Statelessness, 1954 Convention on the Status of Stateless Persons, 1961 Convention on the Reduction of Statelessness. See *List of Multilateral Treaties Applying to Hong Kong* (1 January 1990).

not to be deprived of their nationality or of the right to change their nationality nor to be rendered stateless. Yet, the realization of these entitlements has been made particularly doubtful following the arrangements for the transition of sovereignty over the territory. The status of persons who are currently British Dependent Territories citizens (BDTCs) is the subject of two memoranda which were formally exchanged between the British and Chinese governments as part of the Sino-British Agreement on the Future of Hong Kong. In accordance with the United Kingdom Memorandum, since Hong Kong will no longer be a British dependent territory after 1997, BDTCs by virtue of such a territorial/constitutional connection will cease to have that status as from 1 July 1997. People thus affected will be 'eligible [provided they hold or are included in BDTC passports prior to July 1997][9] to retain an appropriate [non-transferrable] status which, without conferring the right of abode in the United Kingdom, will entitle them to continue to use passports issued by the Government of the United Kingdom'.

Pursuant to its Memorandum and the undertaking to provide Hong Kong's BDTCs with an 'appropriate status', the UK government has proclaimed in the Hong Kong (British Nationality) Order 1986 the creation of a new form of British nationality to be known as 'British National (Overseas)' [BN(O)]. Under the Order, '[a]ny person who is a British Dependent Territories citizen by virtue (wholly or partly) of his having a connection with Hong Kong and who, but for his having a connection with Hong Kong, would not be such a citizen shall be entitled, before 1st July 1997 (or before the end of 1997 if born in that year before that date), to be registered as a British National (Overseas) and to hold or be included in a passport appropriate to that status' [Section 4(2)].

As stated in the Chinese Memorandum, 'all Hong Kong Chinese compatriots, whether they are holders of the "British Dependent Territories citizens' Passport" or not, are Chinese nationals.' But, '[t]aking account of the historical background of Hong Kong and its realities, the competent authorities of the Government of the People's Republic of China will, with effect from 1 July 1997, permit Chinese nationals in Hong Kong who were previously called "British Dependent Territories citizens" to use travel documents issued by the Government of the United Kingdom for the purpose of travelling to other states and regions.' Such 'Chinese nationals' could not, however, avail themselves of British consular protection in the HKSAR and others parts of the PRC.

Forced into a difficult position by the uncompromising Chinese posture (particularly, the objection to the transferability of the new status for

---

[9] This effectively excludes holders of Certificates of Identity (CIs), who make up half of those people who possess some sort of a travel document.

ex-BDTCs) on the one hand and its own international commitments on the other, the UK government has constructed a rather awkward formula. It has opted to sidestep the issue altogether by assigning[10] yet another category of nationality — British Overseas Citizenship [BOC] — to children of former HK BDTCs born on or after 1 July 1997, if these children would be otherwise stateless as well as to what is expected to be a very small number of non-Chinese persons who are BDTCs on 30 June 1997 but who, for some special reason, could not by then obtain a passport entitling them to the BNO status. Like its BN(O) counterpart, BOC offers no abode rights in the United Kingdom and is non-transferable by descent.[11]

Of further relevance to the issue are provisions in the Sino-British Joint Declaration[12] concerning the categories of persons entitled to a 'right of abode' in the HKSAR and, consequently, are qualified to obtain 'permanent identity cards' and passports issued by the HKSAR government. Also applicable to the territory as of 1 July 1997 is the 1980 Nationality Law of the PRC[13] which, inter alia, 'does not recognise dual nationality for any Chinese national' (Article 3). While the status of most of the territory's residents for fifty years after 1997 is addressed to some extent in the various instruments, serious gaps and ambiguities remain which give rise to claims of infringement of international rights and obligations. Nor is the confusion attenuated by pragmatic strategies such as the creation of new categories of nationality, an occasional elevation from one category to another when 'necessary', utilization of ad hoc 'assurance schemes', employment of legal terms of art like the 'right of abode', or the use of discretionary power to grant passports.

Thus, it has been contended[14] that Hong Kong people have been arbitrarily deprived of their nationality and compulsorily naturalized. Specifically, the parties to the Sino-British Agreement, disregarding the inhabitants' right to freely determine their political status, have acted to repudiate the inhabitants' distinct nationality grounded in a 'real and effective link' to the territory.[15] Nor has the Agreement conformed to the customary

---

[10] Under the Hong Kong (British Nationality) Order 1986, Sec. 6.

[11] British Overseas citizenship may, however, be acquired at any time by registration.

[12] See JD, Annex I, Art. XIV.

[13] See Basic Law, Annex III: 'National Laws to be Applied in the Hong Kong Special Administrative Region.'

[14] See, e.g. Nihal Jayawickrama, 'A Right to Nationality: Its Application to Hong Kong' in J. Arthur McInnis, ed., *Legal Forum on Nationality, Passports & 1997* (Hong Kong: The Canadian Chamber of Commerce & the Faculty of Law of the University of Hong Kong, 1990), pp. 83–106.

[15] See Chapter 1 for a discussion of the case for a 'Hong Kong nationality'.

international legal obligation to grant the right of option to the population concerned.[16] Rather, in a manner reminiscent of the no-longer permissible mode of a cession — as well as contrary to China's own past practices of allowing option of nationality[17] — the accord has sought to impose Chinese nationality on all Chinese compatriots[18] in Hong Kong, absent any form of consent on the latter's behalf.[19]

At the same time, an attempt by the territory's ethnic Chinese to exercise their right to change their nationality or renounce such compulsorily-acquired nationality hinges on complying with the vague conditions stipulated in the Nationality Law of the PRC[20] or satisfying other 'hidden

---

[16] On the right of option as a rule of customary international law, see Karl M. Meesen, 'Option of Nationality' in Rudolf Bernhardt, ed., *Encyclopedia of Public International Law* (1981–), Instl. 8 (1985), p. 424ff. For relevant state practice and juridical decisions, see also Ruth Donner, *The Regulation of Nationality in International Law* (Helsinki: The Finnish Society of Sciences and Letters, 1983) pp. 196–215.

[17] e.g. under the 1955 Sino-Indonesian Treaty on Dual Nationality and in an agreement to redraw the boundary with Burma in 1960.

[18] 'Compatriotism' — which does not appear to constitute a required element under the PRC Nationality Law — is not explicated in the Memorandum. The term 'compatriots' is commonly taken to mean 'fellow-countrymen' so that it may have been used here to avoid saying 'Chinese nationals are Chinese nationals'. It may, however, 'imply a test to exclude those who are politically unsound.' See Robin M. White, 'Hong Kong: Nationality, Immigration and the Agreement with China' (1987) *International & Comparative Law Quarterly* 483, 493 n. 40.

[19] It may be noted that, apart from being a fundamental element of human dignity in which human rights is grounded, the freedom to shape one's own fate (including one's nationality) is given special emphasis in the context of territorial transfer. See, for example, Art. 4 of the 1969 American Convention on Human Rights which provides: 'In case of the transfer of a portion of territory on the part of one of the States signatory hereof to another of such States, the inhabitants of such transferred territory must not consider themselves as nationals of the State to which they are transferred, unless they expressly opt to change their original nationality.'

[20] Under Article 9: 'Any Chinese national who has settled abroad and who has been naturalized there or has acquired foreign nationality of his own free will automatically lose Chinese nationality.' Article 10 states: 'Chinese nationals may renounce Chinese nationality upon approval of their applications provided that: 1) they are close relatives of aliens; or 2) they have settled abroad; or 3) they have other legitimate reasons.'

'*Settled abroad*' is nowhere defined. In practice, as observed by one commentator, especially during international crises (like the massacre of Chinese residents in Indonesia or persecution of overseas Chinese after the North Vietnamese took over the South or more recently during Iraqi hostilities in Kuwait), China 'treated and accepted overseas Chinese as Chinese nationals'. In a similar vein, foreign nationals of Chinese descent themselves tend to assume that 'by virtue of their Chinese blood, other countries concede China degree of informal jurisdiction.' See Frankie Fook-Lun Leung, 'The Problem of Being Chinese' *Asian Wall Street Journal*, 2 June 1994, at p. 6. Neither is any indication provided of the reasons considered '*legitimate*' in the context of renunciation of Chinese nationality.

requirements'.[21] Particularly problematic is the conjugated 'settlement abroad/free acquisition of foreign nationality' prerequisite (coupled with non-recognition of dual nationality) for Hong Kong's Chinese who have obtained foreign nationality by virtue of employment, marriage, purchase, investment or under a special 'nationality package', without residing overseas.

Even more grave is the potential violation of the right of the local population not to be rendered stateless. Notwithstanding the construction by the UK government of the special category of BN(O), it is questionable whether such a 'unique' status would be regarded as 'nationality' under internationally accepted criteria. Clearly, it[22] is incongruous with the perception of nationality in state practice, arbitral and judicial decisions and the opinion of writers as a 'legal bond having as its basis a social fact of attachment, a genuine connection of existence, interests and sentiments, together with the existence of reciprocal rights and duties'.[23] Nor can the BN(O) be said to 'constitute the juridical expression of the fact that the individual upon whom it is conferred . . . is in fact more closely connected with the population of the State conferring nationality than with that of any other State'.[24]

In practical terms, the BN(O) fails to convey a 'real and effective' link to *any* state or territory. It carries no right to reside and live in the UK, its dependent territories or, for that matter, in Hong Kong.[25] By the same token, it does not offer any non-territorial means, such as transmission to one's offspring, for the maintenance of what is viewed as 'a continuing legal relationship' between the state and its national.[26] Furthermore, doubts are cast on the ability of the holders of such 'nationality' to benefit from that which is generally considered one of the most significant attributes of nationality, namely diplomatic protection. Besides the pre-imposed restrictions on British consular protection in the HKSAR and any part of China, third countries,

---

[21] For a critical analysis of the PRC's renunciation rules and their inconsistency with the right to expatriation see: Johannes Chan, 'Nationality' in Raymond Wacks, ed., *Human Rights in Hong Kong* (Hong Kong: Oxford University Press, 1992) pp. 470, 487–495.

[22] The following critical observations in relation to the BN(O) apply with equal (or more) force to BOC.

[23] *Nottebohm Case (Liechtenstein v Guatemala)*, [1955] ICJ Rep. 4.

[24] Loc.cit.

[25] Rather, the British government has obtained the PRC's permission to insert into the BN(O) passport a statement to the effect that the holder has a HK identity card which grants him/her the right of abode in Hong Kong.

[26] See judgment of the British-Mexican Claims Commission in *Re Lynch (1929–1930) Annual Digest of Public International Law Cases* 221 at p. 223.

acting under prevalent international norms,[27] may refuse any British intervention on a BN(O)'s behalf for lack of a 'genuine link'.

In fact, the BN(O) may be viewed as anomalous under Britain's own law which requires a 'real link' and close personal connection with the United Kingdom for the acquisition of British nationality.[28] Evidently, the Mainland authorities do not consider the BN(O) status as nationality, otherwise they would have not agreed to what is manifestly inconsistent with China's legally sanctioned policy of non-recognition of dual nationality.[29]

Nor does the issuance of BN(O) passports necessarily denote the conferring of the status of nationality. While a duly authorized passport may be *prima facie* evidence of nationality, there have been judicial decisions to the effect that a passport is not conclusive proof of nationality, except in conjunction with other evidence. Basically, a passport is an identity document for travel purposes and identity may be certified by non-national as well as by the national states. In theory, a state may even issue a passport to an alien, although it is unlikely to do so, especially since passports are taken to imply acceptance of responsibility for, meeting temporary financial demands on behalf of, or arranging the repatriation of a passport holder who encounters difficulties while visiting a foreign country. It is in this regard that additional reservations are voiced pertaining to the effectiveness or recognition by other countries of a passport not backed by 'real' links of nationality.

Yet, if with respect to the ethnic Chinese holders of BDTC, the BN(O) status represents a possible denial of the claim to a meaningful British nationality, for the non-Chinese BDTCs it may signify becoming effectively statelessness. Unlike their Chinese brethren, they would not be 'bestowed' with Chinese nationality on 1 July 1997 and — given the doubtful nature of the BN(O) as nationality — 'will, after 1997, live on Chinese territory as aliens, but without any country which they could call their own and to which

---

[27] See references to state practice and jurisprudence in the *Nottebohm Case*. Based on such authorities, the International Court of Justice held that Guatemala was entitled to treat a naturalized Liechtenstein citizen as German, even though he had forfeited German citizenship on naturalization, because he had no genuine link with Liechtenstein. Note also that under Article 5 of the Hague Convention on Certain Questions Relating to the Conflict of Nationality Laws, a third State 'shall recognize exclusively in its territory either the nationality of the country in which he is habitually and principally resident, or the nationality of the country with which in the circumstances he appears to be in fact most closely connected'.

[28] See Home Office, *British Nationality Law Outline of Proposed Legislation* (1981), paras. 11, 18, 37, 39.

[29] See infra (notes 77, 78); 'The People's Republic of China does not recognize dual nationality for any Chinese national.' Art. 3, 1980 Nationality Law of The People's Republic of China, reprinted in 23 *Beijing Review* 17 (No. 40, 6 October 1980).

they could return should the need arise'[30] (irrespective of general assurances that 'any *forced* to leave Hong Kong can settle in Britain').[31] In principle, like any other 'aliens or stateless persons' they may be able to apply for naturalization as Chinese nationals under the Nationality Law of the PRC, if they are 'willing to abide by China's Constitution and laws' and provided that: '(1) they are close relatives of Chinese nationals; or (2) they have settled in China; or (3) they have other legitimate reasons' (Article 7). Needless to say, the acquisition of Chinese nationality by non-Chinese BDTCs is by no means assured when subject, as it is, to governmental discretion and approval guided by racially-based nationality principles.

The potential statelessness faced by Hong Kong's 'persons not of Chinese nationality' is not mitigated by an entitlement to a 'right of abode' — unattached to any grant of nationality [BN(O), BOC or Chinese nationality] and circumscribed by requirements of continuous residence of at least seven years combined with the taking of the territory as a place of permanent residence. Basically, a 'right of abode' — that is, the right to enter, re-enter, live, and work — is quite distinct from the concept of nationality, and does not preclude statelessness under international norms. In all probability, third countries deliberating the admission of a non-Chinese BN(O) or BOC (with account taken of repatriation prospects) would be inclined to judge such persons stateless.

Finally, no attempt has been made under the applicable nationality arrangements to regularize the position of asylum-seekers, former residents of Vietnam, who are detained in Hong Kong (and are likely to be still in the territory in 1997). After 30 June 1997, members of this group — which includes persons who are *de facto* stateless, having been recognized as nationals by no state (and, hence, refused repatriation)[32] — will not be eligible for any form of British nationality.[33] Not being 'Hong Kong Chinese compatriots', they will not become Chinese nationals.[34] Nor, for that matter, would they be entitled to a right of abode in the HKSAR, given their inability

---

[30] Jayawickrama, supra (note 14), at p. 101.

[31] As restated by British Prime Minister, John Majors; see 'Pledge of Honour' *South China Morning Post*, 5 March 1996, at 18.

[32] See discussion in Chapter 3.

[33] Unless they are BDTCs, having been born in Hong Kong prior to the entry into effect, in 1983, of the British Nationality Act of 1981. It may be pointed out that under the 1961 Convention on the Reduction of Statelessness (Article 1), nationality must be granted to a person born in the territory who would otherwise be stateless.

[34] As noted above, aliens and stateless persons may acquire Chinese nationality under certain prescribed conditions, although approval of applications from the group in question may not be forthcoming, especially in view of the PRC's hard-line policy vis-à-vis Vietnam.

to comply with the requirement of 'ordinary residence'.[35] Indeed, it has been speculated by a UNHCR official that 'China would not wish to keep them in Hong Kong after the handover and they could be moved to jails or re-education camps on the mainland' or 'forced back into Vietnam from China'.[36]

In the light of the above analysis, it is legitimate to conclude that, to the extent that a 'right to nationality' is provided under international law, Hong Kong people have not been duly afforded the respective entitlements. They have been denied their right to a nationality which genuinely reflects their real and effective connection with a country of their own choice, while subjected, contrary to international norms, to a compulsory change of nationality and 'collective naturalization'. It is, moreover, arguable that the British government has not complied with its obligation to 'reduce statelessness', particularly the duties to secure in the appropriate treaty that 'no person shall become stateless as a result of the transfer' of a territory and to 'confer its nationality on such persons as would otherwise become stateless as a result of the transfer'.[37]

A 'right of abode' for Hong Kong people?

Generally, for international law purposes, nationality and citizenship are inextricably bound. Distinctions have nonetheless been drawn by some countries, especially in colonial contexts.[38] Most notably, English law recognizes six categories of UK nationals,[39] of which only one — 'British citizens' — provides its holders with the right of entry to Britain. Yet, since nationality defines a person's political status and denotes a broad spectrum of rights that flow from an individual's belonging to a certain territorial community, arbitrary differentiations cease to be an internal matter of

---

[35] Under Hong Kong's Immigration Ordinance, arrivals from Vietnam who are determined to be 'refugees' are granted permission to stay pending resettlement elsewhere, while those 'screened out' are detained pending repatriation.

[36] See Scott McKenzie, 'Viets to Face Mainland Jail After '97, Says UN' *South China Morning Post*, 20 July 1995, at p. 3 (citing the UNHCR Director for Asia and Oceania).

[37] Article 10, 1961 Convention on the Reduction of Statelessness.

[38] Thus, e.g. persons born in the Dutch possessions were Dutch subjects and not citizens of the Netherlands. Some residents in US posessions are American nationals but do not enjoy full citizenship rights such as voting.

[39] British citizen [BC]; British Dependent Territories citizen [BDTC]; British Overseas citizen [BOC]; British Subject [BS]; British Protected Person [BPP]; British National (Overseas) [BN(O)].

immigration control and regulation but are to be judged by reference to international standards of justice as embodied in human rights law.

Special protection is accorded by the international community to what is deemed to be '[o]ne of the functions inherent in the concept of nationality [namely,] the right to settle and to reside in the territory of the State of nationality or, conversely, the duty of the State to grant and permit such residence to its nationals'.[40] In fact, as observed by the author of an extensive study on *The Right to Leave and Return in International Law and Practice*,[41] '[t]his right does not stem solely or even primarily from its more recent expressions in the Universal Declaration of Human Rights,[42] Covenant on Civil and Political Rights,[43] and other international human rights instruments[44] but is part of customary international law'. It is formally proclaimed in the constitutions of more than 80 states[45] and respected 'in a meaningful way' by the majority of countries.[46]

In terms of its scope, the 'right of return' extends to nationals/citizens born outside the country and who have never lived therein.[47] Nor are formal

---

[40] Paul Weis, *Nationality and Statelessness in International Law* (Germantown, MD: Sijthoff & Noordhoff, 2d ed., 1979), p. 45.

[41] Hurst Hannum, *The Right To Leave and Return in International Law and Practice* (Dordrecht: Martinus Njihoff, 1987) p. 60.

[42] Art. 13(2): 'Everyone has the right to leave any country, including his own, and to return to his country.'

[43] Art. 12(4): 'No one shall be arbitrarily deprived of the right to enter his own country.'

[44] e.g. the 1965 International Convention on the Elimination of All Forms of Racial Discrimination, Art. 5: '. . . State Parties undertake to prohibit and to eliminate racial discrimination in all its forms and to guarantee the right of everyone, without distinction as to race, colour, or national or ethnic origin, to equality before the law, notably in the enjoyment of the following rights: (d)(ii): 'The right to leave any country including one's own, and to return to one's country; European Convention on Human Rights: Protocol No. 4 (1968), Art. 3(2): 'No one shall be deprived of the right to enter the territory of the State of which he is a national;' 1981 African Charter on Human Rights and People's Rights, Art. 12(2): 'Every individual shall have the right to leave any country including his own, and to return to his country . . .'. The right is also incorporated and elaborated in the Helsinki *Final Act* and the Concluding Documents of its compliance review conferences. Note also specific pronouncements such as the 1972 Declaration on the Right to Leave and the Right to Return (adopted by Uppsala Colloquium) and the 1986 Strasbourg Declaration on the Right to Leave and Return (adopted by Strasbourg Meeting of Experts) cited, respectively, in Hannum, ibid., pp. 150, 154.

[45] See list in Hannum, ibid., pp. 139–141.

[46] See ibid., pp. 125–127.

[47] See Hannum, ibid., pp. 56–60 (observing that the change from the formulation in Article 13 of the Universal Declaration — which refers to the right to 'return' to one's country — to the right to 'enter' one's country was made in order to include nationals of a country who could not have a right to 'return' to it in view of the fact that they had never been there).

governmental determinations of nationality/citizenship a final arbiter of whether the right exists: 'Governments come and go, and their political fluctuations and vagaries should not affect the fundamental right of human beings, such as the right to return to one's own country and to have a homeland.'[48] At the same time, the right to enter/return need not imply a right to settle in a specific location within the country, and a state may, possibly, discharge its respective duties if a right of abode is ensured in any part of the country or in territories under its sovereign control.

In this vein, the Commonwealth Immigration Act of 1962 — which imposed immigration control on all Commonwealth citizens (except those born in the UK[49]) — cannot be strictly said to have constituted a breach by the United Kingdom of its international legal obligation, given the presumed security of residence enjoyed by such persons as citizens of independent Commonwealth countries or inhabitants of territories progressing towards independence. The UK's compliance with international human rights law might have been tainted, however, by its differential treatment among nationals/members of the same 'class of citizenship'. It is thus arguable that by granting a right of abode in the UK to the people of the Falkland Islands and not to their Hong Kong brethren,[50] the British government has acted contrary to the general international law principle of non-discrimination[51] and the specific provision in the Convention on the Elimination of All Forms of Racial Discrimination.[52] Similar sentiments have been echoed by the UN Committee on the Elimination of Racial Discrimination, which observed[53]

---

[48] From the papers of the Uppsala Colloquium, cited in Hannum, ibid., at p. 58.

[49] Also excepted were those who held UK passports issued by the government of the UK (as opposed to the government of the colony).

[50] Under a special statute — British Nationality (Falkland Islands) 1983 — BDTCs of the Falkland Islands were granted full British citizenship, including the right of abode in Britain. Given that the citizenship classification is purportedly based on a 'genuine link with the Kingdom', there appears to be no reasonable justification for drawing a distinction between rights attached to the status enjoyed by citizens of British dependent territories which exhibit an identical 'link'.

[51] By the end of 1989, 129 states (more than three quarters of the membership of the UN) had ratified or acceded to the International Convention on the Elimination of All Forms of Racial Discrimination and have taken the necessary legislative means to implement it. See Centre for Human Rights, *The First Twenty Years. Progress Report of the Committee on the Elimination of Racial Discrimination* (New York: United Nations, 1991) pp. 55–56 (list – pp. 72–75). Generally, see Warwick A. McKean, *Equality and Discrimination under International Law* (Oxford: Clarendon Press, 1983).

[52] The United Kingdom ratified the Convention and extended it to Hong Kong on 7 March 1969.

[53] See Committee on the Elimination of Racial Discrimination, 48th session, 26 February-15 March 1996, *Concluding Observations,* D(20).

as a 'matter of concern' that the status of British National Overseas (BNO) or British Overseas Citizen (BOC) 'does not entitle the bearer the right of abode in the United Kingdom and contrasts with the full citizenship status conferred upon a predominantly white population living in another dependent territory'. The Committee noted that 'most of the persons holding BNO or BOC status are Asians and that judgments on applications for citizenship appear to vary according to the country of origin, which leads to the assumption that this practice reveals elements of racial discrimination'.

It may be further contended that divesting Hong Kong BDTCs of their status and its abode entitlement in the territory, and its replacement by another form of British nationality, has reactivated the duty imposed on the British government to admit its nationals for residence in the United Kingdom, irrespective of any internal classification of citizenship. This was the view expressed by both the Foreign Affairs Committee[54] and the International Commission of Jurists Mission to Hong Kong.[55] Particularly compelling is the case of non-Chinese BDTCs who, unlike their Chinese counterparts, would not become Chinese nationals upon the transfer of sovereignty nor be entitled to abode in Hong Kong as a matter of [internationally protected] right.[56] Rather, upon fulfilling prescribed requisites, they would be granted — *qua* aliens — a non-transferrable right of abode in the HKSAR according to a Chinese domestic statute [the Basic Law] which is discriminatory in nature[57] and is subject to interpretation and amendment by the PRC's National People's Congress.[58] Moreover, like any other aliens, they may be expelled or deported, should the authorities consider their presence in the territory a threat to '*ordre public*'.[59] Indeed, it has been suggested that denial of the

---

[54] See House of Commons, Foreign Affairs Committee, *Relations Between the United Kingdom and China in the Period up to and Beyond 1997,* Vol. I (London: HMSO, 1994) [FAC Report 1994] pp. lx–lxi.

[55] See International Commission of Jurists, *Countdown to 1997. Report of a Mission to Hong Kong* (Geneva: ICJ, 1992) pp. 60–67. Specific recommendations include an immediate grant of British citizenship and a right of abode in the UK to Hong Kong BDTCs of non-Chinese descent with no right of abode outside Hong Kong, and to Hong Kong BDTCs under 18 who would have been British citizens if born on or after the 1st January 1983.

[56] Although the right of abode in the HKSAR is dealt with under the Sino-British Agreement (Annex I, Art XIV), its effect on the individuals depends on the applicability within the municipal law (i.e. the Basic Law).

[57] Note, e.g. the preclusion of non-Chinese from senior positions in government, civil service and police (BL, Arts. 44, 61, 71, 90, 101. It may be pointed out that the PRC is a party to the 1965 International Convention on the Elimination of All Forms of Racial Discrimination, having ratified the Convention on 29 December 1981.

[58] See Basic Law, Articles 158 & 159.

[59] See, generally, Guy Goodwin-Gill, *International Law and the Movement of Persons Between States* (Oxford: Clarendon Press, 1978) pp. 262ff.

right of abode in Britain to this group may be tantamount to a 'degrading treatment' which is prohibited under the International Covenant on Civil and Political Rights (Article 7).[60]

For its part, the British government — propelled by the Tiananmen Square massacre and the ensuing confidence crisis in Hong Kong, as well as its undertaking to maintain the stability and prosperity of the territory in the run-up to 1997 — has enacted the British Nationality (Hong Kong) Act of 1990. Under the Act, 50 000 heads of household in Hong Kong (and their families), selected according to an approved scheme,[61] will be registered as British citizens with a right of abode in the United Kingdom, subject to no residential requirement. Explaining the rationale underlying the 'nationality package', the Secretary of State for Home Affairs stated: '. . . the selection of 50,000 key personnel who are essential to the good government of Hong Kong and the management of its economy will stabilise Hong Kong, keep it prosperous and thus provide an incentive for the rest of the people to stay'.[62]

However, the arrangement — which has been criticized as elitist, discriminatory and a probable breach of Article 26 of the International Covenant on Civil and Political Rights[63] — is clearly inadequate[64] and, as concluded by the International Commission of Jurists, 'falls far short' of

---

[60] See Johannes M.M. Chan, 'Hong Kong: An Analysis of the British Nationality Proposals' (1990) 4 *Immigration and Nationality Law & Practice* 57, 59. The author refers, *inter alia*, to the *East African Asians* case [(1973) 3 *European Human Rights Reports* 76] wherein the European Commission of Human Rights held that the refusal of entry to East Africans constituted 'degrading treatment' contrary to Article 3 of the European Convention on Human Rights [which is identical to Article 7 of the ICCPR].

[61] Eligibility is determined by a points system based mainly on the value of the individuals' service to Hong Kong and the extent to which people in their category of employment are emigrating.

[62] 170 *Parliamentary Debates, H.C.* (6th ser., 1990) 1571.

[63] See analysis in Chan, supra (note 60); Article 26 of the ICCPR states: 'All persons are equal before the law and are entitled without discrimination to the equal protection of the law . . . the law shall prohibit any discrimination and guarantee to all persons equal and effective protection against discrimination on any grounds such as property, birth or other status.' It may also be noted that PRC government attacked the scheme as a violation of the UK's 'solemn commitment under the Joint Declaration' and indicated that it would refuse to honour passports distributed under the scheme. See Saith Faison, 'China Makes New Threat on Passports' *South China Morning Post*, 2 March 1990, at 1; Saith Faison, 'China Launches Fresh Attack on Passports Scheme' *South China Morning Post*, 13 April 1990, at 1. Note, however, that 'in [the UK] Memorandum, the United Kingdom never undertook not to grant British citizenship to people in HK before 1997.' 170 *Parliamentary Debates, H.C.* (6th ser., 1990) 1569.

[64] Under the scheme the right of abode is granted to only 50 000 households (or about 225 000 people), representing less than four percent of Hong Kong's residents and less than seven percent of those who hold British passports.

meeting Britain's obligation to 'provide for those BDTCs in Hong Kong who want them rights of residence in the UK itself or in third countries acceptable to them'.[65] Neither is this responsibility absolved by the pledge that 'if any solely British citizen came under pressure to leave Hong Kong the British Government of the day would consider with particular sympathy their case for admission to the United Kingdom'.[66] Finally, although the right of abode in Hong Kong may be assured[67] to '*Chinese citizens* born in Hong Kong before or after the establishment of the Hong Kong Special Administrative Region' and to '*Chinese citizens* who have ordinarily resided in Hong Kong for continuous period of not less than seven years before or after the establishment of the Hong Kong Special Administrative Region' [emphasis added], no definition of 'Chinese citizens' has been provided. Thus, it is not clear, for instance, whether Chinese beneficiaries of the British 'nationality scheme' — whose British nationality is not recognized by the PRC — would be entitled to a right of abode in the HKSAR.

Uncertainty also surrounds the position of Hong Kong's 'returning emigrants' (i.e. those returning from abroad after acquiring a foreign passport). Attempting to 'set hearts at ease', Lu Ping, director of China's Hong Kong and Macao Affairs Office proclaimed:[68] 'Our basic principle is that we welcome overseas immigrants to return to Hong Kong and that they will not be discriminated against or unfairly treated.' The particulars, however, are more blurred. Thus, according to Mr Lu, 'foreigners' who under existing Hong Kong immigration rules do not enjoy a right of abode (even though they have lived in Hong Kong for over seven years), can become permanent residents in the territory upon performance of a 'simple procedure'. Such procedure 'will likely include a declaration that they wish to treat Hong Kong as their permanent residence; that they have a permanent place of stay in Hong Kong, a permanent job or source of income; that the majority of their family members live in Hong Kong; that they pay taxes according to the Laws of Hong Kong'. Yet, as pointed out by one observer,[69] not only is such a procedure not 'simple' but the validity of some of its stipulations (especially the linking of residency right to job security or the presence of relatives in Hong Kong) is questionable. With respect to Hong Kong's

---

[65] Countdown to 1997, supra (note 55) at p. 62.

[66] See 96 *Parliamentary Debates, H.C.* (6th ser., 1986) 148; The statement was recited on 13 June 1990: 174 *Parliamentary Debates, H.C.* (6th ser., 1990) 294.

[67] Under the Basic Law, Article 24.

[68] In a luncheon talk on 18 May 1995, entitled *Towards 1997 and Beyond — Enhancement of Hong Kong's Role as an International Financial Centre* (a written copy of the talk was supplied).

[69] See Frank Ching, 'Hazy Chinese Laws Spell Trouble' *Far Eastern Economic Review*, 6 July 1995, at 34.

Chinese residents who 'emigrated overseas and have obtained a foreign nationality', they are, in Mr Lu's words,[70] 'no longer Chinese citizens' and should be 'treated as persons not of Chinese nationality', namely 'would be required to reside in Hong Kong for a continuous period of not less than seven years and take Hong Kong as their place of permanent residence before they would become permanent residents of Hong Kong'. A special dispensation — which finds no basis in law[71] — would, nonetheless, be given to those who return to Hong Kong before 30 June 1997.

More recently, in a move designed to 'resolve effectively' the issue of 'Hong Kong residents' nationality and right of abode',[72] proposals were submitted by the Preparatory Committee for the HKSAR to the National People's Congress Standing Committee[73] calling for a 'flexible interpretation of the practical implementation of the Chinese Nationality Law, having taken into consideration Hong Kong's historical background and present situation'. Accordingly, it was proposed that 'Hong Kong residents who are of Chinese descent[74] or born in Chinese territory (including Hong Kong)' be considered 'Chinese nationals'. Nationality thus acquired would not be lost by mere possession of foreign passports.[75] Moreover, the so-categorized 'HKSAR Chinese nationals who have overseas right of abode' 'can use documents issued by foreign governments to travel to other countries or places' but 'will not be entitled[76] to consular protection in the HKSAR and other parts

---

[70] Supra (note 68).

[71] The Basic Law draws no date-related distinctions. As noted above, under the PRC Nationality Law (Article 9), '[a]ny Chinese national who has settled abroad and who has been naturalized there or has acquired foreign nationality of his own free will automatically loses Chinese nationality'. The vagueness of 'settlement abroad' notwithstanding, the loss of Chinese nationality cannot be said to be affected by date of return.

[72] Unless otherwise indicated, the following citations are from a speech made by Lu Ping at a conference on Hong Kong's Economic Development, held in Hong Kong on 12 April 1996, reprinted in *South China Morning Post*, 13 April 1996, at p. 6.

[73] The proposals have now been incorporated as 'Explanatory Notes' by the NPC in a resolution passed on 15 May 1996.

[74] Although inconsistent with strict application of the Nationality Law of the PRC, the 'racial' criterion was said to have been preferred for pragmatic reasons, namely to 'allow Hong Kong people to know clearly whether they have Chinese nationality in a simple way without the need to trace back generations before generations.'

[75] Note the observation by one commentator that the proposal overlooks acquisition of foreign nationality (e.g. Singaporean or Malaysian) involving express renunciation of Chinese nationality. See Johannes Chan, 'Right of Abode, Permanent Residents and Consular Protection' *Ming Pao*, 12 April 1996.

[76] It may be noted that diplomatic/consular protection is not a matter of individual entitlement but the right of the state which confers the nationality. By the same token, third states need not accept intervention by the 'state of nationality' on behalf of its nationals if the nationality of the latter is not based on 'genuine link' with the [conferring] state.

of the PRC'.[77] Should such persons, nevertheless, 'experience a change of nationality',[78] they 'can make a declaration [with valid documentation to the appropriate authority responsible for nationality applications]', in which case they will not be able to enjoy rights extended to Chinese nationals under the Basic Law nor retain previous status as permanent residents. Pragmatism aside, it is evident that notions of sovereignty have yet again prevailed over considerations grounded in individual choice or 'acquired rights'. Of particular relevance ought to have been the established doctrine that acquired rights (including rights which accrue, for example, upon possession of permanent residence) survive incidents of transition of power.[79]

A 'right to a passport' for Hong Kong people?

As observed in earlier discussion, Hong Kong people are entitled to a right to leave and return to their 'own country'. Their freedoms of travel and movement are further enshrined in the Sino-British Agreement,[80] in the 'mini-constitution' of the HKSAR,[81] and in the territory's Bill of Rights.[82] These entitlements embody an 'ancillary' right to be provided with the appropriate documents, including a passport, required for the effective exercise of their rights and freedoms.[83] As a corollary, confirmed by the UN Human Rights

---

[77] Presumably, by merely acknowledging the travel qualities of a foreign 'nationality', the apparent conflict with China's rule of 'no-recognition of dual nationality' may be circumvented.

[78] As pointed out by Lu Ping, no nationality change incurs by virtue of possession of BDTC, BNO or BNSS [British Nationality Selection Scheme] which are not recognized by the Chinese government ('the Chinese Government opposes the BNSS because it is a wrong act by the British Government').

[79] See discussion in Chapter 1. See also Chan's suggestion that the question of 'permanent residence' be separated from 'nationality' and that all Hong Kong permanent residents who had obtained such a status before 1997 be allowed to retain it irrespective of their nationality. Supra (note 75).

[80] Joint Declaration, Art. 3(5); Annex I, Art. XIII.

[81] Basic Law, Article 31: 'Hong Kong residents shall have freedom of movement within the Hong Kong Special Administrative Region and freedom of emigration to other countries and regions. They shall have freedom to travel and to enter or leave the Region. Unless restrained by law, holders of valid travel documents shall be free to leave the Region without special authorization.'

[82] Hong Kong Bill of Rights Ordinance of 6 June 1991, Article 8: '(1) Everyone lawfully within Hong Kong shall, within Hong Kong, have the right to liberty of movement and freedom to choose his residence. (2) Everyone shall be free to leave Hong Kong . . . (4) No one who has the right of abode in Hong Kong shall be arbitrarily deprived of the right to enter Hong Kong.'

[83] See conclusion of detailed study of international treaties, jurisprudence of human rights bodies, and state practice in Hannum, supra (note 41), p. 122.

Committee,[84] a duty is imposed under international law on the State of Nationality/Citizenship or residence to furnish the necessary documents. Thus, notwithstanding common (mistaken) perceptions, or the lack of a widespread formal expression of the right to passport in domestic legislations,[85] the guarantees of Article 12 of the International Covenant on Civil and Political Rights are a matter of individual rights rather than government's prerogative.

To effectively secure freedom of international movement, it is also imperative that the travel documents issued are internationally recognized and subject to minimal bureaucratic restrictions. Recognition is generally accorded upon compliance with the so-called 'three-Rs': Respectability, Returnability and Reciprocity.[86] In this respect, questions have been raised regarding post-1997 travel documents to be available to Hong Kong residents. Doubted, in particular, is the credibility of a British issued BN(O) passport[87] which does not guarantee right of abode in Hong Kong. Although the passport may carry a statement to the effect that the holder is in possession of a Hong Kong Permanent Identity Card, and hence allowed a right of return to the territory, not all BN(O)s qualify for the status of 'permanent residence' which, in turn, has not been officially defined.

Treated with even greater suspicion is the yet unissued SAR passport (to which only Chinese residents of the SAR are eligible). As stipulated in the Sino-British Agreement,

> [t]he Central People's Government shall authorise the Hong Kong Special Administrative Region Government to issue, in accordance with the law, passports of the Hong Kong Special Administrative Region of the People's Republic of China to all Chinese nationals who hold permanent identity cards of the Hong Kong Special Administrative Region, and travel documents of the Hong Kong Special Administrative Region of the People's Republic of China to all other persons lawfully residing in the

---

[84] For references to decisions of the UN Human Rights Committee holding Uruguay in breach of Article 12 of the ICCPR for denial of passports, see Hannum, ibid., pp. 20–1.

[85] Evidently, a formal enunciation of the right to a passport often creates an individual entitlement sufficiently strong to ensure that the refusal to grant a passport may be judicially as well as administratively reviewable.

[86] 'Is it a recognised document from a country so rich its citizens return home voluntarily, without overstaying their visas? Does it guarantee the holder can be unceremoniously deported back to his home port in case he commits a crime, overstays his welcome or otherwise breaches the terms of his visa? If we let you in visa-free . . . , what does your country do for us?' See Jonathan Braude, 'Passports, Pride and Prejudice' *South China Morning Post*, 21 May 1994, at 18.

[87] Held by about 3 million people in Hong Kong. Other travel documents used by 'non-British' Hong Kong residents include Certificate of Identity (CI) and Document of Identity (DI) which are allowed to straddle 1997 but will no longer be issued by the Hong Kong government.

> Hong Kong Special Administrative Region. The above passports and
> documents shall be valid for all states and regions and shall record the
> holder's right to return to the Hong Kong Special Administrative Region.[88]

Not only is it difficult to ascribe 'respectability' to a document that does not
exist,[89] neither China nor Britain — who both bear responsibility to facilitate
the implementation of rights/freedoms pledged in an internationally binding
agreement — has started lobbying for its acceptance as a *bona fide* document,
let alone one which ensures returnability or reciprocity.

In addition, whereas at present about 80 countries grant visa-free status
to holders of BN(O) passport, the maintenance of the current position beyond
1997 is not certain, given especially that only three countries have formal
accords with the government of Hong Kong, ten countries extend visa-free
status by virtue of agreements with the British government, and that
arrangements with the other 67 countries are based on internal administrative
understandings 'due to the territory's economic power and the BNO's good
track record'.[90] While Britain has announced it would grant visa-free entry to
all SAR passport holders — as well as lobby other countries to follow suit —
the British and Chinese governments are yet to 'cooperate'[91] to negotiating
with third countries visa abolition agreements in relation to SAR passports.

ACCESS TO INTERNATIONAL REMEDIES

What international remedies are available to Hong Kong people whose human rights are violated?

Were a Hong Kong person aggrieved by denial of a right to nationality or
any other human right to seek remedy or enforcement of rights in international
fora, s/he is likely to find limited satisfaction. Apart from the more general

---

[88] Annex I, Art. XIV; see also BL, Art. 154.

[89] As observed by Braude, supra (note 86), 'respectability' of the SAR passport hinges largely
on 'who' the issuing authorities are or whether it will be seen as a 'Hong Kong or a Chinese
document', namely whether 'damned by association' with Chinese passports which are
'unpopular with many Western governments' or 'blessed by association with the British
system'.

[90] See Fanny Wong, 'The Passport Time-Bomb Ticks Away' *South China Morning Post*, 11
January 1995, at 17.

[91] In accordance with the obligations stipulated in JD, Arts. 4,5. See also undertaking by the
Central People's government to 'assist or authorise the Hong Kong Special Administrative
Region Government to conclude visa abolition agreements with states or regions' — Annex
I, Art. XIV; BL, Art. 155.

impediment of lack of standing before the International Court of Justice (whose jurisdiction is confined to states), the territory's inhabitants are further hampered by unavailability of the relevant international mechanisms designed to allow individual complaints against a government in respect of personal violation of human rights. The British government — which has recognized the right of individual petition to the European Commission of Human Rights and accepted the compulsory jurisdiction of the European Court of Human Rights — has not extended such facilities to Hong Kong. Nor has the UK ratified the First Optional Protocol to the International Covenant on Civil and Political Rights, under which individuals who claim that any of their rights enumerated in the Covenant have been violated and who have exhausted all available domestic remedies may submit written communications to the UN Human Rights Committee for consideration.

Clearly, with regard to post-1997, the obligation undertaken by the PRC under the Sino-British Joint Declaration — whereby '[t]he provisions of the International Covenant on Civil and Political Rights and the International Covenant on Economic, Social and Cultural Rights as applied to Hong Kong shall remain in force'[92] — 'cannot . . . as a matter of strict law encompass an obligation to introduce something which did not previously exist, namely, the right to individual access to the Human Rights Committee under the optional protocol'.[93]

Should allegations, however, pertain to a 'consistent pattern of gross and reliably attested violations of human rights and fundamental freedom' (i.e. 'situations' as distinct from individual complaints), communications may be submitted by any individual, group or organization to the UN Secretary General for the attention of the Sub-Commission on Prevention of Discrimination and Protection of Minorities,[94] and ultimate[95] consideration by the Commission on Human Rights, in accordance with ECOSOC Resolution 728 and the established procedure under Resolution 1503. Specific allegations of 'disappearances', summary or arbitrary executions, torture, or religious intolerance may be forwarded to the relevant 'theme mechanisms'[96]

---

[92] JD, Annex I, art XIII, para 4.

[93] FAC Report 1994, pp. lviii.

[94] Notwithstanding its name, the Sub-Commission — established by the UN Commission on Human Rights under the authority of the Economic and Social Council [ECOSOC] and constituted of 26 members elected by the Commission — deals with a wide-range of human rights topics.

[95] Initial review of communications is done by a Working Group of five members of the Sub-Commission.

[96] Including: Working Group on Enforced or Involuntary Disappearances; Special Rapporteur on Summary or Arbitrary Executions; Special Rapporteur on Torture; Special Rapporteur on Religious Intolerance.

erected by the Commission on Human Rights. A special investigative procedure may also be initiated under the 1984 UN Convention Against Torture, on receipt by the Committee Against Torture of 'reliable information which appears to it to contain well-founded indications that torture is being systematically practised in the territory of a State Party'.[97]

Other 'specialized agencies' too provide avenues for victims of certain violations of human rights. Thus, for example, 'industrial associations of employers or workers' may avail themselves of the 'representation' procedure under the Constitution of the International Labour Organization (ILO) with regard to failure by the government to observe applicable[98] ILO conventions. Additionally, submissions in respect of deprivation of the right to freedom of association may be made by 'organizations of employers or workers' (national or international) to the Committee on Freedom of Association of the ILO Governing Body. In a similar vein, complaints of infringements of rights in the fields of education, science, culture and information may be filed with UNESCO's Committee on Conventions and Recommendations and, when declared 'admissible', could result in a call by the Director General upon the government concerned for a 'satisfactory solution'.

While it has been observed that large number of individuals have petitioned the UN Commission of Human Rights pursuant to Resolution 728, and have obtained relief, the low, complex and secretive nature of the '1503 process' — as well as its vulnerability to political influences at many junctures — are obvious drawbacks, especially where the aim is to obtain prompt publicity or public action. Such an objective may nevertheless be gained through statements related to set agenda of the Human Rights Commission or Sub-Commission made on behalf of affected individuals by non-governmental organizations (NGOs) enjoying 'consultative status'. Bodies instituted to monitor the observance of major human rights conventions[99]

---

[97] Article 20; An inter-state complaint machinery is also available under Article 21. Note, however, that the continuation of such facilities after 1997 has been doubted since China has not accepted the competence of the Committee Against Torture in this regard.

[98] Note that 47 ILO conventions currently applicable to Hong Kong will continue to apply after 1997. See *Achievements of the Joint Liaison Group and its Sub-Group on International Rights and Obligations* (1985-May 1990), p. 15.

[99] The conventions applicable in Hong Kong and their respective monitoring bodies are: 1966 International Convenant on Civil and Political Rights [ICCPR]: the Human Rights Committee; 1966 International Covenant on Economic, Social and Cultural Rights [ICESCR]: the Committee on Economic, Social and Cultural Rights; 1965 International Convention on the Elimination of All Forms of Racial Discrimination [ICERD]: the Committee on the Elimination of Racial Discrimination; 1984 Convention Against Torture and Other Forms of Cruel, Inhuman or Degrading Treatment or Punishment [CAT]: the Committee Against Torture; 1989 Convention on the Rights of the Child [CRC]: Committee on the Rights of the Child).

also facilitate international 'exposure'. Specifically, parties to these conventions are required[100] to submit periodic reports on the implementation of the proclaimed rights to the established committees which examine the reports at public meetings in the presence of government representatives. Although not involving condemnation or sanction nor designed to enforce realization of human rights in the territory concerned, the reporting system is said to be a 'very effective tool in securing [both *a priori* and *post facto*] compliance with human rights obligations'.[101]

Indeed, there is little doubt that an enduring commitment to report to the relevant international human rights committees is essential for the protection of human rights in Hong Kong. Questions have been raised, however, with respect to who should bear the reporting duty after the transfer of sovereignty over the territory, given the particular predicament that the PRC is not a party to the International Covenants on Civil and Political Rights [ICCPR] and Economic, Social and Cultural Rights [ICESCR].[102] The UK's stand (supported by its international law advisers) is that the pledge by the government of the PRC under the Sino-British Agreement[103] — to ensure that the provisions of the two International Covenants (the ICCPR and the ICESCR), as applied in Hong Kong, remain in force on and after 1 July 1997 — 'means that China must accept not only the substantive legal provisions . . . but also follow the relevant reporting procedures'.[104] In fact, as contended,[105] 'the essence of international human rights treaties is the international procedure and the international mechanisms' (whereas it is the 'function of domestic Bills of Rights and constitutions to spell out list of rights').

Further reinforcement for this view could be found in the position adopted by the UN Commission on Human Rights in a resolution entitled *Succession of States in Respect of Human Rights Treaties*.[106] The Commission

---

[100] See ICCPR, Art 40; ICESCR, Art 16; ICERD, Art 9; CAT, Art 19; CRC, Art 44.

[101] Rosalyn Higgins, 'Some Thoughts on the Implementation of Human Rights' in Centre for Human Rights, *Implementation of International Human Rights Instruments* (New York: United Nations, 1990), pp. 60, 62–3.

[102] Note that the PRC ratified ICERD, ICERD, the 1979 Convention on Elimination of Discrimination Against Women [CEDAW], CAT, CRC, and submitted reports for examination by the respective committees. See Andrew Byrnes & Johannes Chan, eds., *Public Law and Human Rights — A Hong Kong Sourcebook* (Hong Kong: Butterworths, 1993) pp. 284–5; 298–9; 316–7; 330.

[103] JD, Annex I, art XIII, para. 4; echoed in BL, Art. 39.

[104] See FAC Report 1994, p. lvii (relaying the interpretation assumed by the Foreign and Commonwealth Office).

[105] Loc. cit. (citing evidence given by international lawyers).

[106] See UN ECOSOC, Commission on Human Rights, *Succession of States in Respect of International Human Rights Treaties. Report of the Secretary-General*, E/CN.4/1995/80 (28 November 1994).

emphasized the special nature of human rights treaties which are not merely obligations between states but are designed primarily to protect the rights of individuals. As such, 'human rights treaties devolve with the territory'[107] and 'all the people within the territory of a former State party to the Covenant remained entitled to the guarantees of the Covenant'.[108] On their part, the 'successors' 'were bound by the obligations under the Covenant as from the date of their independence [whether or not a formal declaration of affirmation has been issued by the successors]' and, consequently, 'reports under article 40 became due'.[109] Heed may also be paid to the 'Guidelines on the Recognition of New States in Eastern Europe and in the Soviet Union',[110] which refers to acceptance of the 'appropriate international obligations' (including international monitoring mechanisms on human rights)[111] among the basic conditions for recognition.

As observed by one commentator, '[b]ecause great social upheavals, and the peaceful break-ups of states, are . . . very painful events, it becomes especially urgent for the international community to monitor closely the human rights situation in various countries. The non-extension of the international human rights obligations of a predecessor state to its successor states would weaken considerably the possibility of such a control'.[112] Nor is this observation less true in relation to a [peaceful] transfer of sovereignty

---

[107] See Fausto Pocar, 'Enhancing the Universal Application of Human Rights Standards and Instruments,' UN Doc. A/CONF.157/PC/60/Add.4 of 8 April 1993. See also Nihal Jayawickrama, 'Human Rights in Hong Kong: The Continued Applicability of the International Covenants' (1995) *Hong Kong Law Journal* 171, 176–7 (contending that a new rule of international succession law has been established whereby '[o]nce it is formally acknowledged by multilateral treaty that the inhabitants of a particular territorial unit are entitled to enjoy certain defined rights and freedoms, that enjoyment cannot be interrupted, suspended, or terminated by reason of new arrangements that may be made in relation to the governance of that territory').

[108] Statement by the Human Rights Committee at its 47th session (March/April 1993), cited in the Report supra (note 106).

[109] Loc. cit.

[110] Adopted by the Council of the European Community on 17 December 1991, repr. in Hurst Hannum, *Documents on Autonomy and Minority Rights* (Dordrecht: M. Nijhoff, 1993) p. 85.

[111] Note, e.g. the finding by the Arbitration Commission of the Conference for Peace in Yugoslavia that the Republic of Slovania in its request for recognition had accepted to succeed to respective treaties of Yugoslavia and *had promised to accept international monitoring mechanisms on human rights*. See 'Opinion No. 7 Concerning International Recognition of the Republic of Slovania by the European Community and Its Member States Conference for Peace in Yugoslavia' (11 January 1992) repr. in (1992) 31 *International Legal Materials* 1512.

[112] Rein Mullerson, 'New Developments in the Former USSR and Yugoslavia' (1993) 33 *Virginia Journal of International Law* 299, 320.

over a territory whose inhabitants have been guaranteed protection of what are in a sense their 'acquired' international rights and freedoms (not to be taken away by the new sovereign).[113]

Acknowledging the supervisory imperative in the specific situation of Hong Kong, the UN Committee on Economic, Social and Cultural Rights has called upon the government of the United Kingdom 'to inform the Committee as soon as possible of the modalities arrived at in agreement with the Government of China by which the reporting obligations under Covenant will continue after 1997'.[114] In its consideration in November 1995 of the forth periodic report of the UK relating to Hong Kong, the Human Rights Committee reaffirmed that — by virtue of the Sino-British Agreement that the Covenant as applied to Hong Kong shall remain in force after 1 July 1997 — 'reporting obligations under article 40 of the Covenant will continue to apply', and 'the Committee will be competent to receive and consider reports that must be submitted in relation to Hong Kong'.[115]

The issue may be 'simplified' if the PRC were to accede to the two Covenants, thereby assuming a duty of reporting for the whole country. Alternatively, a reservation limiting applicability of the Covenants to parts of its territory (including Hong Kong) may be entered by China upon accession.[116] The third solution — and, arguably, the one most consistent with Hong Kong's international legal personality — is to allow the territory itself to undertake the required reporting on human rights.[117] As elaborated in an earlier chapter, international responsibility — which has been 'disentangled' from sovereignty — is grounded in jurisdictional competence and effective control. Notably, the various human rights instruments, including the Covenants, enjoin parties to respect the rights of people 'within their jurisdiction' — a concept understood[118] to cover all areas and individuals subject to their effective control. It is submitted, therefore, that the Hong

---

[113] See Chapter 1, note 170.

[114] Committee on Economic, Social and Cultural rights, Consideration of the Reports Submitted by States Parties Under Articles 16 and 17 of the Covenant, Concluding Observations of the Committee on Economic, Social and Cultural Rights, UN Doc E/C.12/1994/19, repr. in (1995) 2 *International Human Rights Reports* 454.

[115] See 'Concluding Observations of the Human Rights Committee', UN Doc. CCPR/C/79/Add. 57 of 3 November 1995 [hereafter: the November '95 Observations], para. 4.

[116] Such an option is likely to be rejected by China since it may imply lower standards of human rights on the mainland.

[117] As pointed out by one commentator, the Human Rights Committee 'has indicated that it is flexible on the "modalities" of reporting, leaving open the door for China to authorize the HKSAR to compile and submit such reports.' See Frank Ching, 'UN Speaks Out on Hong Kong. Human-Rights Panel Asks for Reports on Territory After 1997' *Far Eastern Economic Review*, 23 November 1995, at 40.

[118] See, for example, Manfred Nowak, *CCPR Commentary* (Kehl: NP Engel, 1993) pp. 41–2.

Kong government, which is responsible for the protection of rights in the territory, should also discharge any associated procedural duties.[119]

THE 'LOCAL REMEDIES' ROUTE

While access to international fora and the appraisal by international independent bodies are instrumental to securing the implementation of international human rights, the 'routine' and systematic award of remedies by domestic courts, administrative tribunals and other organs of authority is held to be the 'most effective guarantee'.[120] In fact, the duty to provide local practicable remedies is mandated under all human rights treaties,[121] and hence failure in this regard constitutes a breach of an international legal obligation.

In Hong Kong, recourse to judicial proceedings to enforce international human rights has been largely facilitated by the 'incorporation'[122] of the ICCPR (as applied to the territory[123]) into the 1991 Bill of Rights Ordinance (BoRO). To enable the ICCPR's effective supervening function in respect of subsequent legislation, Hong Kong's constitutional document, the Letters Patent has been amended to read:

> [t]he provisions of the International Covenant on Civil and Political Rights, adopted by the General Assembly of the United Nations on 16 December 1966, as applied to Hong Kong, shall be implemented through the laws of Hong Kong. No law of Hong Kong shall be made after the coming into operation of the Hong Kong Letter Patent 1991 (No. 2) that restricts the rights and freedoms enjoyed in Hong Kong in a manner which is inconsistent with that Covenant as applied to Hong Kong.

---

[119] It may be noted that, in actual terms, components of the reports pertaining to human rights in the territory are prepared by the Hong Kong administration.

[120] See Higgins, supra (note 101), at p.64.

[121] See, e.g. ICCPR, Art 2; ICERD, Art 6; CAT, Art 13.

[122] In order to be made justiciable in Hong Kong courts, international treaties must be transformed into municipal legislation (further discussion is offered in Chapter 6). Notwithstanding a contention by the government [see *An Introduction to Hong Kong Bill of Rights Ordinance* (Hong Kong: Government Printer, 1992) 5] — that '[b]efore the enactment of the Bill of Rights Ordinance, the two Covenants were implemented in Hong Kong, as in the United Kingdom, through a combination of common law, legislation and administrative measures' — formal 'incorporation' is 'dated' to BoRO's coming into operation on 8 June 1991.

[123] That is, subject to reservations made by the UK upon signature and ratification of the Covenant, regarding the right to self-determination, custodial procedures, freedom of movement, immigration restrictions, expulsion of aliens, policies concerning acquisition of nationality or right of abode, and the right to free election.

The Chinese initiative to ensure maintenance of the ICCPR's 'entrenched' status[124] after the transfer of sovereignty is reflected in Article 39 of the Basic Law which stipulates:

> The provisions of the International Covenant on Civil and Political Rights, the International Covenant on Economic, Social and Cultural Rights, and international labour conventions as applied to Hong Kong shall remain in force and shall be implemented through the laws of the Hong Kong Special Administrative Region. The Rights and freedoms enjoyed by Hong Kong residents shall not be restricted unless as prescribed by law. Such restrictions shall not contravene the provisions of the preceding paragraph of this Article.

Criticisms have nonetheless been levelled at BoRO's limited scope, temporal restrictions, undue exemptions from its application, and its unmodified adoption of unwarranted reservations.[125] Nor is the enumeration of rights in a Bill of Rights a guarantee of their implementation or effective enforcement. In spite of the large number of criminal law challenges under BoRO and the increasing volume of BoRO cases in administrative law,[126] the exclusion from its ambit of 'inter-citizen rights' is a serious flow[127] in BoRO's 'remedial' value. The judicial option of the local people is further inhibited by the 'financial obstacles to bringing a Bill of Rights court case'. Doubts have also been raised regarding the effectiveness of the court system to uphold human rights after the transfer of sovereignty.[128]

It is these considerations (and others)[129] that reinforce the need for a

---

[124] See discussion in Chapter 5.

[125] See generally Johannes Chan and Yash Ghai, eds., *The Bill of Rights: A Comparative Approach* (Hong Kong: Butterworths Asia, 1993), pp. 55–69; 71–105; 161–198.

[126] For the respective number of BoRO cases and a statistical analysis see: Johannes Chan, 'The Hong Kong Bill of Rights 1991–1995: A Statistical Overview' (a paper presented at a Seminar on 'Hong Kong's Bill of Rights Two Years Before 1997' on 24 June 1995).

[127] As well as a failure to implement obligations to prevent or provide a remedy for infringements of rights by private individuals. See Andrew Byrnes, 'The Hong Kong Bill of Rights and Relations Between Private Individuals in *The Bill of Rights: A Comparative Approach*, p. 71, at 73–80. See also the Human Rights Committee's November '95 Observations, supra (note 115), para. 10 ('notes with deep concern the absence of legislation providing effective protection against violations of the Covenant rights by non-governmental actors').

[128] For a particularly pessimistic depiction of the prospects for human rights protection beyond 1997 see: Michael Kirby, 'Human Rights: The Role of the Judge' in *The Hong Kong Bill of Rights: A Comparative Approach*, pp. 225, 242–251. See also FAC Report 1994, at pp. lviii–lix.

[129] See detailed presentation in Amnesty International, *Hong Kong and Human Rights: Flaws in the System — A Call for Institutional Reform to Protect Human Rights* (London: International Secretariat, April 1994) [Amnesty 1994].

complementary complaints system to allow all victims of human rights violations the 'effective remedy' to which they are entitled in accordance with the international legal obligations imposed on parties to the relevant conventions. Of particular importance in this respect is the establishment of an independent statutory human rights commission. Such a body 'would provide an informal and inexpensive way to resolve disputes and help in the enforcement of standards necessary to give effect to various rights. It can empower groups who are not easily able to obtain access to courts. It can play a particularly useful role in supervising affirmative action policies. It can, through co-operation with non-governmental organizations, involve the community in the safe-guarding of human rights'.[130]

Yet, notwithstanding the Legislative Council's consensus vote in favour of setting-up an independent human rights commission, numerous public petitions, strong demand by the legal community of Hong Kong, as well as firm recommendations of the House of Commons' Foreign Affairs Committee and the Human Rights Committee,[131] proposals to this effect have encountered objections from both the Hong Kong[132] and the Chinese governments.[133] Specifically, it has been contended[134] that

> Human Rights Commission is not the best way forward in the particular
> circumstances of Hong Kong [since] human rights in Hong Kong are

---

[130] Johannes Chan and Yash Ghai, 'A Comparative Perspective on the Bill of Rights' in *The Hong Kong Bill of Rights: A Comparative Approach*, p. 1, at 10. See also '32 Arguments Supporting the Establishment of an Effective, Independent Human Rights Commission,' Amnesty 1994, pp. 23–31.

[131] See November '95 Observations, supra (note 115), para. 22 ('The Committee recommends that the State party reconsiders its decision on the establishment and competence of a Human Rights Commission').

[132] The Governor has questioned the necessity of a human rights commission — in addition to the Bill of Rights, the Courts, the ICAC [Independent Commission Against Corruption], the legislature, the free press — although he vowed to 'remain open to the arguments, open to persuasion as any accountable Governor should' and to 'welcome further public debate on the issue.' See 'Speech by Governor Christopher Patten at the Foreign Correspondents Club' cited in Amnesty 1994, p. 30.

[133] According to the Director of the Hong Kong and Macau Affairs Office, Lu Ping, 'China would not tolerate a commission which had the power to conduct independent investigations and take action against violations of human rights.' He further stated that such a commission (dubbed a 'new core of power' and 'a monstrous product') is 'against the Basic Law, which has laid down the functions of the legislature, the executive body and the judiciary'. See Linda Choy, 'Human Rights Body Rejected. Vow to Disband Commission After Handover' *South China Morning Post*, 7 May 1994, at 4.

[134] See *Supplementary Report by the United Kingdom of Great Britain and Northern Ireland in Respect of Hong Kong Under the International Covenant on Civil and Political Rights*, 31 May 1996 ['Supplementary Report'], paras. 14, 15.

founded on the rule of law, an independent judiciary and a justiciable
Bill of Rights. There is a sound and comprehensive legal aid system; an
effective ombudsman ... and a range of other institutions for the
investigation and redress of complaints; a fairly elected legislature; and
a progressive approach to human rights education. The Hong Kong
Government also operates in the full view of a free and active press, and
its policies and practices are subject to rigorous monitory by local and
international NGOs. This system has served Hong Kong well and provides
a suitable framework for securing and enhancing the protection of human
rights in the territory.

No consideration has been given, however, to 'contingency planning'
should the assumptions relied upon be found wanting. Nor have arguments
been advanced to rebut the well grounded case of citizens of Hong Kong for
an 'accessible, affordable, speedy and effective' internal mode of redress,[135]
especially when deprived of international litigation avenues and facing
formidable challenges to their human rights.

---

[135] It was reported nonetheless that 'the Hong Kong Government has made legal aid more
readily available in cases involving the BoRO, has given the judiciary additional resources
to reduce court waiting-times, and has improved the ombudsman system. It is establishing
a statutory Equal Opportunities Commission to tackle discrimination on the grounds of
sex and disability and a Privacy Commissioner to promote and enforce compliance with
new data protection laws'. Supplementary Report, para 16.

Chapter 5

Problems of Treaty Law

'UNEQUAL TREATIES'

How 'unequal' is Hong Kong's origin?

Hong Kong affords discussion of several interesting questions in international treaty law, including notably the controversial issue of 'unequal treaties'. The view propounded under this concept is that treaties concluded between parties of incomparable strength or conferring non-reciprocal obligations are invalid and can be unilaterally abrogated at any time. Hence, treaties between economically powerful and much weaker states whereby the latter grants extensive privileges and facilities to the former do not impose legally binding obligations. In this vein, China considers as 'unequal', and hence null and void, all treaties it was 'compelled' (because of military disadvantage) to enter in the 19th and early 20th centuries relating to consular jurisdiction, [one-sided] most-favoured nation treatment, restrictive tariff regulations, and territorial cessions or leases,[1] including the three treaties signed with Great Britain in respect of Hong Kong.[2]

---

[1] See Hungdah Chiu, *People's Republic of China and the Law of Treaties* (New Haven, Conn: Harvard University Press, 1972), pp. 60–71; see also William Lin Tung, *China and Foreign Powers: The Impact of and Reaction to Unequal Treaties* (Dobbs Ferry, NY: Oceana Publications, 1970).

[2] Treaty of Peace, Friendship, Commerce & Idemnity Great Britain-China, Nanking, 29 August 1842 repr. in Peter Wesley-Smith, 'British Dependent Territories: Hong Kong' in Albert P. & Phyllis M. Blaustein, eds., 5 *Constitutions of Dependencies and Special Sovereignties* (Dobbs Ferry, NY: Oceana Publications, 1985), p. 21; Convention of Peace and Friendship Between Great Britain and China, Peking, 24 October 1860, ibid., at p. 23; Convention Respecting the Extension of the Hong Kong Territory, Peking, 9 June 1898,

Yet, the concept of 'unequal treaties' — extended under the Communist regime in China to treaties which are 'incompatible with the new social system'[3] — is nowhere defined or delimited with any precision. In fact, since no qualifying statements have been made to indicate the degree of inequality necessary to invalidate a treaty — and given that the bargaining strength of parties invariably differs and that benefits conferred are rarely identical — a literal deployment of the doctrine would render all international agreements invalid. Contributing to the ambiguity of the doctrine is its inconsistent application by the Chinese authorities. While many of the treaties explicitly identified as 'unequal' did involve instances of extreme inequality, both in terms of the bargaining power of the parties and the distribution of benefits and burdens under the treaties, other agreements which could not be described as truly 'equal' appear to be acceptable to the PRC.[4]

It is similarly unclear which 'unequal treaties' are regarded merely voidable as distinct from void *ab initio*. Thus, for example, despite repeated claims that it was not bound by the 'unequal' treaties concerning the Hong Kong area signed between the British government and the government of the Qing Dynasty, the PRC has not challenged the validity of measures — including the conclusion of international agreements on behalf of Hong Kong — undertaken by Britain in exercising responsibility for and administration over the territory.[5] In practice, the PRC has formally acknowledged the accreditation by the British government of foreign consular representatives to Hong Kong and has also recognized the right of the UK to issue currency in Hong Kong (one of the most important attributes of sovereignty). Evidently, as contended by students of Chinese politics, political expediency, rather than international legal considerations, determines China's variable application of the unequal treaty doctrine. Cynics also add that — not unlike a common international phenomenon of cloaking otherwise questionable acts in a mantle of legality — a machinery has been conveniently constructed to

---

ibid., at p. 25. For a detailed study see: Peter Wesley-Smith, *Unequal Treaty 1898–1997. China, Great Britain and Hong Kong's New Territories* (Hong Kong: Oxford University Press, 1980).

[3]   See Tiqiang Chen, 'The People's Republic of China and Public International Law' (1984) 21 *Dalhousie Law Journal* 4, 29.

[4]   Note, however, the view that the PRC considers all unequal treaties as null and void but that in 'special cases involving territorial questions, status quo will be preserved until the settlement in an appropriate way through peaceful negotiations' — Wang Tieya, 'Unequal Treaties and China: A Note' (paper presented at a conference on 'International Law of Macao and the Conventional Practices between China and Portugal' held in Macao, 13–15 November 1995).

[5]   See discussion in Anthony Dicks, 'Treaty, Grant, Usage or Suffrance? Some Legal Aspects of the Status of Hong Kong' (1983) 95 *China Quarterly* 727, 737ff.

allow the PRC government to extricate itself from difficult or unmitigable situations.[6]

As a matter of state practice, notwithstanding support and political usage among some non-Western countries, the concept of unequal treaty cannot be said to have gained general acceptance as a rule of international law. At most, it is regarded as a political principle which may justify a moral condemnation of historical events but has no binding legal effect. Evidently, the 1969 Convention on the Law of Treaties, which largely codifies existing customary international law pertaining to treaties, contains no reference to inequality in bargaining power or in obligations assumed by the parties as grounds of invalidity. Although a non-binding declaration issued by the UN Conference on the Law of Treaties condemned the 'threat or use of pressure in any form, whether military, political, or economic by any state in order to coerce another state to perform any act relating to the conclusion of a treaty in violation of the principles of the sovereign equality of states and the freedom of consent'[7] — the 1969 Convention itself went no further than to stipulate that '[a] treaty is void if its conclusion has been *procured by the threat or use of force in violation of the principles of international law embodied in the Charter of the United Nations*'.[8]

A focus on military, political or economic disparities is moreover incongruous with contemporary perceptions of pluralistic international law-making, given the 'multitude of structures and institutions that share in political and legal authority'[9] and the growing participation of non- or sub-state entities[10] in the conduct of international relations. Indeed, Hong Kong is a case in point. In any event, the question whether or not the territory's

---

6   See Gary L. Scott, *Chinese Treaties: The Post Revolutionary Restoration of International Law and Order* (Dobbs Ferry, NY: Oceana Publications, 1975), pp. 96–7.

7   See Declaration on the Prohibition of Military, Political or Economic Coercion in the Conclusion of Treaties, annexed to the Final Act of the United Nations Conference on the Law of Treaties, Vienna, 23 May 1969, UN Doc. A/Conf.39/27, repr. in (1969) 8 *International Legal Materials* 679.

8   Article 52 (emphasis added).

9   See Mark W. Janis, 'International Law?' (1991) 32 *Harvard International Law Journal* 363 [discussing the decline of the sovereign state and the rise of alternative structures (e.g. regional orders 'above' traditional sovereign states: EU; regional trade zones: NAFTA; regional human rights structures: Council of Europe Court & Commission of Human Rights) competing to regulate international activity. Note also the author's 'commonplace' observation that 'multinational corporations have more global importance than do scores of small and poor sovereign states with seats in the UN' (at 369).

10 For example, provinces, cantons, regions or states in federal unions, which are generally endowed with competence to conclude international agreements. See Christoph Schreuer, 'The Waning of the Sovereign State: Towards a New Paradigm for International Law?' (1993) 4 *European Journal of International Law* 447, at 450.

origin has been 'unequal' has been overtaken[11] by another issue of treaty law, namely the validity of the agreement 'giving birth' to Hong Kong's 'successor' — the HKSAR.

THE SINO-BRITISH JOINT DECLARATION

Is it a valid treaty under international law?

There is little doubt that the Sino-British Joint Declaration satisfies the 'formal' requirements of a 'treaty' under international law. It unambiguously falls within the generally accepted definition of a treaty, incorporated in the 1969 Convention on the Law of Treaties, as 'an international agreement concluded between states in written form and governed by international law, whether embodied in a single instrument or in two or more related instruments and whatever its particular designation'. Clearly, it is an 'expression of concurring wills by two subjects of international law', taking the common (though not exclusive) form of a written agreement 'with an intention to produce legal effects under the rules of international law'.[12]

That the parties themselves consider the Joint Declaration and its Annexes[13] as creating legally binding rights and obligations was conveyed by both the PRC and UK representatives in statements pertaining to the effectiveness of the agreement as an international guarantee for Hong Kong's future prosperity and stability.[14] The parties' sincere intention to contract an enforceable international legal agreement is also underscored by their meticulous observance of the established practices regarding treaty-making, namely accreditation of negotiators, negotiations and adoption of the text (26 September 1984), exchange of ratification instruments and entry into force (27 May 1985) and, most significantly, registration by both governments at the UN in accordance with Article 102 of the UN Charter (13 June 1985).

It may be added that the designation of the Sino-British accord as a 'Declaration' does not detract from its status as a legally binding instrument

---

[11] It is also arguable that the PRC's willingness to conclude an agreement on the future of Hong Kong with Great Britain is a *de facto* recognition of British rights under the 1860–1898 conventions.

[12] See elaboration of the Convention definition in the classical work of Paul Reuter, *Introduction to the Law of Treaties* (London: Pinter Publishers, 1989) pp. 22–29.

[13] Note the stipulation that the 'Joint Declaration and its Annexes shall be equally binding.' JD, Article 8.

[14] See references in Roda Mushkat, 'The International Legal Status of Hong Kong Under Post-Transitional Rule' (1987) 10 *Houston Journal of International Law* 1, 9, 53n.

under international law. As laid down in the Convention on the Law of Treaties and aptly supported by relevant commentaries, the international juridical validity of a treaty is unaffected by its title and in this respect 'convention', 'declaration', 'protocol' or a 'general act' are all interchangeable. Nor for that matter does the choice of a treaty-making 'technique' impact on the international legal force of the parties' commitments under the treaty. Thus, the transfer of sovereignty over the territory and the establishment of the HKSAR are valid international obligations notwithstanding the special declaratory form adopted by the governments of the PRC and the UK whereby the former declares that it has 'decided to resume the exercise of sovereignty' and the later declares that it 'will restore Hong Kong to the People's Republic of China'.

The validity of the Sino-British accord should also be distinguished from the question of its effectiveness. The absence of stipulated sanctions in the event of violation, the lack of agreed means of dispute settlement or the fact that access to the International Court of Justice may be precluded (for non-acceptance by the PRC of the compulsory jurisdiction of the Court) may render the accord less effective but do not diminish its valid legal character. Indeed, the status of the Joint Declaration as a legally binding international document, as well as the potential availability of international means of redress for breach of its terms, have been forcefully reaffirmed by the British Prime Minister in a recent visit to the territory.[15]

Having established the 'formal' validity of the Joint Declaration, it remains to consider whether there may be any 'substantive' grounds for its impeachment. A potential reason for holding the agreement void is its alleged conflict with a 'peremptory norm of general international law' (*jus cogens*).[16] Specifically, it is argued[17] that as a 'cession of territory' by a colonial administrator to another state, without the freely expressed will of the people in the colony, the Sino-British agreement explicitly contradicts the peremptory norm of self-determination and hence has no legal force under international law. Yet, while 'self-determination has undoubtedly attained that status of a "right" in international law', it is 'debatable whether the right of self-

---

[15] See extract from speech by John Major in *South China Morning Post*, 5 March 1996.

[16] Under Article 53 of the Convention on the Law of Treaties, '[a] treaty is void if, at the time of its conclusion, it conflicts with a peremptory norm of general international law. For the purposes of the present Convention, a peremptory norm of general international law is a norm accepted and recognised by the international community of States as a whole as a norm from which no derogation is permitted and which can be modified only by a subsequent norm of general international law having the same character.'

[17] See, e.g. Nihal Jayawickrama, 'The Right of Self-Determination' in Peter Wesley-Smith, ed., *Hong Kong's Basic Law Problems & Prospects* (Hong Kong: Faculty of Law, University of Hong Kong, 1990) pp. 85, 96–7.

determination is *jus cogens*'.[18] As summarized by a reviewer of major works on the subject,[19] skepticism rests on the observations that 'the history of self-determination is one of periodic transformation and perversion'; that the UN has been 'radically inconsistent in articulating the norm and selective in enforcing it'; that nor could customary understanding of the right of self-determination be inferred from the erratic recognition policies of states; and that 'to the contrary, the concept of self-determination has been equally honoured as deployed in efforts to destabilise an adversary or to provide a pretextual basis for expansionism, ethnic exclusiveness and repression'.

Given the lack of consensus about the status and meaning of the doctrine as well as recurrent controversy over the preferred institutional outcome of self-determination (independent statehood, lesser forms of association and autonomy, federalism, participatory or consociational democracy, ethnic homogeneity, or systematic protection of individual and collective human rights), an attempt to invalidate the Sino-British Joint Declaration for derogation from *jus cogens*, in accordance with the Convention on the Law of Treaties, is unlikely to elicit firm support in international law and practice. (This, however, should not deflect the cogency of the claim of Hong Kong people to the right to self-determination under international law).[20]

IMPLEMENTATION AND BREACH OF TREATIES

Embodied in the commitment to a valid international agreement is the parties' duty to 'perform the treaty in good faith' as prescribed under the fundamental rule of international law *pacta sunt servanda*.[21] Consequently, their will is

---

[18] Hurst Hannum, 'Rethinking Self-Determination' (1993) 34 *Virginia Journal of International Law* 1, 31. The author contrasts (132n) the writings of Ian Brownlie (*Principles of Public International Law*) and Hector Gros Espiell ('The Right to Self-Determination, Implementation of United Nations Resolutions') — who assert that self-determination has achieved the status of *jus cogens* — with views expressed (respectively) by special UN rapporteur Aurelieu Cristescu ('The Right to Self-Determination, Historical and Current Developments on the Basis of United Nations Instruments') and J.H.W. Verzijl (*International Law in Historical Perspective*) that 'no United Nations instrument confers such an imperative character [as that of *jus cogens*] to the right of peoples to self-determination' and that self-determination is even 'unworthy of the appellation of a rule of law'.

[19] See review article by Ralph G. Steinhardt in (1994) 88 *American Journal of International Law* 831, 832.

[20] See Chapter 1.

[21] See codification in Article 26 of the Convention on the Law of Treaties: 'Every treaty in force is binding upon the parties to it and must be performed by them in good faith.'

expected to produce the effects it has openly sought and they must be considered effectively bound, in accordance with their declarations. In fact, the principle of 'good faith' — which governs the creation and performance of legal obligations 'whatever their source'[22] — determines both the legal effects of the parties' pronouncements and the extent of their respective responsibilities.

Particular attention is paid on the application of 'good faith' to treaty interpretation. Specifically, as laid down in the Convention on the Law of Treaties,[23] an interpreter exercising good faith must search for the ordinary meaning of terms in the context of the whole treaty and its purpose, read the entire text of the treaty (including its preamble and annexes), examine any subsequent related agreements and the conduct of the parties following ratification, and attach a special meaning to any treaty term if it can be established that the parties intended it to be so defined. Significant weight is to be attributed to the objectives pursued by the contracting parties and, by implication, to the principle of 'effectiveness' (*ut res magis valeat quam pereat*) whereby a treaty must be given an interpretation which enables its provisions to be 'effective and useful', that is to have the appropriate effect.

A British or Chinese interpretation?

Bearing in mind that the Joint Declaration is a reciprocal undertaking by Britain and China to join their [opposing] individual wills in a common enterprise governed by international law, the function of any interpretation should be to seek the common intention of the parties as synthesized in the text rather than ascertaining their individual wills *per se*.[24] Such an emphasis on the treaty text is also evinced in the relegation of negotiators record or

---

[22] *Nuclear Tests Case* [1974] ICJ Reports 253, 268. 'Good faith' is said to constitute the 'postulate upon which the international legal order rests in its entirety.' See Michel Viraly, 'Review Essay: Good Faith in Public International Law' (1983) 77 *American Journal of International Law* 130, 132 (reviewing E. Zoller's *La Bonne Foien Droit International Public,* 1977).

[23] See Articles 31–33. Note that these rules of treaty interpretation are considered 'customary international law' and as such are binding on all states regardless of whether or not they are parties to the Convention on the Law of Treaties: *Guinea v Guinea-Bissau* (1986) 25 *International Legal Materials* 251, 271; *Guinea-Bissau v Senegal* (1991) ICJ Reports 53, 70.

[24] The approach of looking specifically for the intention of the parties was rejected both by the International Law Commission which drafted the Vienna rules and by the Conference which adopted the Convention. See Ian Sinclair, *The Vienna Convention on the Law of Treaties,* 2nd ed., (Manchester: Manchester University Press, 1984), at p. 115. Note, however, that '[a] special meaning should be given to a term if it is established that the parties so intended' [Article 31(4)].

preparatory work to the status of 'supplementary means', to be resorted to only if other means fail or lead to a 'result which is manifestly absurd or unreasonable'. By the same token, due cognisance ought to be given to the fact that words are often ambiguous and can have meaning only within the particular context in which they are used. 'Context', under international treaty law, comprises, in addition to the text (which includes preamble and annexes), '[a]ny *agreement* relating to the treaty which was made between all the parties in connection with the conclusion of the treaty' and [a]ny instrument which was made by one or more parties in connection with the conclusion of the treaty and *accepted* by the other parties as an instrument related to the treaty'.[25]

Clearly, not every subsequent diplomatic correspondence between the parties nor any subsequent practice in the application of the treaty are to be 'taken into account together with the context' unless they constitute or establish the parties' *agreement* regarding the interpretation of the treaty or application of its provision.[26] Thus, for example, an exchange of letters in 1990 between the UK Foreign Secretary and the Chinese Foreign Minister related to the 'development of political structure in Hong Kong' represents 'merely a record of a series of proposals which both sides made with inconclusive results',[27] and is not tantamount to an 'agreement' which ought to affect the interpretation of the Sino-British Joint Declaration. Similarly, a 'deal' reached in a purported 'spirit of co-operation'/'attempt to defuse tension'[28] or as 'part of a package of compromises'[29] falls short of a 'subsequent agreement' which may act to divest a treaty provision of an ordinary meaning which is consistent with the object and purpose of the treaty. *A fortiori*, a 'subsequent practice' which is contrary to the clear meaning of the relevant article cannot be considered an amendment or modification of the original pact unless a later treaty is concluded in accordance with applicable rules.

Also to be excluded from the interpretative process is the domestic law of one party to which the other party did not give (or did not have to give)

---

[25] See Convention on the Law of Treaties, Art. 31(2) [emphasis added].

[26] See Convention on the Law of Treaties, Art. 31(3) [emphasis supplied].

[27] See 'Memorandum submitted by the Foreign and Commonwealth Office' in House of Commons, Foreign Affairs Committee, *Relations Between the United Kingdom and China in the Period Up to and Beyond 1997* (London: HMSO, 3 November 1993), 'Minutes of Evidence', p. 39.

[28] See Shui-hing Lo, 'The Politics of the Court of Final Appeal Debate in Hong Kong' (1993) 29 Issues & Studies 105, 119, 124 (referring to arrangements for the composition of the Court of Final Appeal announced by the JLG at the end of September 1991).

[29] See Stacy Mosher, 'Court of Contention' *Far Eastern Economic Review*, 19 December 1991, at 10.

its agreement. Although, for internal legal purposes, a statute implementing a treaty is deemed authoritative[30] and binding (as municipal public law) upon the country and any person within the limits of its jurisdiction — at the international plane, however, such a statute is not a definitive interpretation of the treaty for international purposes (indeed, it may, in some instances, amount to a breach of the treaty). Fundamentally, in accordance with the principle of judicial equality of states, no state is to be placed under the jurisdiction of another or subjected to interpretation of treaty asserted by another state. Nor are there any reasonable grounds for imposing a unilateral interpretation of a contract which is essentially bilateral. The formal sanctioning of a particular interpretation by the legislature, judiciary or any other authority of one of the parties does not infuse it with binding force over the other party.

In this vein, the Basic Law of the Hong Kong Special Administrative Region of the People's Republic of China — which may be said to 'implement' the Joint Declaration — is a Chinese domestic law[31] and does not constitute a mutually accepted interpretation of the international agreement. While it will be[32] the *de facto* constitution of the HKSAR, and as such of binding force on the territory and its people, the Basic Law has no status in international law, no international legal effect with regard to the interpretation of the Sino-British accord, and clearly may not be invoked as a 'justification for failure to perform' it.[33]

Does the Basic Law 'implement' the Sino-British Joint Declaration?

The implementation of the Sino-British Joint Declaration may be examined from two main perspectives: formal/institutional and substantive. In relation to the former, several 'implementing' developments are discernable, including the respective enactment by the parties of enabling/incorporating domestic legislation and the establishment of prescribed joint working institutions. Specifically, the Hong Kong Act of 1985 provides for the termination as from 1 July 1997 of 'Her Majesty's sovereignty or jurisdiction over any part of Hong Kong' and authorizes the government to make changes in British

---

[30] So far as it is not inconsistent with the treaty.
[31] Adopted at the Third Session of the Seventh National People's Congress of the PRC and promulgated by a Decree of the President of the PRC on 4 April 1990.
[32] When it comes into force on 1 July 1997.
[33] See Article 27 of the Convention on the Law of Treaties ('Internal law and observance of treaties').

law, in consequence of, or in connection with, the ending of sovereignty. Appropriate powers are also granted under the Act to the Hong Kong authorities to pass legislation with extraterritorial effect and repeal or amend British statutes insofar as they are part of the law of Hong Kong. At its end, the Chinese government has promulgated the Basic Law of the HKSAR, which is expected, as stipulated in the Joint Declaration,[34] to incorporate and give [domestic] legal effect to the PRC's policies regarding Hong Kong in accordance with statements and elaborations made under the Sino-British agreement.

Institutionally, pursuant to a declared 'common aim' of ensuring a 'smooth transfer of government in 1997' and 'with a view to the effective implementation of the Joint Declaration',[35] a Sino-British Joint Liaison Group [JLG] was set up on 27 May 1985. To date its record[36] of 'achievements' comprises of agreements: on continued application of international rights and obligations affecting Hong Kong, including participation and membership of the territory in international organizations and conventions; on matters of the defence of Hong Kong and the maintenance of its public order; on the territory's bilateral treaties pertaining to air services, investment promotion and protection, and the surrender of fugitive offenders; as well as on localization of laws. By the same token, '[t]here remains, however, much ground that the Joint Liaison Group [needs] to cover before 1 July 1997'.[37] It has also been suggested that a 'lack of cooperation' in the JLG amounts, in fact, to a breach of the terms of the Joint Declaration, which mandates 'cooperative relationship' (to be 'intensified' in the second half of the period between the establishment of the JLG and 1 July 1997).[38]

Yet, whereas the 'formal' implementation of the Sino-British accord has been largely unquestioned, several controversies mark its 'substantive'

---

[34] See Article 3(12).

[35] See JD, Annex II.

[36] See *White Paper on the Annual Report on Hong Kong to Parliament,* 1984/85–1994.

[37] *White Paper on the Annual Report on Hong Kong 1994 to Parliament* (March 1995), para. 16 (reference is made in particular to the progress required on the clearance of bilateral agreements between Hong Kong and third countries; precise arrangements for the Court of Final Appeal; issues of right of abode, travel documents for the HKSAR and visa abolition agreements; the substance and practicalities of the adaptation of Hong Kong laws to the Basic Law.

[38] See conclusion and recommendation of the Foreign Affairs Committee, Report on *Relations Between the United Kingdom and China in the Period Up to and Beyond 1997* (London: HMSO, 23 March 1994 [FAC Report 1994], para. 180: 'We recommend that if China continues to block further negotiations in the Joint Liaison Group, *thereby breaching the Joint Declaration,* there can be no choice but for the Hong Kong Government to put before LegCo the necessary legislation to adapt and localise legislation prior to the transfer of sovereignty' [emphasis supplied].

implementation. Doubts are raised, in particular, regarding 'convergence' between the Basic Law and the treaty it purports to implement. Viewed as inconsistent with the Joint Declaration — and as 'grave potential threats to the autonomy of the Hong Kong SAR after 1997'[39] — are Basic Law provisions such as Articles 18 and 158. Thus, contrary to stipulations in the Joint Declaration[40] that the maintenance of public order in the HKSAR will be the responsibility of the HKSAR government, Article 18 confers on the Standing Committee of the National People's Congress power to decide that the SAR is in a state of emergency 'by reason of turmoil within the Hong Kong SAR which endangers national unity or security and is beyond the control of the government of the region' (entitling the issue of 'an order applying the relevant national laws in the Region'). Article 158, which vests the National People's Congress with the ultimate power of the interpretation of the Basic Law, is arguably incongruous with the 'independent judicial power, including that of final adjudication', guaranteed the HKSAR courts under the Joint Declaration.[41]

Other articles in the Basic Law which are cited[42] as a failure to implement both letter and spirit of the Joint Declaration pertain, *inter alia*, to the right given the NPC Standing Committee to invalidate HKSAR legislation;[43] the ousting of the HKSAR's jurisdiction over 'act of state, *such as* defence and foreign affairs';[44] the requirement imposed on the SAR to proscribe, among other matters, 'subversion against the Central People's Government' and 'prohibit political organizations or bodies of the Region from establishing ties with foreign political organizations or bodies';[45] and the provision that the Chief Executive of the SAR 'shall be accountable to the Central People's

---

[39] See FAC Report 1994, ibid., p. lvi.

[40] See JD, Art. 3(11); Annex I, Art. XII.

[41] See JD, Art. 3(3); Annex I, Art. III.

[42] For a list of articles which contain inconsistencies with the Joint Declaration, see: International Commission of Jurists, *Countdown to 1997. Report of a Mission to Hong Kong* (Geneva: ICJ, 1992) [ICJ Report 1992], pp. 110–115.

[43] BL, Art. 17; 'The power to determine whether a law of the SAR is consistent with the Basic Law is a judicial power which, under Article III of Annex I to the Joint Declaration, should ultimately be vested in the court of final appeal of the SAR.' ICJ Report 1992, p. 110.

[44] BL, Art. 19 (emphasis added); 'This goes beyond the exclusion of foreign and defence affairs from the judicial power of the SAR, as provided by Article I of Annex I to the Joint Declaration, both by treating defence and foreign affairs as merely examples of excluded "acts of state" and by making the certificate of the Chief Executive binding on issues of fact.' ICJ Report 1992, p. 111.

[45] BL, Art. 23; 'Such prohibitions would be contrary to the Articles of the International Covenant on Civil and Political Rights relating to freedom of expression and freedom of association and therefore to Article XIII of Annex I to the Joint Declaration.' ICJ Report 1992, p. 111.

Government and the Hong Kong Special Administrative Region in accordance with [the Basic Law)'.[46]

It should nonetheless be emphasized that the ultimate point of reference in ascertaining compliance with an international treaty is the treaty itself and that the fundamental governing norm is its observance in good faith. Furthermore, since implementation invariably entails a process of 'interpretation', conflicts and indeterminacies must be resolved[47] in the light of international maxims of treaty interpretation. It may also be argued that, given the special nature of the Sino-British Joint Declaration as an agreement on the 'future' of a territory and its people, a broad intellectual approach should be employed which takes heed of the 'basic constitutional policies of the larger global community, including the policies of the United Nations Charter and the human rights prescriptions'.[48] Guided by such principles, an attempt will be made below to ascertain the compatibility with the Joint Declaration of selective disputed issues.

Are democratic reforms a 'violation' of the Sino-British Joint Declaration?

One of the most contentious issues in the course of 'implementing' the Sino-British accord has been a package of electoral changes introduced by Governor Patten in 1992 and enacted into Hong Kong law in 1994. Following 17 rounds of unsuccessful talks between the UK and the PRC in 1993, and over Beijing's strong objections, the Legislative Council approved, on 24 February 1994, the lowering of the voting age from 21 to 18; adoption of single-seat, single-vote method for the Legislative Council, Municipal Council and the District Board geographical constituency elections; abolition of appointed District Board and Municipal Council membership; and an increase in the number of elected Municipal Council seats. Additional legislation was passed on 30 June 1994 to provide for the creation of nine new Legislative

---

[46] BL, Art. 43; 'This conflicts with Article I of Annex I to the Joint Declaration, which provides: "The executive authorities shall abide by the law and shall be accountable to the legislature".' ICJ Report 1992, p. 111.

[47] See, however, doubts expressed about the 'resolvability' of the 'overall indeterminacy' afflicting any interpretative enterprise or the achieving of an 'unbiased' application between parties dedicated to different ideologies in Richard L. Falk, 'On Treaty Interpretation and the New Haven School: Achievements and Prospects' (1968) 8 *Virginia Journal of International Law* 323.

[48] For a powerful advocacy of such an approach see: Myres S. McDougal, Harold D. Lasswell & James C. Miller, *The Interpretation of International Agreements and World Public Order. Principles of Content and Procedure* (Dordrecht: M. Nijhoff Publishers, 1994).

functional constituencies; an expansion in the franchise of five existing professional functional constituencies; and the establishment of an Election Committee to elect ten Legislative Council members.

There is little doubt that such electoral arrangements fall within the 'ordinary meaning' of the terms in the Joint Declaration stipulating that the legislature of the HKSAR shall be 'constituted by election'.[49] They may be further regarded as a legitimate and reasonable step in the implementation of obligation imposed on the British government under the Joint Declaration[50] to administer Hong Kong in the transition period (1984-1997) 'with the object of maintaining and preserving its economic prosperity and social stability'. Clearly, as contended in the *White Paper on Representative Government* in Hong Kong, 'at the heart of this [object] . . . is the rule of law' and [i]t is difficult to envisage the maintenance of the rule of law in a community where the legislative body is neither fairly elected nor free from the possibility of manipulation'.[51] The reforms are also fully consistent with the central tenets of the Sino-British Joint accord, namely, retainment by the territory of its [capitalist] way of life under a 'one country-two systems' concept, a 'high degree of autonomy' and 'Hong Kong people ruling Hong Kong'.

Nor are the electoral arrangements incompatible with the Basic Law (to the extent that the it has been 'accepted' as an instrument related to the Joint Declaration, and hence part of its 'context'). In fact, while reaffirming the ultimate aim of electing all of the SAR's legislature through universal suffrage,[52] as well as approving the creation of new constituencies (up to 30),[53] the Basic Law does not prescribe any voting system, does not define 'functional constituency', does not stipulate who should be included or who should be represented in the functional constituency electorate, and does not specify the composition of the election committee. The Basic Law is equally silent on the composition of the District Boards and Municipal Councils, and the manner of election of their members.

By the same token, no attempt should be made to supplant any perceived *lacuna* by reference to assumed intentions by the drafters. Rather, in line with acceptable principles of constitutional interpretation, the Basic Law should be construed as an 'organic' document designed to grow 'with the

---

[49] JD, Annex I, Art. III.

[50] JD, Art. 4.

[51] *White Paper on Representative Government in Hong Kong* (Hong Kong: Government Printer, February 1994), para. 83.

[52] See BL, Art. 68.

[53] See BL, 'Decision of the National People's Congress on the Method for the Formation of the First Government and the First Legislative Council of the Hong Kong Special Administrative Region,' adopted at the Third Session of the Seventh National People's Congress on 4 April 1990, para. 6.

changing political and moral ideas of the community it governs'.[54] That this community strongly endorses, indeed demands, democratization of its political institutions and a greater say in the running of its own affairs, is unequivocally demonstrated. Such aspirations on the part of the territory's residents have been evidenced, *inter alia*, in numerous presentations related to the drafting of the Basic Law, the favourable response to the reform proposals, and most clearly in elections conducted on the basis of the new electoral arrangements.[55]

In their quest, moreover, Hong Kong people are substantially reinforced by prevailing international legal prescriptions that form the normative background against which the Sino-British Joint Declaration had been concluded and in respect to which it ought to be constructed. Support may be grounded, in particular, in the 'right to democracy' or 'democratic governance' enshrined in all major human rights instruments and practised (in a variety of shades) by the majority of states.[56] In fact, not only is the right to democracy part of the relevant international 'context' but is contained in the 'text' itself by virtue of a provision in the Joint Declaration ensuring a continued application to Hong Kong of the Covenant on Civil and Political Rights. As formulated in the Covenant, it denotes the right and opportunity, without discrimination and without unreasonable restrictions to 'take part in the conduct of public affairs directly or through freely chosen representatives'; 'vote and be elected at genuine elections which shall be by universal and equal suffrage and shall be held by secret ballot, guaranteeing the free expression of the will of the electors'; and 'have access, on general terms of equality, to public services'.[57]

Their full consistency with the Sino-British Joint Declaration notwithstanding, could the democratic reforms be held in breach of the accord because of the unilateral manner in which they had been introduced? The answer should be negative unless the party's conduct failed the 'good faith' test. Evidently, in the particular circumstances, the British government may

---

[54] See Peter Wesley-Smith, 'Originalism and Akers-Jones' (1994) 24 *Hong Kong Law Journal* 5, 8 (rejecting suggestions by 'originalists' that drafters' intentions should dictate interpretation of the Basic Law).

[55] See Kevin Murphy, 'Hong Kong Voters Back Self-Rule Slate' *International Herald Tribune,* 6 March 1995, at 4 (commenting on elections to the Municipal Councils held on 5 March 1995); Philip Bowring, 'A Signal to Beijing About Transition in Hong Kong' *International Herald Tribune,* 19 September 1995, at 8; Editorial, 'Hong Kong's Voice' *International Herald Tribune,* 20 September 1995, at 8 (comments on elections to the Legislative Council held on 17 September 1995).

[56] See discussion in Chapter 1.

[57] CCPR, Art. 25.

not be faulted for want of effort to reach an agreement with their Chinese counterparts.[58] It is also apparent that the divisions between the side were not reconcilable.[59] Yet, an arbiter presented with the protagonists' separate ['double vision'] accounts[60] of their talks is likely to find it difficult to ascertain whether Britain 'lacked sincerity and deliberately complicated the issue' (as charged by China) or (as portrayed by Britain) China was 'rigid and uncooperative'. Nonetheless, as dictated by the 'principle of effectiveness', individual incriminations ought to give way to the decisive factor of implementing the objectives both parties had agreed to observe.

On the other hand, the obligation of 'good faith' would be clearly undermined by retaliatory acts which themselves constitute breaches of the treaty. The dismantling of three tiers of government (the last Legislative Council, Urban Council, Regional Council and District Boards)[61] composed of duly-elected representatives, and the institution of a selectively-appointed legislative body[62] ('provisional' or otherwise) — are such acts. They contravene the terms of the Joint Declaration 'in their context and in the light of its object and purpose'. They are also contrary to provisions in the

---

58 At least in terms of length of time invested: official talks which started on 22 April 1993 were carried on over a period of eighteen months (17 rounds; 160 hours of discussions).

59 Issues cited as 'intractable' include the size of the electorate (whether the functional constituencies should incorporate the entire working population of Hong Kong or merely 130 000); election methods (the application of the "single-seat, single-vote" principle in elections for the legislature); and the conditionalities on a "through train" to the first SAR legislature. See Kathleen Cheek-Milby, *A Legislature Comes of Age. Hong Kong's Search For Influence and Identity* (Hong Kong: Oxford University Press, 1995) p. 244 (and references therein).

60 See, respectively, *White Paper on Representative Government in Hong Kong,* supra (note 51); 'China's Version of the Talks' *South China Morning Post*, 1 March 1994, at 12.

61 A resolution to terminate Hong Kong's present political structure on 1 July 1997 was adopted by the Standing Committee of the National People's Congress on 31 August 1994. See 'China to Abolish Hong Kong's Legislature' *International Herald Tribune*, 1 September 1994, at 1.

62 See proposal by the political subgroup of the China-appointed Preliminary Working Committee [PWC], reported in Linda Choy, Chris Yeung & So Lai-fun, 'Selected Caretakers to Run SAR for a Year' *South China Morning Post*, 8 October 1994, at 1. More recently, the decision to set up a 'Provisional Legislature' was endorsed by the Preparatory Committee [a body — whose 150 members were chosen by Beijing without open deliberations or formal consultations with Hong Kong and do not include any members of the Democratic Party, the largest political party in the legislature, enjoying broad popular support among HK people — charged with the responsibility to prepare for the establishment of the HKSAR and prescribe the specific method for forming the first Government and first Legislative Council]. See 'Beijing Panel Votes to Scrap HK's Legislature' *International Herald Tribune*, 25 March 1996, at 3.

Basic Law,[63] — as well as at variance with its 'spirit'[64] insofar as this law is designed to implement the Joint Declaration and particularly pledges in respect of the territory's high degree of autonomy and the proclaimed goal of Hong Kong's stability and prosperity. Furthermore, such 'undemocratic' measures deviate from internationally established norms and the legitimate expectations of the local people.

Does the Bill of Rights Ordinance infringe the Sino-British Joint Declaration?

Another vociferously contested 'unilateral' move by one of the parties to the Sino-British Joint Declaration has been the enactment in 1991 of the Bill of Rights Ordinance [BoRO]. Yet, when subjected to the customary modes of international legal scrutiny outlined earlier, attacks pertaining to BoRO's congruity with the Joint Declaration find no grounds of support. Regardless of its long 'gestation' period,[65] or the immediate impetus behind its legislation,[66] the BoRO represents a necessary (albeit insufficient)[67] endeavour to implement international legal duties arising out of the application to Hong Kong of the International Covenant on Civil and Political

---

[63] See BL, Arts. 66, 68 and 'Decision of the National People's Congress on the Method for the Formation of the First Government and the First Legislative Council of the Hong Kong Special Administrative Region,' supra (note 53), para. 6 (setting-out, *inter alia*, the basis on which members of the Legislative Council elected in 1995 could serve through 1997 to 1999); note also that the formation of the first government and the first Legislative Council should be in accordance with the principle of 'smooth transition' (para. 1). See in this connection Denis Chang, QC, 'Provisional Legislature Boundaries Must Be Drawn' *Hong Kong Standard,* 13 April 1996 (criticizing the 'constitutional' illegitimacy of a 'provisional legislature' in the absence of necessary basis in the Joint Declaration, Basic Law and the Decision of the NPC; neither document empowers the Preparatory Committee to establish a 'provisional legislature').

[64] The concept is recognized neither under domestic or international legal systems.

[65] Taking account of the fact that the ICCPR and the ICESCR were extended to the territory already in 1976.

[66] Identified as the 'events of June 1989 in Beijing' or the need to 'reassure the people of Hong Kong as they contemplated the transfer of sovereignty to China in 1997, and to restore investment confidence in the territory.' See Johannes Chan and Yash Ghai, 'A Comparative Perspective on the Bill of Rights' in Johannes Chan and Yash Ghai, eds., *The Hong Kong Bill of Rights: A Comparative Approach* (Hong Kong: Butterworths Asia, 1993), 1, at p. 2.

[67] See criticisms referred to in Chapter 4.

Rights [ICCPR].[68] It is also an imperative act if substance is to be given to commitment made by China in the Joint Declaration[69] that provisions of the Covenant shall *remain in force*.[70]

The 'incorporation'[71] of the ICCPR in the Bill of Rights Ordinance clearly accords with the Joint Declaration's[72] 'object and purpose', as reflected in the mutual pledges to enshrine in Hong Kong law provisions of the ICCPR and ICESCR, to preserve Hong Kong's 'life-style',[73] and guarantee protection of fundamental rights and freedoms of its people. Equally legitimate are the legislative measures undertaken to ensure the effectiveness of the BoRO as the mechanism through which the controlling function of the ICCPR is facilitated. In fact, the 'ingenious solution'[74] adopted — whereby it is the ICCPR (or its provisions 'as applied to Hong Kong'), rather than the BoRO itself,[75] which is 'entrenched' — should serve to deflect objections that a Hong Kong law has been endowed with special status thus derogating from the Basic Law's own elevated position[76] or that the system which had prevailed at the time of the Joint Declaration's conclusion has been deviated from.[77]

---

68 '. . . to take the necessary steps, in accordance with its constitutional processes and with the provisions of the present Covenant, to adopt such legislative or other measures as may be necessary to give effect to the rights recognized in the present Covenant' (ICCPR, Art. 2).

69 See JD, Annex I, Art. XIII, para. 4.

70 As pointed out by one observer, '[b]efore 1991 the ICCPR had been "applied" to Hong Kong only upon the international plane . . . since China has not acceded to the ICCPR, it is difficult to see how the ICCPR can "*remain* in force" after 1997 *unless* it has been incorporated into domestic law.' Richard Swede, 'One Territory — Three Systems? The Hong Kong Bill of Rights' (1995) 44 *International & Comparative Law Quarterly* 358, 361.

71 See discussion in Roda Mushkat, 'International Human Rights and Domestic Hong Kong Law' in Raymond Wacks, ed., *Hong Kong's Bill of Rights. Problems & Prospects* (Hong Kong: Faculty of Law, University of Hong Kong, 1990), 25, at pp. 34–36.

72 As well as with the Basic Law which, in Article 39, obliges the HKSAR to implement the ICCPR through its laws.

73 See JD, Art. 3(5); The term is explained in context by what follows, namely: 'Rights and freedoms . . . will be protected by law.'

74 See Yash Ghai, 'The Bill of Rights Ordinance and the Basic Law of the Hong Kong Special Administrative Region: Complementaries and Conflicts' (1995) 1 *Journal of Chinese and Comparative Law* 30, 38.

75 The BoRO remains an ordinary legislation, unable by its own terms to control or override subsequent legislation of either the Hong Kong legislature or the HKSAR legislature.

76 As secured under Article 11 of the Basic Law.

77 It may be added in this connection that while the parties stipulated that the 'current social and economic systems will remain unchanged' [JD, Art. 3(5)], a period of 'transition' between 1984 and 1997 is clearly envisaged, in which an action by the responsible administrative authorities designed to implement guarantees stipulated in the accord, would not be considered 'deviation', even if it involves certain changes from the 1984 state of affairs.

Like other ordinances, and in accordance with the *lex posterior* rule, the BoRO may repeal laws antedating its enactment to the extent of any inconsistency. Moreover, judicial review of legislation has long been a feature of Hong Kong's legal system, which under its constitution limits the territory's lawmaking authority.[78] Consequently, local judges, as the 'guardians of the constitution', are empowered to interpret laws (including constitutional documents like the Letters Patent, Royal Instructions, the New Territories Order in Council 1898, and the Bill of Rights Ordinance),[79] and strike down (by way of declaration, injunction or other appropriate relief) any legislation which is repugnant, for example, to an Act of Parliament or is 'unconstitutional'.[80] Indeed, such judicial power is assumed to be present beyond 1997 to allow the repeal of laws which breach the Basic Law. By the same token, the BoRO has not altered the balance between the legislature and the executive, which would continue to be maintained in line with Basic Law prescriptions.[81]

The protractors' stand is further weakened by the fact that the amendment to the Letters Patent — employed to effect the 'indirect entrenchment' in accordance with Hong Kong's 'constitution' — mirrors Article 39 of the Basic Law which itself (following the Joint Declaration) provides for the supervening authority of the ICCPR'.[82] In fact, despite some divergencies between the individual articles in the BoRO and the Basic Law, no fundamental conflict can be said to exist which may render the BoRO invalid by reason of inconsistency with the Basic Law.[83] Finally, questions pertaining to the 'good faith' aspect of the 'unilateral' enactment of the BoRO should be assessed against apparent attempts by drafters and legislators to anticipate

---

78 See Peter Wesley-Smith, 'Legal Limitations upon the Legislative Competence of the Hong Kong Legislature' (1981) *Hong Kong Law Journal* 3.

79 See, e.g. *R v Godber* [1975] HKLR 326; *R v Cheung Son-yat* [1979] HKLR 630; *Lam Yuk-ming v Attorney General* [1980] HKLR 815; *Winfat Enterprises (HK) Co. Ltd. v Attorney General* [1984] HKLR 32; [1985] 2 WLR 786; *R v Sin Yau-ming* [1991] 1 HKPLR 88; *R v To Kwan-hand and Tsoi Yiu-cheong* [1994] 4 HKPLR 356.

80 See *Rediffusion (HK) Ltd v Attorney General* [1970] AC 1136 (per Lord Diplock); Most recently, the Court of Appeals reaffirmed that '[t]he [BoRO] is the embodiment of the [ICCPR] as applied here. Any legislative inroad into the bill is therefore unconstitutional and will be struck down by the courts as the guardians of the constitution.' See *Lee Miu-ling and Law Piu v Attorney General,* 24 November 1995 (per Bokhary J), reported in Cliff Buddle, 'Poll Plea Dismissed' *South China Morning Post*, 25 November 1995, at 2.

81 See Ghai's contention that the Basic Law's postulate of 'executive-led government' has not been affected by the BoRO and is preserved through rules pertaining to the mode of election and dismissal of the Chief Executive and her relationship with the legislature, etc., supra (note 74) at 55.

82 Ghai, supra (note 74).

83 See analysis in Ghai, ibid.

potential opposition and ensure compatibility with the Basic Law.[84] By the same token, the BoRO as an act aimed at the fulfilment of Britain's international obligations should not be construed as discrediting the adequacy of protection offered by China under its implementing tool.

The conclusion to be derived from the above analysis is that the Bill of Rights Ordinance is fully consistent with the Joint Declaration and the Basic Law. Consequently, any attempt to repeal or modify the provisions of the BoRO so as to restrict the application of any of those provisions to the HKSAR[85] would constitute a breach of both the Joint Declaration and the Basic Law.[86] Equally unlawful would be a 'resurrection' of laws which had been invalidated by reference to the ICCPR as incorporated in the BoRO.[87] Furthermore, apart from engendering uncertainty regarding China's compliance with its express undertaking to respect Hong Kong's autonomy within the declared basic policy of 'one country-two systems', such illicit moves would inevitably cast doubts on China's adherence to the fundamental rule of *pacta sunt servanda*[88] and to international human rights law.

---

[84] See Philip Dykes, 'The Hong Kong Bill of Rights 1991: Its Origin, Content and Impact' in *The Hong Kong Bill of Rights: A Comparative Approach*, op.cit., pp. 39–49; see also James Allan, 'A Bill of Rights for Hong Kong' (1991) *Public Law* 175, 179 (describing the 'influence' of the Chinese government prior to the enactment of BoRO, as reflected in the 'noticeable softening of the Bill' which occurred between the March 1990 and July 1990 drafts).

[85] See, e.g. advice tendered by the legal subgroup of the Preliminary Working Committee [PWC] ('Beijing-appointed think-tank on Hong Kong's future') to delete BoRO's articles 2(3), 3 & 4 (which are central to the incorporation of the ICCPR into Hong Kong law). Reported in Connie Law & Chris Yeung, 'PWC Asks China to Bury Bill of Rights' *South China Morning Post*, 18 October 1995, at 1. It should be noted, however, that neither the removal of these articles nor a repeal of the BoRO itself could abrogate the applicability to Hong Kong of the ICCPR. See discussion in Chapter 6.

[86] See also conclusion by the International Commission of Jurists, ICJ Report, supra (note 42), pp. 99, 101.

[87] See proposals of PWC's legal subgroup, reported in Sam Mok, 'PWC Moves to Resurrect Severe Laws' *South China Morning Post*, 18 October 1995, at 2. Note that the six laws targeted for reinstatement (including the pre-1995 version of the Public Order Ordinance, which allowed widespread restrictions to be imposed on public meetings, processions and gatherings; Emergency Regulations, which provided for the censorship and suppression of publications, detention and deportation of undesirables, and requisition of land property; the pre-1992 version of the Societies Ordinance; pre-1993 legislation relating to television, telecommunications and the Broadcasting Authority) are clearly incompatible with provisions of the Basic Law (e.g. Articles 27 & 39), and could be subject to challenge before the HKSAR courts as breaching the Basic Law.

[88] Notwithstanding official statements such as: 'it is important that Hong Kong enjoys the autonomy we have promised because we want to show the world that China can be relied upon to implement agreements on these important matters' (Lu Ping). Cited in Nigel Holloway, 'Don't Worry Be Happy. China Reassures US About HK's Future' *Far Eastern Economic Review*, 6 April 1995, at 21.

Is the agreement on the 'Court of Final Appeal' consistent with the Sino-British Joint Declaration?

Whereas the discord surrounding the issues hitherto investigated stemmed in part from the unilateral nature of the disputed acts, the question featured in the present discussion relates to controversy triggered by a 'mutual' deed. More specifically, it concerns an 'agreement' reached in 1991 in the Sino-British Joint Liaison Group (JLG) on the composition of the Court of Final Appeal (CFA)[89] — as well as a later 'Agreement between the British and Chinese Sides on the Question of the Court of Final Appeal in Hong Kong'[90] — seeking to limit to one the number of overseas judges on the five-members' court (the 'four to one formula').· Although centred mainly around one provision in the Joint Declaration,[91] the 'CFA debate' (aside from its political significance)[92] may serve to illustrate the parties' [mis]perceptions and [mis]understandings of key elements in the treaty.

As indicated at the outset of this section (on the 'implementation and breach of treaties'), and in line with the applicable international rules of treaty interpretation, the respective terms in the Joint Declaration must be interpreted 'in good faith in accordance with the ordinary meaning to be given to the terms of the treaty in their context and in the light of [the treaty's] object and purpose'. Thus approached, it is doubtless that the 'ordinary meaning' to be assigned to the relevant article[93] confers on the Court of

---

[89] [Hereafter: the 1991 agreement]. A text of the 'agreement' has not been published.

[90] The agreement, concluded on 9 June 1995 [hereafter: the 1995 agreement], consists of five clauses, reaffirming *inter alia* the 'four to one formula'. Reprinted in (1996) 35 *International Legal Materials* 207.

[91] JD, Annex I, Art. III, para. 4.

[92] See Lo Shiu-hing, supra (note 28), (highlighting the unprecedented local concern about Hong Kong's future judicial independence, China's lingering suspicion of Britain's political motives in Hong Kong, the reluctance of Britain's Foreign Office to alienate mainland China on the composition of the CFA, the need to seek approval from LegCo). See also Jackie Sam, 'New Power Balance in Territory' *Hong Kong Standard*, 10 June 1995, at 1 (alluding to the 'shift in power from British to Chinese hands' as reflected in Section 5 of the 1995 Agreement: '. . . the Hong Kong Special Administrative region shall, *with the British side . . . participating in the process and providing its assistance,* be responsible for the preparation for the establishment of the Court of Final Appeal . . .'); and Chris Yeung, 'Accord Bodes Well for Future Talks' *South China Morning Post*, 10 June 1995, at 1 (opining that '[a]lthough it is dangerous to read too much into the political significance of the outcome of a single issue, it does show that China can be conciliatory and flexible over matters of sovereignty when there is a need').

[93] Stipulating that '[t]he power of final judgment of the Hong Kong Special Administrative Region shall be vested in the court of final appeal in the Hong Kong Special Administrative Region, which may as required invite judges from other common law jurisdictions to sit on the court of final appeal.'

Final Appeal discretion to decide *when* does a requirement arise to invite judges from other common law jurisdictions, *whom* and *how many* to invite. There is no qualification or proviso which could support other than an intention to grant the Court full discretion regarding the exercise of its power. Such an interpretation is also induced by the principle of 'institutional effectiveness', favouring wide powers for institutions to perform their functions in the most effective manner.

Further substantiation is equally drawn when the terms are examined 'in the light of the object and purpose' of a treaty aimed at preserving the stability and prosperity of a region endowed with a high degree of autonomy, including final power of adjudication. Indeed, the importance to Hong Kong's stability and prosperity of maintaining the current advantages derived from an international judicial link and ensuring the CFA's true independence and membership of the highest standard, has also been recognized by the drafters of the Basic Law, who reaffirmed that the Court 'may as required invite judges from other common law jurisdictions'.[94] Basically, as delineated by one observer,

> '[t]he setting up of a Court of Final Appeal in Hong Kong was to provide for continuity in the legal system and the rule of law even while ending the link to the Privy Council, ensuring the territory's stability. The provision for overseas judges to serve on the Court of Final Appeal was clearly intended to lend that court greater stature, so that domestic and foreign investors would continue to have confidence in the judicial system, thus ensuring the territory's prosperity. That being the case, too great a restriction on the court's right to invite overseas judges — both when they might be invited and how many might be invited — would work against giving the court the independence it is meant to enjoy and could, in fact, detract from the territory's stability and prosperity'.[95]

Whether account should be taken of the 1991 or 1995 agreements hinges on either constituting an 'agreement between the parties regarding the interpretation or the application of its provisions', under the Convention on the Law of Treaties [Art. 31(3)(a)]. As suggested in an earlier context,[96] the 1991 agreement is more appropriately viewed as a 'deal', reflecting compromises designed to diffuse political tension that had developed between the parties (following the 'Tiananmen crackdown'), and justified on pragmatic

---

[94] BL, Art. 82.

[95] Frank Ching, 'The Vienna Convention on the Law of Treaties and the Joint Liaison Group's Agreement on Hong Kong's Court of Final Appeal', a paper presented at a Zonta Club Forum on the Court of Final Appeal, 21 October 1994.

[96] See supra (notes 28, 29).

grounds (such as 'workability' and the benefits of erecting a Court of Final Appeal before 1997).[97]

Neither does the 1995 agreement — which contains no direct reference to the Joint Declaration, and has been depicted by British officials as the 'best possible deal under the circumstances',[98] by political commentators as 'capitulation/acquiescence to Chinese demands'[99] and by critics as a 'sell-out'[100] — amount to an agreement on interpretation or application of provisions in the Joint Declaration, sufficiently authoritative to displace an 'ordinary meaning' that is consistent with the Declaration's 'object and purpose'. In a similar vein, unless expressly provided in a later agreement concluded in accordance with applicable rules, the 'mutuality' of conduct by itself bestows no amending or modifying effect on the 'subsequent practice' of the parties, particularly when it contradicts the clear meaning of the article at question.

Also of doubtful validity is a line of argument paraphrasing the issue as one, not of interpretation or modification but, of 'subsequent elaboration of a general principle'. Specifically, it has been contended[101] that the Joint Declaration lays down a *general principle* that the CFA is to have *a power* to invite judges from other common law jurisdictions to sit on the court, but leave the *precise scope of that power* to be defined in the course of implementation of that general principle. In other words, the relevant articles in the Joint Declaration (as well as in the Basic Law) are said to be merely 'framework provisions which are intended to be fleshed out by more detailed legislative provisions'.

Yet, it remains true that the mode of implementation (for example, through legislative prescription) must not circumvent the primary international obligation to 'perform' the treaty in 'good faith' (namely in accordance with the 'ordinary meaning to be given to the terms of the treaty in their context

---

[97] See speech by Secretary for Constitutional Affairs (Mr Michael Sze) on the motion debate on the Court of Final Appeal in the Legislative Council on 4 December 1991. Note that the early establishment of the CFA, regarded as probably the most important consideration underlying the 1991 agreement, forms no part of the 1995 agreement (the agreed date for setting-up the Court is 1 July 1997).

[98] See Louise de Rosario, 'A Court Too Far' *Far Eastern Economic Review*, 22 June 1995, at 20.

[99] See 'Britain Gives in on CFA' *Hong Kong Standard*, 10 June 1995, at 1.

[100] See report by Lily Mak, 'Hong Kong "Sold Out" Says Lee' *Hong Kong Standard*, 10 June 1995, at 4; see also Martin Lee, 'Courting Disaster' *South China Morning Post*, 14 June 1995, at 19.

[101] In a letter dated 17 November 1994 from the Attorney General (J F Mathews) to the Chairman of the Hong Kong Bar Association, enclosing a British government's statement on 'Hong Kong: Court of Final Appeal'.

and in the light of its object and purpose'). An arrangement that denies the Court of Final Appeal flexibility in the choice of judges and unduly inhibits its power to invite overseas judges does not fully comply with one of the Joint Declaration's cornerstone promises of judicial autonomy'.[102]

Of greater concern perhaps is the issue of the CFA's jurisdiction, or more specifically, the stipulation inserted into the Hong Kong Court of Final Appeal Ordinance, pursuant to the 1995 agreement, that '[t]he Court shall have no jurisdiction over acts of state such as defence and foreign affairs'.[103] Although this clause merely replicates Article 19 of the Basic Law, its compatibility with the Joint Declaration should still be assessed in light of the applicable international treaty rules. An evaluation conducted within such a framework would, arguably, yield the conclusion that a severe restriction is imposed on the CFA which is inconsistent with both the judicial power postulated in the Joint Declaration and the constitutional doctrines affecting the decision-making process by local judges under a system internationally guaranteed to be maintained. In particular, the incorporation in the CFA Ordinance of undefined [or loosely defined][104] constraints, combined with a lack of explicit reference to interpretative sources[105] and a failure to identify the determining authorities,[106] cast serious doubts on the implementation of the commitment in the Joint Declaration to vest the Court with the 'power of final adjudication'. Whereas under the present common law system, the 'acts of state' exclusion is most narrowly construed and rarely invoked,[107] should other reference contexts prevail or defining power removed from the

---

[102] See conclusion in ICJ Report, supra (note 42), at 91 ('The agreement reached by the Joint Liaison Group on the composition of the Court of Final Appeal is contrary to the Joint Declaration and the Basic Law and is constitutionally invalid; the Court of Final Appeal itself should be allowed to determine the number and identity of foreign judges to sit as temporary members').

[103] Hong Kong Court of Final Appeal Ordinance (No. 79 of 1995), s4(2).

[104] In fact, the term '*such as*' — rather than illustrate — has introduced an additional element of imprecision and vulnerability to an expansive interpretation. Note also that in the Chinese text of the 1995 agreement, the CFA 'shall have no jurisdiction over acts of state, that is, defence and foreign affairs, *etcetera*.' See Martin Lee, supra (note 100).

[105] It may be queried, for example, whether the term should be interpreted by reference to English common law or — given its 'adoption' in the present context from the Basic Law — be regarded as a matter of interpretation of the Basic Law.

[106] As a general rule in common law countries, the courts determine what constitutes an 'act of state'. It has been argued, however, that — as in respect of other provisions in the Basic Law — the final arbiter regarding 'acts of state' in the HKSAR would be the Standing Committee of the National People's Congress, in accord with Art. 158 of the Basic Law.

[107] Not even all acts related to foreign affairs and defence are beyond the scope of judicial power. Nor can the 'act of state' exception be relied upon to usurp court authority over events on home territory. Clearly, acts of the Executive affecting private rights would be subject to review if they are amenable to the judicial process.

judicial domain, the 'act of state' exemption may arbitrarily expand at a heavy cost to judicial independence, citizens rights and the rule of law in Hong Kong.

Similar misgivings may be directed at any attempt to totally oust the judicial function in respect of 'questions of fact concerning [the undefined] acts of state'.[108] It is generally expected that where certain questions arise in the course of proceedings related to facts, circumstances, or events which are 'peculiarly within the cognisance of the Executive'[109] (for example, extent of territory, existence of a state of war, belligerency/neutrality, determination of status that entitles one to immunity from process, or recognition of a state/government), judges would seek the executive's statement or certification. Yet, the legal effects of the certified 'facts of state' (as well as the interpretation of the certificate itself) is a matter that falls solely within the province of the judiciary.[110] Indeed, to preserve the judicial independence bestowed upon them in the Joint Declaration, HKSAR judges must not permit the expression of executive policy to usurp entirely the judicial function and must guard against the 'trap' of 'what may begin by guidance as to the principles to be applied and end in cases being decided irrespective of any principle in accordance with the view of the Executive as to what is politically expedient.[111]

Independent judges in an autonomous regime may also be trusted not to 'embarrass or interfere with the Executive'[112] or hurt the national interest, by applying 'judicial restraint and abstention' which is said to be 'inherent in the very nature of the judicial process'.[113] That the curtailment of judicial autonomy is gravely perceived by the local community needs no restatement.[114] Concerns have also been voiced outside the territory.[115] The

---

[108] CFA Ordinance, s(4)3. Clause 4(3).

[109] See F.A. Mann, *Foreign Affairs in English Courts* (Oxford: Clarendon Press, 1986), p. 23.

[110] Mann, ibid., p. 52. It may also be noted that English courts have tried to mitigate effects of the rigid certification — ibid.

[111] Mann, ibid., quoting Lord Cross of Chelsea in *The Philippine Admiral* [1977] AC 373, 399.

[112] The rationale underlying the 'Act of State' doctrine: see the leading American decision in *Baker v Carr* 369 US 186 (1962).

[113] *Buttes Gas v Hammer* [1982] AC 888, 932 (per Lord Wilberforece). For further discussion and criticism of 'judicial abstention' see Chapter 6.

[114] The 1991 agreement was vehemently rejected by members of the Legislative Council and the legal profession: See *LegCo Proceedings,* 4 December 1991 and 3 May 1995. For reactions to the 1995 agreement see reports by Louis Won & Lok Wong, 'From Politicians: Outrage. Parties Line Up Against a "Sellout" '; Connie Law & Catherine Ng, 'Bar Chairman Attacks "Unhappy Compromise" ' *South China Morning Post,* 10 June 1995, at 3. The approval of the CFA Bill by the Legislative Council on 26 July 1995 was described as a 'pragmatic (but reluctant) vote', amidst continuing objections: see editorial, 'Defining Acts of State' *South China Morning Post,* 27 July 1995, at 16.

impartial adjudicator guided by the relevant international norms should caution against unduly constraining a court upon which rests the preservation of the integrity of Hong Kong's legal system after 1997.

---

[115] See, for example, statement by the US Lawyers Committee for Human Rights that 'the failure of the June 9 agreement to protect the jurisdiction of the CFA is likely to have serious repercussions on the rights of Hong Kong citizens, as well as of foreign nationals', cited in Martin Lee, 'CFA: The Opening Arguments' *South China Morning Post*, 26 July 1995, at 19; comment by the executive chairman of the International Commission of Jurists, Justice Kirby (also President of the New South Wales Court of Appeal) that 'any reference to an Act of State exemption in a society such as the People's Republic of China is fraught with danger,' cited in Robin Fitzsimons, 'Is Hong Kong Facing a Legal Sell-Out?' *London Times*, 1 August 1995; editorial, 'Hong Kong's Unappealing Court' *The Economist*, 17 June 1995, at 18 (observing that 'the rule of law, after 1997, looks ever more doubtful,' and 'justice is blind, and crippled'). See, however, report of comments by diplomatic representatives in Hong Kong in Neville de Silva, 'International Community Welcomes Agreement' *Hong Kong Standard*, 10 June 1995, at 5 (noting, in particular, the positive aspect of an *agreement* being reached).

Chapter 6

Interrelationship Between International Law and Hong Kong Domestic Law

THE PLACE OF INTERNATIONAL LAW IN THE HONG KONG LEGAL SYSTEM

An overview

As seen in earlier chapters, notwithstanding the territory's non-sovereign status, the Hong Kong legal system has had to address several issues in the field of international law, including the scope of local jurisdictional powers, extradition matters, treatment of aliens, obligations under the international laws of human rights and the environment, succession to membership in international organizations and agreements, as well as the effect and interpretation of treaties in domestic law. To facilitate comprehension of the extent to which international law is applied and enforced in Hong Kong, a review of the general relationship between international law and the domestic law is undertaken.

Like its British counterpart, Hong Kong's 'constitution' lays down no rules or principles regarding the international/domestic law interrelationship, although established British practices are invariably followed. Thus, the traditional common law distinction between customary international law and treaty-based law — said to be warranted by 'separation of powers constraints'[1] — is largely maintained. Accordingly, customary international

---

[1] Under British constitutional law and practice, treaty-making is the prerogative of the Crown (i.e. the conclusion of treaties by the executive branch of the government requires no

law forms part of the law of the land, hence binding without the need for legislative transformation, whereas conventional international law — consisting of treaties, conventions and other international agreements — requires formal incorporation. In this vein, customary international law, as part of the law of the land enjoys no special rank under the local hierarchy of legal norms, and would give way in the face of a later conflicting law. Similarly, treaties once incorporated become legislation like any other, to be trumped by subsequent contrary statutes.

At the same time, the application of international law within the Hong Kong legal system is not confined to enforcement by the judiciary but impacts also on other organs of government,[2] either under the legislature's responsibility to implement international obligations or the executive's duty to abide by them. Indeed, given the well-established[3] rule of construction that the legislature is presumed not to have derogated from the state's international obligations, it may be contended that the powers of the executive are *prima facie* delimited by international law, and 'should also be exercised in accordance with the selfsame international obligations, particularly when fundamental rights are involved'.[4] Such a view appears to have been adopted

---

formal sanctioning by parliament), hence direct applicability of treaties would have allowed government the power to introduce norms into the domestic legal system, thereby usurping the legislative function. Arguably, however, the separation of powers principle need not be compromised since the legislature may still exercise a supervisory or supervening power. Nor is a distinction between customary international law and treaty-based law with reference to the principle of separation of powers justified given that customary international law is also the outcome of governmental action or inaction.

[2]   It may be noted that 'state' responsibility is engaged as a result of breach of international law by *all* organs of state.

[3]   The 'compatibility rule' is applied by courts in the Commonwealth — including Australia [*Lim v Minister of Immigration* (1992) 176 CLR 1, 38], Canada [see Hugh M. Kindred et al., *International Law Chiefly as Interpreted and Applied in Canada,* 5th ed. (Toronto: Emond Montgomery Publications, 1993) pp. 157–160], India [*Kubik Darusz v Union of India* (1993) 92 *International Law Reports* 540 (SC)], Namibia [*Minister of Defence, Namibia v Mwandinghi* (1993) 91 *International Law Reports* 341 (HC)], United Kingdom [*R v Chief Immigration Officer, Ex parte Salamat Bibi* (1981) 61 *International Law Reports* 267 (C.A.)], Zimbabwe [*State v Ncube et al.* (1993) 91 *International Law Reports* 580 (SC)] — and in Europe, including Denmark, Germany, Italy [see Francis G. Jacobs and Shelly Roberts, eds., *The Effect of Treaties in Domestic Law* (London: Sweet & Maxwell, 1987), pp. 36, 68–9, 100–1 respectively].

[4]   Andrew J. Cunningham, 'The European Convention on Human Rights, Customary International Law and the Constitution' (1994) *International Comparative Law Quarterly* 537, 557 (and references therein).

by courts in some Commonwealth countries.[5] Yet, Hong Kong judges have been reluctant to draw the necessary inference from the 'presumption of compatibility' or to attempt an alignment between the territory's international obligations and its domestic law,[6] although 'progressive' pronouncements are available.[7]

In general, the attitude of the local judiciary pertaining to the relevance of international law in the domestic context may be characterized as overly conservative. Partly, such conservatism is attributable and justified by reference to limitations arising from the acts of state/facts of state doctrine. As commonly perceived, municipal courts will 'accept' acts of the executive performed as a matter of policy in the course of its relations with another state (for example, a declaration of war, an annexation of territory or an act of reprisal) and will not question their validity despite an apparent breach of international law. Also accepted as binding by the courts is the executive affirmation of certain legal situations in the international sphere (for example, recognition of foreign states or governments, territorial sovereignty, existence of a state of war, entitlement to diplomatic status, etc.), irrespective of whether or not the executive's certificate accurately reflects the international legal stance.

---

[5]   See Australian decision: *re Minister of Foreign Affairs,* 37 Federal Court Reports 298, 112 Australian Law Reports 529 (1992) (HC); New Zealand case: *Birds Galore Ltd. v Attorney-General et al.*, 90 *International Law Reports* 567 (1992); India: *Kubik Darusz v Union of India,* supra (note 3) (qualified as applicable only with respect to interactions with foreign nationals). Note, however, that in the UK a claim from the bindingness of the executive by international law was rejected (despite its 'considerable persuasive force') due to its novelty: *R v Home Secretary, Ex parte Brind* [1991] 1 AC 696, 748, 761–2. On the other hand, there are dicta in UK cases to the effect that where discretion is 'extra-statutory', the executive ought to have regard to its international obligations, even though contained in unenacted treaties; for citations see Cunningham, ibid., at 558.

[6]   See editorial comment, (1993) 2 *Bill of Rights Bulletin* 61–2 (alluding, in particular, to a sweeping statement made by a Justice of the Court of Appeal in *R v Director of Immigration, ex parte Li Jin-fei and others* (1993) 3 Hong Kong Public Law Reports [HKPLR] 565, 575: '. . . it is axiomatic that the municipal courts of the territory do not exist for the enforcement of international obligations incurred by the United Kingdom Government on behalf of Hong Kong').

[7]   See *R v Director of Immigration, ex parte Simon Yin Xiang-jiang* (1994) 4 HKPLR 265, 273 (per Bokhary JA): 'Naturally, it is not to be assumed that Hong Kong has no respect at all for its treaty obligations, especially those pertaining to fundamental human rights of an international dimension. It is at least potentially arguable, therefore, that where Hong Kong has a treaty obligation not to expel stateless persons except on grounds of national security or public order, then, even though that obligation has not been incorporated into our domestic law, it is nevertheless a factor which our immigration authorities ought to take into account when exercising a discretion whether or not, in all the circumstances, to insist upon the departure from this territory of any stateless person even though his departure is not required by national security or public order.'

While it is acknowledged that since all states are sovereign equals, each state must respect the public acts of every other state it recognizes,[8] it needs not follow that domestic courts are precluded from determining how and how far to give effect to such acts of the foreign government[9] (particularly, where such acts are manifestly in violation of international law).[10] Clearly, a complete judicial abstention over transactions of sovereign states, known as the 'English acts of state doctrine', finds little support amongst international jurists and commentators.[11] Held as particularly flawed is the premise that courts should refrain from rendering a judgment which would offend a foreign state, so as to avoid retaliation by the foreign state against the national interests of the forum state or cause embarrassment to the national executive.[12] Unsurprisingly, a 1993 resolution adopted by the Institut de Droit International recommends that national courts assert their competence to examine the compatibility of foreign laws with international law and 'decline to give effect to foreign public acts that violate international law'.[13]

---

[8] See *locus classicus* decision *Underhill v Hernandez* (1897) 168 US 250, 252 (per Fuller CJ): 'Every sovereign state is bound to respect the independence of every other sovereign state, and the courts of one country will not sit in judgment on the acts of the government of another done within its own territory. Redress of grievances, by reason of such acts must be obtained through the means open to be availed of by sovereign powers as between themselves.'

[9] The reference is mostly to acts by the foreign government against its own subjects in respect of property situated on its own territory.

[10] Although judging the acts of another by the forum's national laws may be an abuse of the other's sovereignty, no such infringement occurs if the validity of those acts is determined by international law. Note the flexible case-by-case approach encouraged in *Banco Nacional de Cuba v Sabbatino* (1964) 376 US 398, 428. Note also that in what is known as the 'Hickenlooper Amendement' (to the Foreign Assistance Act of 1961), the US Congress directed the courts not to give effect to foreign acts of state that violated international law by taking without compensation the property of US nationals. In the United Kingdom, a court held that Iranian legislative acts of nationalization were contrary to international law (*The Rose Mary* [1953] 1 Weekly Law Reports 246) and in *Oppenheimer v Cattermole* [1976] Appeal Cases 249, at 277–8, Lord Cross, speaking for the majority said: 'A judge should, of course, be very slow to refuse to give effect to the legislation of a foreign state in any sphere in which, according to accepted principles of international law, the foreign state has jurisdiction . . . But I think . . . that it is part of the public policy of this country that our courts should give effect to clearly established rules of international law.'

[11] See Benedetto Conforti (Rapporteur), 'The Activities of National Judges and the International Relations of their State, Preliminary Report' (1993) 65 *Yearbook of the Institute of International Law* 328, at 393–406.

[12] See, e.g. the observation that the risk of the forum state being embarrassed by a decision is negligible, and that the executive actually may prefer judicial intervention that relieves it from the necessity to make a politically difficult choice, cited ibid., at 361.

[13] Article 3, Resolution on 'The Activities of National Courts and the International Relations of their State' (Milan, 7 September 1993).

Nor for that matter can justification be adduced for any 'avoidance doctrine' grounded in a 'general principle . . . inherent in the very nature of the judicial process' or on a 'lack of judicial or manageable standards'.[14] Similar reservations may be expressed with regard to what is considered an embedded reluctance by judges to review governmental and legislative action in the light of international legal norms,[15] and frequently subsumed under the doctrine of 'non-justiciability of political questions'.[16] Whether through a change of 'legal culture'[17] or by adhering to international calls 'not to decline competence on the basis of the political nature of the question'[18] whenever international law provides criteria for examining the legality of executive acts — local judges are urged to discharge their responsibility to uphold the territory's international obligations.[19]

Customary international law — a 'part of Hong Kong law'?

Customary international law may form part of the law of Hong Kong on the basis of two possible grounds. It can be held to be adopted into the local legal system by way of the Application of English Law Ordinance 1966 which stipulates that 'the common law and rules of equity shall be in force in Hong Kong, so far as they may be applicable to the circumstances of Hong Kong or its inhabitants and subject to such modifications thereto as circumstances may require' (Sec. 3). Consequently, English law received by

---

[14] See *Buttes Gas and Oil Co. v Hammer and Occidental Petroleum Corp.* [1981] 3 All ER 616, at 628, 633 (per Lord Wilberforce).

[15] See Eyal Benvenisti, 'Judicial Misgivings Regarding the Application of International Law: An Analysis of Attitudes of National Courts' (1993) 4 *European Journal of International Law* 159.

[16] For a forceful attack on the doctrine see: Thomas Franck, *Political Questions/Judicial Answers: Does the Rule of Law Apply to Foreign Affairs?* (Princeton: Princeton University Press, 1992)

[17] The term is used by Rosalyn Higgins to describe the lack of background in international law amongst judges which manifest itself in ways varying from contempt for everything to do with international law to strenuous efforts 'not to decide points of international law, but to locate the *ratio decidendi* of the judgment on more familiar ground' — *Problems and Process. International Law and How We Use it* (Oxford: Clarendon Press, 1994), pp. 206–7.

[18] Article 2, Resolution, supra (note 13).

[19] As indicated above (note 2), '[t]he Judiciary and the courts are organs of the State and they generate responsibility in the same way as other categories of officials . . . Like the executive organs and the legislature, the courts may be instrumental in the misapplication of treaty standards [and international law in general].' See Ian Brownlie, *System of the Law of Nations — State Responsibility,* Part I (Oxford: Clarendon Press, 1983) at p. 144.

the territory includes the common law doctrine, to which Blackstone gave expression in the often-quoted passage from his *Commentaries on the Laws of England,* that 'the law of nations, in its fullest extent, was part of the law of the land'.[20]

Under this doctrine, rules of international law are incorporated into English law automatically and are considered to be part of English law unless they are in conflict with an Act of Parliament. As stated in a recent edition of the authoritative text on Oppenheim's *International Law,* the 'incorporation doctrine' has been 'repeatedly acted upon by the courts and can be regarded as an established rule of English law'.[21] Most notable among the categorical affirmations of the doctrine[22] is Lord Denning's pronouncement in *Trendtex Trading Corporation v Central Bank of Nigeria* that 'the rules of international law, as existing from time to time, do form part of our English law'.[23]

Evidently, were the reception of customary international law in Hong Kong to stem exclusively from the Application of English Law Ordinance, local courts would be compelled to espouse the definitions and interpretations given to international customs by English judges. They would, additionally, be precluded from incorporating customary rules rejected by English courts for being contradictory to English legislation. However, should it be acknowledged that as an international legal entity Hong Kong is under obligation to observe international law, it may be argued that the reception of customary international law into the territory's legal system is thereby mandated. Although international law does not demand automatic incorporation of custom by municipal law, it has been observed by a noted international jurist,[24] that subject to differing *internal* constitutional or statutory provisions regarding priority, international law is 'everywhere part

---

[20] Blackstone, *Commentaries on the Laws of England* (15th ed., 1809), Book IV, Chapter 5, p. 67.

[21] Sir Robert Jennings & Sir Arthur Watts, eds., *Oppenheim's International Law,* 9th ed., Vol. I (London: Longmans, 1992) pp. 56–7.

[22] See, e.g. *Buvot v Barbuit* (1737) 25 ER 777 (per Lord Talbot); *Triquet v Bath* (1764) 3 Burr 1478 (per Lord Mansfield CJ); *West Rand Central Gold Mining Co v R* [1905] 2 KB 391 (per Lord Alverstone CJ: 'whatever has received the common consent of civilized nations must have received the assent of our country, and that to which we have assented along with other nations in general may properly be called international law, and as such will be acknowledged and applied by our municipal tribunals when legitimate occasion arises for those tribunals to decide questions to which doctrines of international law may be relevant').

[23] [1977] 2 WLR 356, 365–6; see also p. 388 (per Shaw LJ).

[24] See Rosalyn Higgins, 'The Relationship Between International and Regional Human Rights Norms and Domestic Law (1992) *Commonwealth Law Bulletin* 1268.

of the law of the land' and 'there is not a legal system in the world where international law is treated as a 'foreign law'.

In accordance with British constitutional law, as effective in Hong Kong, two major constraints overshadow substantial implementation of the 'incorporation doctrine'. First, consistently with the principle of parliamentary sovereignty, incorporation of customary international law will not take place if it conflicts with a statute. Secondly, Hong Kong courts like their British counterparts are limited in their power to eschew precedent and apply new or modified international law, hence English law and international law may take divergent paths. It is a moot question whether local judges will follow the emphatic statement of Lord Denning that '[i]nternational law knows no rule of *stare decisis*' and therefore the courts 'must discover what the prevailing international rule and apply that rule', implementing any changes in international law 'without waiting for the House of Lords to do it'.[25] A degree of scepticism is not unjustified, although such an approach is clearly warranted by the dynamic nature of international law and in light of the overarching obligation to comply with its rules.[26]

As alluded to earlier, there are two other limitations from British 'practice' affecting an automatic incorporation of customary international law by Hong Kong courts, namely the 'acts of state' and 'facts of state' doctrines which are based on the belief that in matters concerning foreign relations the state 'cannot speak with two voices'.[27] Reference was further made to the tradition of British/Hong Kong judges to stay aloof from political questions as much as possible and their general reluctance to rule on questions of international law,[28] ensuing from the [wrong] assumption that international

---

[25] Supra (note 23).

[26] See in this context the section introduced in the 1993 Interim South African Constitution, eliminating any qualification on incorporation by reason of judicial precedent: '231(4) The rules of customary international law binding on the Republic, shall, unless inconsistent with this Constitution or an Act of Parliament, form part of the law of the Republic.'

[27] *Government of the Republic of Spain v SS Arantzazu Mendi* [1939] AC 256, 264 (per Lord Atkin); see also *British Airways v Laker Airways* [1984] QB 142. In Hong Kong such a belief was expressed in respect to assertion of jurisdiction by the Crown in *Re Wong Hon* [1959] HKLR 601, 613 (per Sir Michael Hogan CJ giving the judgment of the Full Court): 'In these matters, the Crown speaks with one voice, and alone delimits the sphere in which, and the extent to which, its various organs of government, legislative, executive and judicial, shall properly function.'

[28] Note, however, the exceptional lack of timidity displayed by a Hong Kong court *In the Matter of an Arbitration Between the Osaka Shosen Kaisha and the Owners of the Steamship "Prometheus"* (1906–8) 2 HKLR 207 (applying customary international law in the interpretation of a term ['contraband of war'] in a contract between private parties).

laws is more like a question of foreign affairs (therefore beyond their supervision) than a matter of law (which they ought to adjudicate).[29]

The incorporation of customary international law into Hong Kong law may also be circumvented by judges' 'legitimate' device of 'classification',[30] resulting on occasions in artificially constructed decisions.[31] There are, of course, problems of incorporation inherent in the nature of customary international law, including the difficulties encountered in determining the existence of rules of customary international law,[32] the vagueness of formulation characterizing such rules (many of which take the form of permissions rather than mandatory rules),[33] as well as their inappropriateness when applied to individuals (as distinct from states).[34]

---

[29] See Colin Warbrick, 'International Law and Domestic Law: Ministerial Powers' (1989) 38 *International & Comparative Law Quarterly* 965, 968 (commenting on the 'Cambodian Embassy Case' and referring [n.18] in particular to Henry J's statement that 'courts should not engage themselves in cases involving questions of international law between states because of the risk of conflict with the Executive, even if this excluded the courts from cases which only affect the rights of individuals in exceptional cases . . . or by a sidewind').

[30] See, e.g. the characterization made by Lord Templeman (HL) in *J H Rayner Ltd. v Department of Trade & Industry* and related appeals ('International Tin Council Case') [1990] 2 AC 418, 475: 'a short question of construction of the plain words of a statutory instrument' — contrasted with Kerr LJ's classification in the Court of Appeals as a case about the status and powers of an international organization so that 'the logical starting point must be international law' [1988] 3 All ER 257, 275.

[31] See *Arab Monetary Fund v Hashim (No. 3)* [1991] 1 All ER 871 (HL) (ruling that although the Arab Monetary Fund as an international organization created under international law could not be accorded legal status in the UK, it may be recognized as a legal person (in line with domestic conflict of law rules) by virtue of its status under the domestic law of another state [UAE].

[32] Particularly cumbersome is the requirement for evidence of 'general practice *accepted as law*' ('*opinio juris*') postulated under Article 38 of the Statute of the International Court of Justice (involving a subjective element of belief that there exist a legal obligation to act).

[33] Note Lord Oliver's statement in the 'International Tin Council Case', supra (note 30) at 513 that automatic incorporation would occur in relation to a rule of international law 'only when it is certain and is accepted generally by the body of civilized nations; and it is for those who assert the rule to demonstrate it, if necessary before the International Court of Justice. It is certainly not for a domestic tribunal in effect to legislate a rule into existence for the purposes of domestic law and on the basis of material that is wholly indeterminate.'

[34] As may be inferred from the 'International Tin Case', incorporation of customary international law does not necessarily mean that rights granted under such law can be enforced directly in municipal courts. Rather, enforcement will only occur if specifically provided for under the rule in question. See also observation that 'customary international law confers none or only the rarest of rights on individuals; accordingly, individuals will seldom, if ever, be in a position to rely on customary law in an English court' — Colin Warbrick, 'The Theory of International Law: Is there an English Contribution' in W.E. Butler, ed., *Perestroika and International Law* (Netherlands: Kluwer Academic Publications, 1990) p. 49.

Whether or not local courts are prepared to fully embrace customary international law as 'part of Hong Kong law', they may be inclined to adopt the 'moderate' approach exhibited by Australian judges[35] and traced to a statement by Sir Owen Dixon in *Chow Hung Ching v The King*[36] that 'international law is not a part, but is one of the sources' of domestic law. As such, customary international law ought to be drawn upon by judges in exercising their duty to interpret and apply the law as well as to fill any gaps in that law.

Treaties and Hong Kong law

In contrast with customary international law, treaties are not directly received into English law[37] and are incapable of constituting a rule of law for the courts in the absence of legislative implementation. As emphatically stated by Lord Oliver in the *International Tin Council Case*, 'a treaty is not part of English law unless and until it has been incorporated into the law by legislation. So far as individuals are concerned, it is *res inter alios acta* from which they cannot derive rights and by which they cannot be deprived of rights or subjected to obligations'.[38]

This basic premise has been transplanted into Hong Kong law. Indeed, as early as 1880, the Supreme Court of Hong Kong, sitting as a Full Court in the *Status of the French Mail Steamers*[39] rejected an attempt to distinguish the position of Hong Kong in respect of domestic application of treaties on the ground that it was a Crown Colony. The Court relied on the *Parliament Belge*[40] to affirm that 'no treaty by the Queen with a foreign Power can affect the rights and privileges of the Queen's subjects within Hong Kong

---

[35] See Report of the Australian Branch to the International Law Association Committee on International Law in National Courts, reprinted in (1994) *Australian Year Book of International Law* 231, 234–7.

[36] (1948) 15 *International Law Reports* 147, 169.

[37] In so far as such reception would require a change in the law, a levy on public funds or an addition to powers of the Crown not already possessed by it. Possible exceptions are treaties of cession, those affecting belligerent rights, and 'declaratory' treaties which merely restate customary international law. Note, however, that by virtue of the 'act of state' doctrine, 'even if in a treaty of cession it is stipulated that certain inhabitants should enjoy certain rights, that does not give a title to these inhabitants to enforce these stipulations in the municipal courts. The right to enforce remains only with the high contracting parties' — *Vajesingji Joravarsingji v Secretary of State for India* (Ind App PC) (1924) LR 51, 360 (per Lord Dunedin).

[38] Supra (note 30), at 500.

[39] *The Daily Press,* 12 January 1880.

[40] (1878–79) 4 PD 129.

except under the sanction of an Act of Parliament or of a local ordinance or probably an order of the Queen in Council'.

More recently the 'rule' that domestic courts will not enforce obligations and rights under international treaties unless incorporated into the local law was restated by the Privy Council in the celebrated case of *Winfat Enterprises (HK) Co Ltd v Attorney General of Hong Kong*.[41] The appellants in the case challenged a refusal by the Hong Kong government of a building permission as well the amount of compensation following compulsory purchase by the government as contrary to the terms of the Peking Convention of 1898. Their appeal was dismissed by the Privy Council which advised that the stipulation against expropriation contained in a bilateral treaty such as the 1898 Peking Convention could not create rights enforceable by individuals in municipal courts. Equally unsuccessful were bids to rely on the 1898 Convention in order to establish a right of way or a licence to mainland Chinese to enter Hong Kong[42] and to oust jurisdiction of local courts over an area in the City of Kowloon.[43]

Also regarded as 'not justiciable' is the 1984 Sino-British Joint Declaration (and its Annexes), which was held not to have been incorporated into the local law. As pronounced by the High Court,[44] neither the Hong Kong Act 1985 nor the Application of English Law Ordinance bestowed upon the Joint Declaration the force of law in Hong Kong. In a similar vein, the Court ruled — with respect to a claim based on a provision in Annex III of the Joint Declaration[45] — that the government's announced intention to implement the Accord had not given rise to a justiciable legitimate expectation (that the applicant's Crown lease would be renewed in accordance with the relevant provision).

By the same token, 'incorporation' of a treaty may take a variety of forms. Most commonly a 'direct' mode is employed whereby a treaty becomes an integral part of the legislation itself (for example by including it in a schedule attached to the statute).[46] A treaty may also, however, be

---

[41] [1985] 1 AC 733; (1988) 77 *International Law Reports* 376.

[42] See decision by Magistrate D'Almada Remedios in *Lau Hong-chung & Others,* reported in Cynthia Chan, 'Entry Right Ruled Out for Illegals' *South China Morning Post,* 20 September 1990.

[43] See *Fung Yuen Mui v Chan Kam Yee* (HC) [1991] 1 Hong Kong Cases 462 (the courts would generally take no notice of treaties until they were embodied in domestic law).

[44] In *Tang Ping-hoi v Attorney General* [1987] HKLR 324, 329 (per Nazareth J).

[45] See *The Home Restaurant Ltd v Attorney General* [1987] HKLR 237, 247 (per Mayo J).

[46] See, e.g. the Carriage By Air (Overseas Territories) Order 1967, setting out in Schedule 1 the 1929 Warsaw Convention and Additional Protocol on Unification of Certain Rules Relative to International Carriage by Air.

incorporated 'indirectly' or 'by reference' (either by mention in the statute[47] or where extrinsic evidence can be adduced to show that the statute was designed to incorporate the treaty[48]).

Evidently, while all treaties which have been incorporated become part of the law of the land and hence justiciable in the courts of the land, 'those that are incorporated in terms — by being appended to a Statute, and forming the substantive part of the Statute — have the most unequivocal status in domestic law'.[49] Yet, in the English legal system — and its Hong Kong counterpart — even 'fully incorporated' treaties have no special position and enjoy no higher status than other legislation.[50] Thus, in line with the *lex posterior* rule of construction, a later statute on the same subject-matter may prevail over an earlier one incorporating an international treaty.

It further appears that although courts pay regard to the presumption that legislation is to be so construed as to avoid inconsistency with international law,[51] they reserve application of this canon to ambiguous statutes. Accordingly, where the provisions of a statute implementing a treaty are 'capable of more than one meaning' and 'one of the meanings which can reasonably be ascribed to the legislation is consonant with the treaty obligations and another or others are not, the meaning which is consonant is to be preferred'.[52] If, however, the terms of the statute are 'clear and unambiguous, they must be given effect to, whether or not they carry out Her Majesty's treaty obligations, for the sovereign power of the Queen in Parliament extends to

---

[47] See, e.g. the Internationally Protected Persons and Taking of Hostages Ordinance (No. 20 of 1995) which states in the preamble: 'An Ordinance to provide for the implementation of both the Convention on the Prevention and Punishment of Crimes against Internationally Protected Persons, including Diplomatic Agents and the International Convention against the Taking of Hostages.'

[48] See, e.g. Nuclear Material (Liability for Carriage) Ordinance (No. 45 of 1995) which contains reference to agreements concerning 'their-party liability in the field of nuclear energy' applicable to Hong Kong (such as the 1960 Convention and 1964 Additional Protocol on Third Party Liability in the Field of Nuclear Energy).

[49] Rosalyn Higgins, 'United Kingdom' in *The Effects of Treaties in Domestic Law*, supra (note 3) at p. 129.

[50] It is commonly perceived that under British constitutional doctrines no 'entrenchment' of laws is possible. It may be pointed out nonetheless that the United Kingdom Parliament had legislated in the past to divest itself of sovereignty (e.g. Section 4 of the Statute of Westminster 1931; the European Communities Act 1972, Sections 2(1), 2(4)) and, as observed by Lord Dening, has not subsequently endeavoured to reclaim it ('freedom once conferred cannot be revoked' — *Blackburn v Attorney General* [1971] 1 WLR 1037, 1040).

[51] See supra (note 3) and respective text.

[52] See *Salomon v Commissioners of Customs and Excise* (CA) [1967] 2 QB 116 (per Diplock LJ).

breaking treaties, and any remedy for such a breach of an international obligation lies in a forum other than Her Majesty's own courts'.[53]

Such an approach may nonetheless be subject to some critical observations. Particularly questionable is its congruity with a notion of 'incorporation' as the admittance into the municipal legal system of a treaty without altering its international and contractual nature. It is furthermore arguable that, apart from incurring responsibility for infringement of specific treaty provisions,[54] the State (via its judicial organ) may be held in breach of the general duty to bring international law in conformity with international law.[55]

In this vein, it may also be contended that judges must not completely eschew reference to 'unincorporated' treaties. As asserted by a renowned expert, F.A. Mann,[56] whether because there can be no fear of conflict with the executive ('speaking with two voices') or since the ultimate aim is to reach 'a decision which protects this country against a possible breach of its international duties', the principle that unincorporated treaties are not justiciable in English courts is no longer tenable.[57] In fact, a substantial body of case law[58] is available to reinforce Mann's observation that when the occasion or necessity arises, English courts are 'in principle neither unable nor unwilling to look at, construe, and give effect [even] to treaties which have not been adopted by Parliament'.[59] Clearly in relation to civil liberties,[60]

---

[53] Loc. cit., following *Ellerman Lines v Murray* [1931] AC 126. See, however, *R v Secretary of State for Transport ex parte Factortame (No 2)* [1990] 3 WLR 818 — for the proposition that the law of the Treaty of Rome (Community Law) must prevail even in the face of a clearly contrary Act of Parliament.

[54] It should be noted that the state cannot seek shelter behind its domestic law: see Article 27, 1969 Convention on the Law of Treaties ('A party may not invoke the provisions of its internal law as justification for its failure to perform a treaty'); Article 13, 1949 Draft Declaration on the Rights and Duties of States (1949) *Yearbook of the International Law Commission* 286.

[55] For references supporting the existence of such a general duty see: Karl Josef Partsch, 'International Law and Municipal Law' in Bernhardt, ed., *Encyclopedia of Public International Law* (Amsterdam: North-Holland Publishing, 1981–), Vol. 10 (1987), pp. 238–257.

[56] F.A. Mann, *Foreign Affairs in English Courts* (Oxford: Clarendon Press, 1986), pp. 94–104.

[57] See also Rosalyn Higgins (supra note 24, at 1274) for the view that '[a]n unincorporated treaty can *always* be looked at, so long as rights of individuals are not founded upon it alone and so long as it is not suggested that it takes away rights existing under common law'.

[58] For an account of recent cases see: Christopher Stalker, 'Decisions of British Courts During 1993' (1993) *British Yearbook of International Law* 455–463.

[59] Supra (note 56), at p. 87. See also Robert Y Jennings, 'An International Lawyer Takes Stock' (1990) 39 *International & Comparative Law Quarterly* 513, 525 (criticizing the rigidity reflected in Lord Oliver's speech in the *International Tin Council Case* — supra

English judges have demonstrated a willingness to consider and be influenced by unincorporated international treaties, or more specifically the European Convention on Human Rights. Admittedly, approaches vary from judge to judge and no consistent judicial view may be said to emerge. Yet, it is doubtless that, concurrently with similar trends in other jurisdictions,[61] unincorporated international human rights treaties will continue be resorted to by English judges as an aid to statutory interpretation or when deciding uncertain points of common law. Reference to such treaties would presumably increase upon awareness of potential engagement of state responsibility.[62]

Hong Kong's rather barren judicial scene in respect to unincorporated treaties renders it somewhat difficult to draw solid conclusions. Attitudes displayed by the local courts range from a wholesale rejection,[63] to 'reserved' acceptance,[64] and susceptibility to the territory's treaty obligations.[65] On

---

note 37 — and repudiating any assumed "doctrine of unjusticiability of unincorporated treaties" as 'contrary to precedent, to reason and to common sense'.

[60] See, e.g. cases concerned with freedom of expression: *Attorney General v Guardian Newspapers (Nos 1 and 2)* [1987] 3 All ER 316; [1990] 1 AC 109; *Derbyshire County Council v Times Newspapers* [1992] 3 WLR 28; [1993] 2 WLR 449 (HL); *Rantzen v Mirror Group Newspapers* (1986) Ltd [1993] 3 WLR 953 (CA); *Attorney General v Associated Newspapers Ltd* [1993] 3 WLR 74 (QBD); See also *R v Secretary of State for the Home Department, ex parte Wynne* [1993] 1 WLR 115 (HL) (right to a fair and public hearing); *R v Brown* [1993] 2 WLR 556 (HL) (right to respect for private and family life).

[61] See discussion infra.

[62] See, e.g. *R v Secretary of State for the Home Dept ex parte Phansopkar* [1976] QB 606 (Lord Scarman LJ suggested that it was the duty of UK courts to have regard to the Convention when interpreting and applying statute and common law); *Attorney General v Guardian Newspapers (No 2)* [1990] 1 AC 109, 283–4 (per Lord Goff): 'I conceive it to be my duty, when I am free to do so, to interpret the law in accordance with the obligations of the Crown under this treaty [the European Convention on Human Rights];' *Derbyshire County Council v Times Newspapers* [1992] 3 WLR 28 (The court is under a duty to decide uncertain questions of common law in a manner consistent with the Convention).

[63] See supra (note 6).

[64] See readiness exhibited by Mayo J in *R v Director of Immigration, ex parte Li Jin-fei and Others* (1993) 3 HKPLR 552 to consider the 'issue of "statelessness" under the [unincorporated] 1962 Convention Relating to the Status of Stateless Persons [subsequently rebuked in the Court of Appeals — supra note 5, at 576, 578 — as 'misplaced'; note, in particular, the observation by Litton, JA that 'the [HC] judge was lured into a blind alley in which the issue of statelessness became, in effect, litigated']. See also supra (note 42) — It may be inferred (upon a most 'liberal' construction of the judgment) that had evidence of 'intention to give the Joint Declaration the force of law' been more convincing, a claim based on 'legitimate expectations' would have received more favourable consideration.

[65] See supra (note 7). See also *Cheung Ng Sheong v Eastweek Publishers Ltd.* (1995) Civ App No 198 of 1995, 20 October 1995 (per Nazareth VP: 'I can see no reason, nor has any been brought to the attention of this Court, why we should not be free to interpret the law in accordance with treaty obligations applying to Hong Kong.)

occasions, judges had even relied on a treaty which has not been extended to Hong Kong,[66] without however offering any jurisprudential illumination (such as the 'declaratory' nature of the treaty). It may nonetheless be reasonable to suggest that Hong Kong's judiciary has yet to overcome their 'cultural' resistance to international law in general, and adopt the declared principle of 'Commonwealth Law' that '[i]t is within the proper nature of the judicial process and well-established judicial functions for national courts to have regard to international obligations which a country undertakes — whether or not they have been incorporated into domestic law — for the purpose of removing ambiguity or uncertainty from national constitutions, legislation or common law'.[67]

It is clear in any event that should the need arise to construe the terms of a treaty binding on the territory,[68] Hong Kong judges are expected to apply international rules of treaty interpretation (as codified in Articles 31–33 in the 1969 Vienna Convention on the Law of Treaties).[69] In embracing such an 'international legal approach', local courts would be supported by a considerable number of authoritative English decisions as well as by the jurisprudence of courts in many other states.[70] They should garner particular

---

[66] See, e.g. references to the definition of 'refugee' in the 1951 Convention and 1967 Protocol Relating to the Status of Refugees in *R v Director of Immigration and the Refugee Status Review Board, ex parte Do Giau & Others* [1972] HKLR 287; *R v Director of Immigration, ex parte Le Tu Phuong & Others* [1993] 3 HKPLR 641.

[67] Principle 4, 'Bangalore Principles' reprinted in (1988) 14 *Commonwealth Law Bulletin* 1196; The Bangalore Principles have been reaffirmed successively by the 'Harare Declaration of Human Rights' (1989); 'The Banjul Affirmation' (1990); and 'The Abuja Confirmation' (1991), reprinted in Commonwealth Secretariat, *Developing Human Rights Jurisprudence* (London: Interights, 1991).

[68] Arguably, no distinction should be drawn between interpretation of incorporated and unincorporated treaties since, as instruments created within the system of public international law, [all] treaties should be interpreted in accordance with the rules of that system.

[69] Note that although the 1969 Convention has not been incorporated into the domestic legislation, its status as 'customary international law' (see supra Chapter 5) renders it part of Hong Kong law.

[70] See, e.g. in Australia — *Shipping Corp of India Ltd v Gamlen Chemical Co (Australasia) Pty Ltd* (1980) 147 CLR 142, 159 (HC) (laying down the rule that when Australian courts are applying the text of a treaty, incorporated by statute into national law, the courts must apply international law rules of interpretation, not municipal rules of statutory interpretation); see also *Commonwealth v Tasmania* (HC) (1983) 68 *International Law Reports* 266, 303 (having accepted that the 1969 Convention on the Law of Treaties was declaratory of customary international law, the court applied the Convention to ascertain the meaning of provisions in the treaty of World Heritage); in Canada — *Re Regina and Palacios* (Ont.CA) (1984) 45 OR (2d) 269, cited in *International Law Chiefly as Interpreted and Applied in Canada,* supra note 3 (holding that the rules of public international law, not domestic law, govern the interpretation of a statute incorporating a treaty, and hence

reinforcement from the House of Lords' landmark judgments in *James Buchanan v Babco Forwarding*[71]*and Fothergill v Monarch Airlines,*[72] subsequently endorsed in several cases.[73]

As reasoned by Lord Diplock,[74]

> The language of an international convention has not been chosen by an English parliamentary draftsman. It is neither couched in the conventional English legislative idiom nor designed to be construed exclusively by English judges. It is addressed to a much wider and more varied judicial audience than is an Act of Parliament . . . It should be interpreted as Lord Wilberforce put it[75] . . . 'unconstrained by technical rules of English law, or by English precedent, but on broad principles of general acceptance'.

Thus, since international courts and tribunals refer to *travaux préparatoires* as an aid to interpretation and

> this practice as regards national courts has now been confirmed by the Vienna Convention on the Law of Treaties[76] . . . where the text is ambiguous or obscure, an English court should have regard to any material which the delegates themselves had thought would be available to clear up any possible ambiguities or obscurities. Indeed, in the case of Acts of Parliament giving effect to international conventions concluded after the coming into force of [the Vienna Convention], I think an English court might well be under a constitutional obligation to do so.[77]

---

the court is not bound by the common law canon of literal construction); in Israel — *Attorney General of the Government of Israel v Eichmann* (Jeru.DC) (1961) 36 *International Law Reports* 5 (applying international rules to the interpretation of a domestic law which did not incorporate an international treaty but was only 'inspired' by it).

[71] [1978] AC 141.

[72] [1981] AC 251.

[73] See, e.g. *R v Home Secretary, ex parte Read* [1989] 1 AC 1014; *IRC v Commerzbank* [1990] STC 285; *Hiscox v Outhwaite* [1992] 1 AC 562; *Antwerp United Diamond v Air Europe* [1993] 4 All ER 469; *Abnett v British Airways,* Times Law Reports, 22 June 1995.

[74] Supra (note 72) at 281–2.

[75] Supra (note 71) at 152.

[76] While noting that the Vienna Convention applies only to treaties concluded after it came into force, Lord Diplock reaffirmed that 'what it says in Articles 31 and 32 about interpretation of treaties . . . does no more than codify already-existing public international law.'

[77] Supra (note 74) at 283. It may be pointed out that at the time the Lords pronounced upon the permissibility of using the *travaux préparatoires* of a treaty as an aid to interpretation, a UK court could not have had regard to the legislative history of 'ordinary' Acts of Parliament when interpreting their terms. (See, however, *Pepper (Inspector of Taxes) v Hart* [1992] 3 WLR 1033 — allowing 'relaxation' of the rule excluding reference to Parliamentary material as an aid to statutory construction).

Notwithstanding the lack of explicit and systematic application of the 'Vienna rules' by English courts and the emergence of no categorical prescription of reference to international rules of treaty interpretation,[78] it is evident that the 'international approach' is accepted as most 'appropriate'. The application of international norms and practice assumes added pertinence when the treaty which falls to be interpreted aims at achieving international legislative uniformity.[79] As cogently expressed in the judgment of the *Cour de Cassation* of Belgium.[80]

The interpretation of an international convention, the purpose of which is the

> unification of law, cannot be done by reference to the domestic law of one of the contracting states. If the treaty text calls for interpretation, this ought to be done on the basis of elements that actually pertain to the treaty, notably its object, its purpose, and its context, as well as its preparatory work and genesis. The purpose of drawing up an international convention, designed to become a species of international legislation, will be wholly frustrated if the courts of each State were to interpret it in accordance with concepts that are specific to their own legal system.

By the same token, where treaties are not concerned with promoting uniform legislation, their uniform interpretation is not an end itself. Ultimately, the treaty (and the statute designed to implement it) should be interpreted in 'good faith . . . in light of its object and purpose'.[81] Thus, for example, international human rights treaties should be given a generous and purposive construction compatible with their aim to protect fundamental rights and freedoms.

Yet, it is important that judges 'avoid parochial constructions which are uninformed (or ill-informed) about the jurisprudence that has gathered around

---

[78] For an analysis and criticism of the 'lack of intellectual coherence' and the 'cherry-picking' nature of references to isolated elements of the Vienna rules see: Richard Gardiner, 'Treaty Interpretation in the English Courts Since *Fothergill v Monarch Airlines* (1980)' (1995) 44 *International & Comparative Law Quarterly* 620.

[79] Notable examples include the 1929 Warsaw Convention for the Unification of Certain Rules relating to International Carriage by Air as amended by the 1955 Hague Protocol; the 1956 Geneva Convention on the Contract for the International Carriage of Goods by Road.

[80] In *Tondriau v Air India* (1977), cited in *SS Pharmaceutical Co Ltd v Quantas Airways (CA)* [1991] 1 LLoyd's Rep 288 (affirming the importance of approaching construction of the international instruments attached to the statute [the Warsaw Convention and the Hague Protocol] with a view to keeping in mind their international character and the desirability so far as possible that they should be given a consistent construction by the courts of the several contracting parties).

[81] Article 31, 1969 Convention on the Law of Treaties.

[the relevant international instruments]'[82] and have regard to judicial decisions of international courts and courts in other countries as well as to the respective 'teachings of highly qualified publicists'.[83] Although there is evidence of some 'internationalization of jurisprudence' in respect of interpretation of human rights legislation in Hong Kong,[84] local judges have been slow to shake off 'parochial' tendencies, even when faced with the need to construe 'uniform' treaties[85] and notwithstanding specific encouragement by the legislature to explore international sources.[86]

The status of International Human Rights Law in the Hong Kong legal system

Although as contended by the Hong Kong government,[87] the International Covenant on Civil and Political Rights [ICCPR] and the International Covenant on Economic, Social and Cultural Rights [ICESCR] were 'implemented in Hong Kong, as in the United Kingdom, through a

---

[82] Per Kirby P in *Shipping Corp of India Ltd.* Supra (note 70); in that case, judges consulted (in aid of interpreting disputed provisions of the Warsaw Convention) decisions of courts from Argentina, Austria, Belgium, France, Greece, India, Italy, Korea, the Netherlands, Switzerland, the United Kingdom, and the United States. Manuals of authority on international air law were also referred to as well as articles in international legal journals.

[83] Note that under Article 38(d) of the Statute of the International Court of Justice (the 'sources of international law'), 'judicial decisions and the teachings of the most highly qualified publicists of the various nations' are to be applied as 'subsidiary means for the determination of rules of law.'

[84] See infra.

[85] See, e.g. *Ka Da Watch Co Ltd v Skyworld Air Express Ltd* (CA) [1991] Hong Kong Cases 184 (adopting interpretation of the Warsaw Convention [set out in Schedule 1 to the Carriage By Air (Overseas Territories) Order 1967] as provided in an English case without undertaking an independent interpretation nor displaying awareness that international rules of interpretation should apply); *Manohar t/a Vinamito Trading House v Hill & Delamain (Hong Kong) Ltd* (CA) [1993] 2 Hong Kong Cases 342 (alluding to the Warsaw Convention but proceeding to interpret the term 'carriage by air' without any reference to the Vienna rules or to the need to apply international rules to maintain uniformity).

[86] See Arbitration Ordinance (Cap 340) which — apart from reproducing the UNCITRAL Model Law in Schedule 5 — provides in Section 2(3) as follows: 'In interpreting and applying the provisions of the UNCITRAL Model Law regard should be had to its *international origin* and to the *need for uniformity* in its interpretation, and regard may be had to the documents specified in the Sixth Schedule [Report of the Secretary General dated 25 March 1985 entitled 'Analytical Commentary on Draft Text of a Model Law on International Commercial Arbitration', UN Doc. A/C N9; Report of the UN Commission on International Trade Law on the Work of its 18th Session). To allow reference to case law of other states a list of signatories is also annextured to the Ordinance.

[87] See *An Introduction to Hong Kong Bill of Rights Ordinance* (Hong Kong, 1992), para. 5.

combination of common law, legislation and administrative measures', the effects on domestic law which are associated with 'incorporation' of treaties may only be said to have materialized with the enactment of the Bill of Rights Ordinance [BoRO]. In particular, by means of purposive interpretation cognizant of the 'international origin of the Covenant',[88] the BoRO was set to serve the implantation of international human rights norms enshrined in the Covenant (and 'in other international agreements'[89]).

Yet, expectations, in line with the 'growing tendency for national courts to have regard to [international norms of human rights]'[90] and the relevant international jurisprudence,[91] have not been fully substantiated. Commentators have observed that the initial 'enthusiasm' and 'receptiveness to international standards' has 'flowed and ebbed'.[92] The 'high water mark'

---

[88] See Hong Kong Government, *Commentary on the Draft Hong Kong Bill of Rights Ordinance 1990* (Hong Kong: March 1990), p. E12: '(2) Interpretation . . . (3) In interpreting and applying this Ordinance, the rules of interpretation applicable to other Ordinances may be disregarded and regard shall be had to — (a) the fact that the purpose of this Ordinance is to implement further the International Covenant on Civil and Political Rights as applied to Hong Kong; and (b) the international origin of that Covenant and the need for uniformity in interpretation of rights recognized in that Covenant and similar rights recognized in other international agreements.'

[89] Loc.cit.

[90] Bangalore Principles, Principle 4, supra (note 67).

[91] See, e.g. Hon Mr Justice Michael Kirby (President of the New South Wales Court of Appeal), 'The Australian Use of International Human Rights Norms from Bangalore to Balliol — A View from the Antipodes' (1992) *Commonwealth Law Bulletin* 1306, 1322 (highlighting the 'rapid progress' and 'firm footing' of the 'Bangalore ideas' in Australia's appellate courts, notwithstanding 'the strength of earlier legal authority; the high conservatism of the judiciary in matters of basic principle; the features of provincialism which are almost inescapable in a legal system now largely isolated from its original sources; the absence of an indigenous Bill of Rights to provide a vehicle for international developments; and the special problems of a Federal State where many matters relevant to fundamental rights still rest within the legislative powers of the States); For numerous references to international conventions and comparative jurisprudence by Canadian courts see: Anne F. Bayefsky, *International Human Rights Law: Use in Canadian Charter of Rights and Freedoms Litigation* (Butterworths, 1992); For examples of an increased judicial reference to international standards following the enactment of the New Zealand Bill of Rights Act of 1990 see: *Parkhill v Ministry of Transport* (1992) 1 NZLR 555 (CA); *Noort v Ministry of Transport* (1992) 1 NZLR 743 (CA); *R v Goodwin* (1993) 2 NZLR 153 (CA); *TV3 Network Ltd v Eveready Newzealand Ltd* (1993) 3 NZLR 435 (CA); See also citations from court practices in Namibia South Africa and Zimbabwe in John Dugard, 'The Role of International Law in Interpreting the Bill of Rights' (1994) 10 *South African Journal of Human Rights* 208, 211–2.

[92] See Andrew Byrnes, 'Killing It Softly? The Hong Kong Courts and the Slow Demise of the Hong Kong Bill of Rights' (a paper presented at a Seminar on 'Hong Kong and the International Covenant on Civil and Political Rights' held at the University of Hong Kong on 30 September 1995).

is invariably traced to the forceful pronouncement by Silke VP in *R v Sin Yau-ming*:[93]

> In my judgment, the glass through which we view the interpretation of the Hong Kong Bill is a glass provided by the Covenant. We are no longer guided by the ordinary canons of construction of statutes nor with the dicta of the common law inherent in our training. We must look, in our interpretation of the Hong Kong Bill, at the aims of the Covenant and give 'full recognition and effect' to the statement which commences that Covenant. From this stems the entirely new jurisprudential approach to which I have already referred . . .
>
> While this court is, in effect, required to make new Hong Kong law relating to the manner of interpretation of the Hong Kong Bill and consequentially the tests to be applied to those laws now existing and, when asked, those laws yet to be enacted, we are not without guidance in our task. This can be derived from decisions taken in common law jurisdictions which contain a constitutionally entrenched Bill of Rights. We can also be guided by decisions of the European Human Rights Commission — 'the Commission'. Further, we can bear in mind the comments and decisions of the United Nations Human Rights Committee — 'the Committee'. I would hold none of these to be binding upon us though in so far as they reflect the interpretation of articles in the Covenant, and are directly related to Hong Kong legislation, I would consider them as of the greatest assistance and give to them considerable weight.

Proceeding to lay down a more specific approach to the interpretation of the BoRO, Silke VP cited Lord Wilberforce's famous dictum in *Ministry of Home Affairs v Fisher*[94] to the effect that a constitutional document like the BoRO calls for a 'generous interpretation, avoiding what has been called the 'austerity of legalism', suitable to give to individuals the full measure of the fundamental rights and freedoms' contained therein. Silke VP has also echoed (without explicit mention of the Vienna Convention) the international rules of treaty interpretation, highlighting the necessity to have regard to the 'context of the Covenant and its aims and objects, [and hence] with a bias towards the interests of the individual'.[95]

---

[93] (1992) 1 Hong Kong Cases 127, at 141.

[94] [1980] AC 319 (PC)(concerning the Constitution of Bermuda which, as emphasized by Lord Wilberforce, had influenced by the European Convention on Human Rights and the Universal Declaration of Human Rights). The dictum was cited with approval by Canadian and South African courts, see Dugard supra (note 91) at 212, 27n; as well as in another Hong Kong case: *R v Town Planning Board, ex parte Auburntown Ltd* (1994) 4 HKPLR 194, at 229 (HC) (per Rhind J).

[95] Supra (note 93) at 145.

It has nonetheless been suggested that Silke's determined 'internationalist' approach was somewhat tempered by concern for local practical feasibility, and that the judgment was a *'creative blend of international human rights law and common law pragmatism'*.[96] Indeed — whether because of 'common law chauvinism'[97] or a perception of the BoRO as mere statutory reaffirmation of fundamental rights long recognized under the common law — Hong Kong's judges have been keen to 'stress the compatibility of their decision with the common law as it existed prior to the passage of [the BoRO)]'.[98] Evidently, to the extent that the common law reflects universal notions of justice and rule of law, conclusions arrived in the light of principles of domestic case law often coincide with international standards. However, where incongruous with international law and jurisprudence, or in the absence of well-settled principles,[99] the 'common law approach' may thwart the BoRO's stated objective of implementing the ICCPR.[100]

Unfortunately, local 'provincial' tendencies seem to have been reinforced following the Privy Council decision in *Attorney General v Lee Kwong-kut/ Attorney General v Lo Chak-man.*[101] Reaffirming the principle that the BoRO should be given a 'generous and purposive construction' — and acknowledging the 'valuable guidance as to the proper approach to the interpretation of the Hong Kong Bill' provided by 'decisions in other common law jurisdictions, including the United States and Canada, and of the European Court of Human Rights' — their Lordships went on to remind the territory's courts that 'decisions in other jurisdictions are persuasive and not binding

---

[96] Richard Swede, 'One Territory — Three Systems? The Hong Kong Bill of Rights' (1995) 44 *International & Comparative Law Quarterly* 358, 367.

[97] Term used by Byrnes, supra (note 92).

[98] Supra (note 96), at 368 (the author cites as examples the following cases: *R v Sin Yau-ming; R v William Hung* [1992] 2 Hong Kong Cases 91; *R v Wong Cheung-bun* [1992] 1 Hong Kong Cases 241; *R v Kevin Barry Egan* [1993] 1 Hong Kong Cases 284.

[99] Arguably, where the common law is unsettled, the courts are *bound* to decide cases in a manner consistent with the Convention as an international legal instrument (namely as an international court would have done). See Derbyshire *County Council v Times Newspapers Ltd* and *Rantzen v Mirror Group Newspapers (1986) Ltd.,* supra (note 60).

[100] See Byrnes, supra (note 92) for an account of 'cases in which the Bill of Rights/Letters Patent have been given an interpretation that is inconsistent with the international jurisprudence'. Cf. the instructive decision of Australia's highest court in *Mabo v Queensland* (1992) 66 ALJR 408, 422 (HCA): 'The common law does not necessarily conform with international law, but international law is a legitimate and important influence on the development of the common law, especially when international law declares the existence of universal human rights. A Common law doctrine founded on unjust discrimination in the enjoyment of civil and political rights demands reconsideration.'

[101] (1993) 3 HKPLR 72.

authority and that the situation in those jurisdictions may not necessarily be identical to that in Hong Kong'.[102] The Council sounded a further general caution that

> While the Hong Kong judiciary should be zealous in upholding an individual's rights under the Hong Kong Bill, it is also necessary to ensure that disputes as to the effect of the Bill are not allowed to get out of hand. The issues involving the Hong Kong Bill should be approached with realism and good sense, and kept in proportion. If this is not done the Bill will become a source of injustice rather than justice and it will be debased in the eyes of the public. In order to maintain the balance between the individual and the society as a whole, rigid and inflexible standards should not be imposed on the legislature's attempts to resolve the difficult and intransigent problems with which society is faced when seeking to deal with serious crime. It must be remembered that questions of policy remain primarily the responsibility of the legislature.[103]

Lord Woolf's 'observations' have been 'respectfully endorsed' in several cases,[104] and appear to have given rise to a resurgence of the 'domestic approach' to statutory interpretation which pays insufficient regard to the 'international origin' of the BoRO and its 'incorporating' purpose. Thus, the Court of Appeal held that the BoRO's provisions should be construed by the 'well-known rules that apply to the interpretation of statutes', and that '[i]n the absence of ambiguity or obscurity, it is neither necessary nor permissible to refer to matters extraneous to the Ordinance, *like the terms of the Covenant* or the *Siracusa Principles on the Limitation and Derogation Provisions in the ICCPR*'.[105] In the appeal case of *R v Director of Immigration, ex parte Le Tu Phuong and another,* the lower court's judge was rebuked for determining standards of fairness without consideration to 'what fairness required in the context of the Hong Kong statutory scheme and local conditions'.[106] Appropriately depicted as the 'low tide' in the receptiveness of Hong Kong courts to international standards, *R v Town*

---

[102] Ibid., at 90–1 (per Lord Woolf).

[103] Ibid., at 100.

[104] See *R v Director of Immigration, ex parte Wong King-lung and others/R v Director of Immigration, ex parte So Kam-cheung and others/R v Director of Immigration, ex parte Lau Shek-to and others* (1993) 3 HKPLR 253, 275 (HC, per Jones J); *R v Director of Immigration, ex parte Hai Ho-tak/ R v Director of Immigration, ex parte Wong Chung-hing and others* (1994) 4 HKPLR 324, 336 (CA, per Godfrey JA); *R v To Kwan-hang and Tsoi Yiu-cheong* (1994) 4 HKPLR 356, 363 (CA, per Macdougal VP).

[105] *R v Director of Immigration, ex parte Hai Ho-tak,* supra (note 104), at 333–4 (per Nazareth JA) [emphasis added].

[106] Supra (note 66) at 352.

Planning Board, ex parte Kwan Kong Co Ltd[107] gives expression to the limited [and wrong][108] view that

> the Court should interpret [the BoRO] in the same way as it interprets any other ordinance of Hong Kong, namely with established rules of interpretation; the proper and primary judicial interpretation of the Ordinance is by concentrating on the text of the Ordinance and the language of the text;
>
> Even if the court should have resort to foreign jurisprudence, the Court would not be justified in importing foreign autonomous meaning interpretation so as to contradict or arrive at an interpretation substantially different, from the normal common law interpretation.[109]
>
> . . . therefore, unless something overwhelming and compelling can be shown in any particular European authority, the Hong Kong Court should very wisely decline to be seduced by the seemingly inexhaustible literature from the European Court of Rights.[110]

The narrowness of approach displayed by the local courts with respect to the interpretative process of the BoRO is also evinced in decisions regarding its 'applicability' to the issues adjudicated,[111] as well as in the inadequate acknowledgement of the CCPR's 'incorporation' as a normative source of public policy. Anxious not to encroach on the 'province of the legislature' ['policy questions'],[112] Hong Kong judges have declined to consider the

---

[107] (1995) HC, MP No 1676 of 1994, 31 July 1995 (Waung J); (1995) 3 *Hong Kong Cases* 254.

[108] See 'Editorial Comment' *Bill of Rights Bulletin,* Vol. 3, No. 4 (December 1995), at 22–3 for criticism of the judgment as 'ultimately flawed' ['seems to ignore the nature of the Bill of Rights, and particularly the aims of the ICCPR as stated in its preamble . . . overlooks the well-established rule that, where a statute gives effect to a treaty, then the terms in the statute should be given the same meaning as they bear in the treaty, and that this meaning is to be determined by applying the normal rules of treaty interpretation set out in the Vienna Convention on the Law of Treaties'].

[109] Supra (note 107) at 291.

[110] Ibid., at 306.

[111] See, e.g. determinations that the entitlements in the BoRO are inapplicable to extradition proceedings in *Ng Hung-yiu v Government of the United States of America* [1992] 2 HKLR 383; *Re Suthipong Smittachartch* [1993] 1 HKLR 93; *Re Thanat Phaktiphat and the Government of the US of America* (1994) CA, extracted in *Bill of Rights Bulletin,* Vol. 3, No. 4 (December 1995) at 26–7.

[112] See *R v Director of Immigration, ex parte Hai Ho-tak,* supra (note 104) at 336 (per Godfrey JA; while expressing concern as to the consequences of the Hong Kong government's immigration policy and urging legislative reform); see also *R v Director of Immigration, ex parte Wong King-lung,* supra (note 104) at 276 (per Jones J; quoting the Privy Council's edict [in *Lee Kwong-kut*] that 'questions of policy remain primarily the responsibility of the legislature' but opining that 'all right-thinking members of society will regard a policy that requires the removal of [young children] decidedly unattractive and unworthy of a government that professes to support human rights').

binding nature of treaty commitments as a legally relevant component (along with laws and applicable legal precedents) in the territory's public policy.

It may be further emphasized that — notwithstanding the *'lex specialis'* status of the BoRO, and the CCPR standards imported through it — customary international law of human rights has not been made redundant. Indeed, since most fundamental human rights antedate conventional instruments and are deemed 'general international law',[113] they form *ipso facto* part of Hong Kong law.[114] Consequently, reference to pertinent international documents and jurisprudence should not be viewed as 'extraneous' nor be contingent on 'ambiguity' or 'obscurity' of domestic legislation.

Post-1997

Leaving aside the question whether the Bill of Rights Ordinance will 'survive 1997'[115] or to what extent a judicial review of statutes' compatibility with the ICCPR would be available in the HKSAR courts,[116] it may be tentatively stated that current principles governing the relationship between international law and Hong Kong law should continue to apply after the resumption of sovereignty by the PRC. Thus, coterminous with the Joint Declaration[117] (and the Basic Law)[118] — which provide for the maintenance of 'laws

---

[113] See 'Interim Report on the Status of the Universal Declaration of Human Rights in National and International Law' in International Law Association, *Report of the Sixty-Fifth Conference* (Cairo, 1993), pp. 446–459 and references therein to state practice and scholarly writings.

[114] Note, however, the decision in *re an Application by Wong Chun-Sing and Ng Fook-yin for Judicial Review* [1984] HKLR 71 (holding that the Universal Declaration of Human Rights did not have the force of law in Hong Kong and therefore rejecting a claim for judicial review based on its provisions; no consideration was given to the relevance of international norms embedded in the Declaration for the purpose of statutory interpretation).

[115] It should be emphasized that under the Basic Law, the Standing Committee of the National People's Congress is empowered to repeal the BoRO only if it is inconsistent with the Basic Law; no such inconsistency has been demonstrated. See Yash Ghai, 'The Hong Kong Bill of Rights Ordinance and the Basic Law of the Hong Kong Special Administrative Region: Complementaries and Conflicts' (1995) 1 *Journal of Chinese and Comparative Law* 307.

[116] Note the contention that, by virtue of the phrase 'as applied to Hong Kong', legislation could be reviewed under Article 39 in the same way as is presently done under the Letters Patent and regardless of whether or not the BoRO itself is repealed. See Swede, *supra* (note 96) at 375.

[117] JD, Annex I, Art II.

[118] BL, Art 8.

previously in force in Hong Kong (i.e. the common law, rules of equity, ordinances, subordinate legislation and customary law)' — customary international law would form part of the HKSAR laws,[119] treaties will be enforceable by the local courts when 'incorporated' into the domestic law by legislative acts, while unincorporated treaties should remain indirectly relevant either through the interpretation of statutes, the development of the common law, and the filling of lacunae or as a source of public policy and executive rules of decision.

Were Chinese conceptions of the international/domestic interrelationship to prevail in the HKSAR, it is arguable that the 'gap-plugging' function of customary international law would be bolstered. Some support for such surmise may be garnered from China's General Principles of Civil Law, which provides [in Article 142(1)] that '[w]here the law of the PRC or international treaties which the PRC has concluded or participated in do not contain a relevant provision, *international custom* may be applied'.[120] Yet, 'international custom' is nowhere defined and — when read in conjunction with another provision [Article 150] that conditions its application upon coherence with the 'public interest of the PRC' — appears to differ significantly from 'customary international law' as commonly understood.[121]

More easily substantiated perhaps is the view that under the Chinese system, 'once they become effective', treaties have a direct internal application (imposing respective obligations on all 'government organs including the executive and the judiciary'),[122] 'without the need for any additional enactments

---

[119] Subject to the constraints discussed above.

[120] *Laws and Regulations of the People's Republic of China Governing Foreign Related Matters (1949–1990)* (Beijing: China Legal System Publishing House, 1991), p. 59 [emphasis added].

[121] See Chinese writings cited in Hungdah Chiu, *Chinese Attitudes toward International Law in the Post-Mao Era, 1978–1987* (Baltimore: University of Maryland School of Law, Contemporary Asian Studies Series, 1988) at 24, 87n for the view that 'customary international law' in the Western sense (being still embedded in colonialism and capitalism as well as too vague) is *not* part of Chinese domestic law.

[122] Wang Tieya, 'The Status of Treaties in the Chinese Legal System' (1995) 1 *Journal of Chinese and Comparative Law* 1, 5–6. Examples relied upon include a Notice on the Accession by China to the Hague Convention and Montreal Convention issued by the State Council in 1980 stating that '[i]t is hoped that every region and every relevant department will conscientiously implement the relevant provisions of the aforesaid international conventions'; a Notice on the Implementation of the Convention on the Recognition and Enforcement of Foreign Arbitral Awards Acceded to by China issued by the Supreme People's Court in 1987, requiring people's courts at various levels to 'earnestly follow and implement' this Convention.

to transform them to domestic law'.[123] Furthermore, it may be suggested that — in light of a considerable number of Chinese legislative illustrations[124] — where treaties and domestic law conflict, the former is given priority.

While it is difficult to speculate on legal proclivities should a situation arise whereby PRC national laws applicable to the HKSAR are inconsistent with China's treaty obligation, it may be reiterated[125] that no shelter can be sought in the municipal order to evade the legal consequences that follow from the basic subordination of domestic law to public international law on the interstate level. Indeed, as declared in the Rules on Certain Questions in the Handling of Foreign-Related Cases, issued by the Ministry of Foreign Affairs in the PRC,

> [w]here a conflict arises between domestic law and certain internal rules on the one hand and treaty obligations which China has undertaken on the other, relevant provisions of the international treaties shall apply. According to general principles of international law, China should not refuse to perform obligations undertaken under the provisions of international treaties on the ground of [different] provisions in domestic law. This is good both for the maintenance of China's prestige and for the protection of lawful rights and interests of Chinese nationals abroad.[126]

---

[123] Li Haopei, *A General Treatise on the Law of Treaties,* cited ibid., at 16, 16n. Note, however, that Regulations have been enacted to implement the 1961 Vienna Convention on Consular Relations and the 1963 Vienna Convention on Consular Relations [Regulations on Diplomatic Privileges and Immunities 1986; Regulations on Consular Privileges and Immunities 1990]; Also presumably, the Basic Law has been promulgated to give effect to the Sino-British Joint Declaration.

[124] Several laws passed since early 1980s contain provisions which affirm treaties' superior status. Most notably, Article 189 of the 1982 Civil Procedure Law ['where an international treaty concluded or acceded to by the People's Republic of China contains provisions differing from those found in this Law, the provisions of the international treaty shall apply, unless the provisions are ones on which China has announced reservations']; Article 142 of the 1986 General Principles of Civil Law (covering 'all civil laws') ['where an international treaty concluded or acceded to by the People's Republic of China contains provisions differing from those in the civil laws of the People's Republic of China, the provisions of the international treaty shall apply, with the exception of those on which the People's Republic of China has declared reservations']; Article 6 of the 1985 Foreign Economic Contract ['where an international treaty which is relevant to a contract, and which the People's Republic of China has concluded or joined, has provisions different from the law of the People's Republic of China, the provisions of the international treaty shall prevail, with the exception of those on which the People's Republic of China has declared reservations']. For these and references to similar provisions in other laws covering a wide range of subject-matters [civil law, civil procedure law, administrative litigation law, fisheries law, postal affairs, trade marks, foreign economic contracts, entry and exit of aliens, frontier health regulation, transport on inland rivers, taxation, environmental protection, and protection of wild animals] see Wang Tieya, supra (note 122) at 8–10.

[125] See supra (note 54).

[126] Cited supra (note 122) at 10–11.

Epilogue

This book focuses on Hong Kong as a highly autonomous territory from an international legal perspective. The approach is grounded in a broad normative framework which transcends constraints imposed by narrowly-based shifting political configurations. The spirit pervading the text is consistently positive in affirming the vision inspired by the 1984 Sino-British Joint Declaration.

It needs to be acknowledged, however, that the implementation of this vision hinges on the political realities unfolding in both China and Hong Kong — perhaps even Taiwan — and the quality of the relationship between Beijing and the outside world. These crucial non-legal factors could either undermine or underpin the vision, or just dilute it sufficiently to render the original blueprint largely irrelevant.

At the time of writing, for instance, one cannot dismiss the prospect of a power struggle in China. Such a destabilizing development might have the effect of redirecting mainland energies inwards in a disruptive manner and plunging Hong Kong into an identity crisis. Even the mere escalation in nationalist sentiment in Beijing, already reflected to some extent in policies vis-à-vis Hong Kong and Taiwan, could materially diminish the prospect of a high degree of autonomy for the territory.

Indeed, it is not altogether clear that China is committed to the 'one country, two systems' formula as construed in this book. Recent events suggest that Beijing is inclined to seize control of the 'commanding heights' of the Hong Kong power structure — the legislature, the civil service, the judiciary, the media and strategic industries such as aviation. The process may possibly be carried far enough to undermine local autonomy.

The transition from British to Chinese rule could also prove not entirely smooth due to resistance from segments of Hong Kong society — such as its vociferous democrats — that Beijing is determined to remove from the political arena. The reaction which this might provoke could rapidly shift the balance from self-rule to central control. A deterioration in the relationship between China and Taiwan, or between the former and major international powers such as the United States, could reinforce the trend.

As the above caveats demonstrate, the 'one country, two systems' concept is easier to grasp at the theoretical than practical level. Two divergent entities — an advanced capitalist society which is driven by the 'rule of law' and a country at early stages of capitalist development which is propelled by the 'rule of man' — are brought within a single political framework, albeit a flexible one. It remains to be seen whether the partial integration with the mainland leaves the foundations of the Hong Kong system intact.

On the positive side, the divergence between the two entities is diminishing. China is evolving into a less centrally controlled society and one which is governed in a less arbitrary fashion. From a long-term perspective, this process, which is nearly two decades old, is bound to continue and even gather further momentum. A feature of the transformation is a greater willingness to abide by established international legal norms. This increases the probability of Hong Kong functioning within the kind of normative framework envisaged in the present book.

If a more pessimistic scenario materializes, our effort would not necessarily be in vain. Such a normative framework is needed to assess actual practices in terms of their deviation from the prescribed international standards. Political realities are a fact of life which cannot be denied, but they need to be critically evaluated in the light of generally accepted legal principles.

Appendix A

THE NATURE AND EXTENT OF HONG KONG'S PARTICIPATION IN MULTILATERAL FORUMS

1. **International organizations in which Hong Kong's continued participation has been agreed in the JLG:**

    Asian Development Bank (ADB)
    Asian and Pacific Development Centre (APDC)
    Asia-Pacific Postal Union
    Asia-Pacific Telecommunity (APT)
    Customs Cooperation Council (CCC)
    Economic and Social Commission for Asia and the Pacific (ESCAP)
    Food and Agriculture Organization (FAO)
    General Agreement on Tariffs and Trade (GATT)
    Intergovernmental Typhoon Committee (ITC)
    International Atomic Energy Agency (IAEA)
    International Bank for Reconstruction and Development (IBRD)
    International Criminal Police Organization (INTERPOL)
    International Development Association (IDA)
    International Finance Corporation (IFC)
    International Hydrographic Organization (IHO)
    International Labor Organization (ILO)
    International Maritime Organization (IMO)
    International Maritime Satellite Organization (INMARSAT)
    International Monetary Fund (IMF)
    International Telecommunications Satellite Organization (INTELSAT)
    International Telecommunication Union (ITU)
    Network of Aquaculture Centres in Asia and the Pacific (NACA)
    Statistical Institute for Asia and the Pacific (SIAP)

United Nations Commission on Narcotic Drugs (UNCND)
United Nations Conference on Trade and Development (UNCTAD)
Universal Postal Union (UPU)
World Health Organization (WHO)
World Intellectual Property Organization (WIPO)
World Meteorological Organization (WMO)
World Trade Organization (WTO)

2. International organizations in which Hong Kong currently participates, but JLG approval for post-1997 participation remains pending:

Asian Productivity Organization (APO)
International Civil Aviation Organization (ICAO)
Multilateral Investment Guarantee Agency (MIGA)*

3. Other organizations in which Hong Kong currently participates, and which JLA agreement is not required for Hong Kong's continued participation:**

Asia Pacific Economic Cooperation Forum (APEC)
Asia-Pacific Metrology Program
International Association of Lighthouse Authorities
International Association of Ports and Harbors
International Organization for Standardization
National Conference of Standards Laboratories
United Nations Development Program
United Nations Environment Program
United National Fund for Drug Abuse Control
United Nations Fund for Population Activities

---

*   The JLA has agreed that the MIGA Convention will apply to Hong Kong after 1997,
      but no decision has yet been reached on Hong Kong's participation as a MIGA member
      after 1997.
**   It has not yet been determined in what capacity Hong Kong will participate in
      organizations listed in Section 3.

4. Organizations in which the HKSAR will be a full member:

Asian Development Bank (ADB)
Asian Productivity Organization (APO)***
Customs Cooperation Council (CCC)
General Agreements on Tariff and Trade (GATT)
Network of Aquaculture Centres in Asia and the Pacific (NACA)
World Meterological Organization (WMO)
World Trade Organization (WTO)

5. Organizations in which the HKSAR will participate as part of the PRC delegation:

Asia-Pacific Postal Union (APPU)
Food and Agriculture Organization (FAO)
International Atomic Energy Agency (IAEA)
International Bank for Reconstruction and Development (IBRD)
International Civil Aviation Organization (ICAO)***
International Criminal Police Organization (INTERPOL)
International Development Association (IDA)
International Finance Corporation (IFC)
International Hydrographic Organization (IHO)
International Labor Organization (ILO)
International Maritime Satellite Organization (INMARSAT)
International Monetary Fund (IMF)
International Telecommunications Satellite Organization (INTELSAT)
International Telecommunication Union (ITU)
United Nations Commission on Narcotic Drugs (UNCND)
United Nations Conference on Trade and Development (UNCTAD)
Universal Postal Union (UPU)
World Intellectual Property Organization (WIPO)

6. Organizations in which the HKSAR will be an associate member:

Asian and Pacific Development Centre (APDC)
Asia-Pacific Telecommunity (APT)

***
*** JLG approval for Hong Kong's participation is pending.

Economic and Social Commission for Asia and the Pacific (ESCAP)
Intergovernmental Typhoon Committee (ITC)
International Maritime Organization (IMO)
Statistical Institute for Asia and the Pacific (SIAP)
World Health Organization (WHO)

Source: United States Hong Kong Policy Act Report as of March 31, 1996.

Appendix B

JOINT DECLARATION OF THE GOVERNMENT OF THE UNITED
KINGDOM OF GREAT BRITAIN AND NORTHERN IRELAND AND
THE GOVERNMENT OF THE PEOPLE'S REPUBLIC OF CHINA
ON THE QUESTION OF HONG KONG [DECEMBER 19, 1984]

The Government of the United Kingdom of Great Britain and Northern
Ireland and the Government of the People's Republic of China have reviewed
with satisfaction the friendly relations existing between the two Governments
and peoples in recent years and agreed that a proper negotiated settlement
of the question of Hong Kong, which is left over from the past, is conducive
to the maintenance of the prosperity and stability of Hong Kong and to the
further strengthening and development of the relations between the two
countries on a new basis. To this end, they have, after talks between the
delegations of the two Governments, agreed to declare as follows:

1. The Government of the People's Republic of China declares that to
   recover the Hong Kong area (including Hong Kong Island, Kowloon
   and the New Territories, hereinafter referred to as Hong Kong) is the
   common aspiration of the entire Chinese people, and that it has decided
   to resume the exercise of sovereignty over Hong Kong with effect from
   1 July 1997.
2. The Government of the United Kingdom declares that it will restore Hong
   Kong to the People's Republic of China with effect from 1 July 1997.
3. The Government of the People's Republic of China declares that the
   basic policies of the People's Republic of China regarding Hong Kong
   are as follows:
   (1) Upholding national unity and territorial integrity and taking
   account of the history of Hong Kong and its realities, the People's
   Republic of China has decided to establish, in accordance with the
   provisions of Article 31 of the Constitution of the People's Republic of

China, a Hong Kong Special Administrative Region upon resuming the exercise of sovereignty over Hong Kong.

(2) The Hong Kong Special Administrative Region will be directly under the authority of the Central People's Government of the People's Republic of China. The Hong Kong Special Administrative Region will enjoy a high degree of autonomy, except in foreign and defence affairs which are the responsibilities of the Central People's Government.

(3) The Hong Kong Special Administrative Region will be vested with executive, legislative and independent judicial power, including that of final adjudication. The laws currently in force in Hong Kong will remain basically unchanged.

(4) The Government of the Hong Kong Special Administrative Region will be composed of local inhabitants. The chief executive will be appointed by the Central People's Government on the basis of the results of elections or consultations to be held locally. Principal officials will be nominated by the chief executive of the Hong Kong Special Administrative Region for appointment by the Central People's Government. Chinese and foreign nationals previously working in the public and police services in the government departments of Hong Kong may remain in employment. British and other foreign nationals may also be employed to serve as advisers or hold certain public posts in government departments of the Hong Kong Special Administrative Region.

(5) The current social and economic systems in Hong Kong will remain unchanged, and so will the life-style. Rights and freedoms, including those of the person, of speech, of the press, of assembly, of association, of travel, of movement, of correspondence, of strike, of choice of occupation, of academic research and of religious belief will be ensured by law in the Hong Kong Special Administrative Region. Private property, ownership of enterprises, legitimate right of inheritance and foreign investment will be protected by law.

(6) The Hong Kong Special Administrative Region will retain the status of a free port and a separate customs territory.

(7) The Hong Kong special Administrative Region will retain the status of an international financial centre, and its markets for foreign exchange, gold, securities and futures will continue. There will be free flow of capital. The Hong Kong dollar will continue to circulate and remain freely convertible.

(8) The Hong Kong Special Administrative Region will have independent finances. The Central People's Government will not levy taxes on the Hong Kong Special Administrative Region.

(9) The Hong Kong Special Administrative Region may establish mutually beneficial economic relations with the United Kingdom and

other countries, whose economic interests in Hong Kong will be given due regard.

(10) Using the name of "Hong Kong, China", the Hong Kong Special Administrative Region may on its own maintain and develop economic and cultural relations and conclude relevant agreements with states, regions and relevant international organisations.

The Government of the Hong Kong Special Administrative Region may on its own issue travel documents for entry into and exit from Hong Kong.

(11) The maintenance of public order in the Hong Kong Special Administrative Region will be the responsibility of the Government of the Hong Kong Special Administrative Region.

(12) The above-stated basic policies of the People's Republic of China regarding Hong Kong and the elaboration of them in Annex I to this Joint Declaration will be stipulated, in a Basic Law of the Hong Kong Special Administrative Region of the People's Republic of China, by the National People's Congress of the People's Republic of China, and they will remain unchanged for 50 years.

4. The Government of the United Kingdom and the Government of the People's Republic of China declare that, during the transitional period between the date of the entry into force of this Joint Declaration and 30 June 1997, the Government of the United Kingdom will be responsible for the administration of Hong Kong with the object of maintaining and preserving its economic prosperity and social stability; and that the Government of the People's Republic of China will give its cooperation in this connection.

5. The Government of the United Kingdom and the Government of the People's Republic of China declare that, in order to ensure a smooth transfer of government in 1997, and with a view to the effective implementation of this Joint Declaration, a Sino-British Joint Liaison Group will be set up when this Joint Declaration enters into force; and that it will be established and will function in accordance with the provisions of Annex II to this Joint Declaration.

6. The Government of the United Kingdom and the Government of the People's Republic of China declare that land leases in Hong Kong and other related matters will be dealt with in accordance with the provisions of Annex III to this Joint Declaration.

7. The Government of the United Kingdom and the Government of the People's Republic of China agree to implement the preceding declarations and the Annexes to this Joint Declaration.

8. This Joint Declaration is subject to ratification and shall enter into force on the date of the exchange of instruments of ratification, which shall take place in Beijing before 30 June 1985. This Joint Declaration and its Annexes shall be equally binding.

ANNEX I

Elaboration by the Government of the People's Republic of China of Its Basic Policies Regarding Hong Kong

The Government of the People's Republic of China elaborates the basic policies of the People's Republic of China regarding Hong Kong as set out in paragraph 3 of the Joint Declaration of the Government of the United Kingdom of Great Britain and Northern Ireland and the Government of the People's Republic of China on the Question of Hong Kong as follows:

I

The Constitution of the People's Republic of China stipulates in Article 31 that "the state may establish special administrative regions when necessary. The systems to be instituted in special administrative regions shall be prescribed by laws enacted by the National People's Congress in the light of the specific conditions." In accordance with this Article, the People's Republic of China shall, upon the resumption of the exercise of sovereignty over Hong Kong on 1 July 1997, establish the Hong Kong Special Administrative Region of the People's Republic of China. The National People's Congress of the People's Republic of China shall enact and promulgate a Basic Law of the Hong Kong Special Administration Region of the People's Republic of China (hereinafter referred to as the Basic Law) in accordance with the Constitution of the People's Republic of China, stipulating that after the establishment of the Hong Kong Special Administrative Region the socialist system and socialist policies shall not be practised in the Hong Kong Special Administrative Region and that Hong Kong's previous capitalist system and life-style shall remain unchanged for 50 years.

The Hong Kong Special Administrative Region shall be directly under the authority of the Central People's Government of the People's Republic of China and shall enjoy a high degree of autonomy. Except for foreign and defence affairs which are the responsibilities of the Central People's Government, the Hong Kong Special Administrative Region shall be vested with executive, legislative and independent judicial power, including that of final adjudication. The Central People's Government shall authorise the Hong Kong Special Administrative Region to conduct on its own those external affairs specified in Section XI of this Annex.

The government and legislature of the Hong Kong Special Administrative Region shall be composed of local inhabitants. The chief executive of the Hong Kong Special Administrative Region shall be selected by election or through consultations held locally and be appointed by the Central People's Government. Principal officials (equivalent to Secretaries) shall be nominated by the chief executive of the Hong Kong Special Administrative Region and appointed by the Central People's Government. The legislature of the Hong Kong Special Administrative Region shall be constituted by elections. The executive authorities shall abide by the law and shall be accountable to the legislature.

In addition to Chinese, English may also be used in organs of government and in the courts in the Hong Kong Special Administrative Region.

Apart from displaying the national flag and national emblem of the People's Republic of China, the Hong Kong Special Administrative Region may use a regional flag and emblem of its own.

II

After the establishment of the Hong Kong Special Administrative Region, the laws previously in force in Hong Kong (i.e., the common law, rules of equity, ordinances, subordinate legislation and customary law) shall be maintained, save for any that contravene the Basic Law and subject to any amendment by the Hong Kong Special Administrative Region legislature.

The legislative power of the Hong Kong Special Administrative Region shall be vested in the legislature of the Hong Kong Special Administrative Region. The legislature may on its own authority enact laws in accordance with the provisions of the Basic Law and legal procedures, and report them to the Standing Committee of the National People's Congress for the record. Laws enacted by the legislature which are in accordance with the Basic Law and legal procedures shall be regarded as valid.

The laws of the Hong Kong Special Administrative Region shall be the Basic Law, and the laws previously in force in Hong Kong and laws enacted by the Hong Kong Special Administrative Region legislature as above.

III

After the establishment of the Hong Kong Special Administrative Region, the judicial system previously practised in Hong Kong shall be maintained except for those changes consequent upon the vesting in the courts of the Hong Kong Special Administrative Region of the power of final adjudication.

Judicial power in the Hong Kong Special Administrative Region shall be vested in the courts of the Hong Kong Special Administrative Region. The courts shall exercise judicial power independently and free from any interference. Members of the judiciary shall be immune from legal action in respect of their judicial functions. The courts shall decide cases in accordance with the laws of the Hong Kong Special Administrative Region and may refer to precedents in other common law jurisdictions.

Judges of the Hong Kong Special Administrative Region courts shall be appointed by the chief executive of the Hong Kong Special Administrative Region acting in accordance with the recommendation of an independent commission composed of local judges, persons from the legal profession and other eminent persons. Judges shall be chosen by reference to their judicial qualities and may be recruited from other common law jurisdictions. A judge may only be removed for inability to discharge the functions of his office, or for misbehaviour, by the chief executive of the Hong Kong Special Administrative Region acting in accordance with the recommendation of a tribunal appointed by the chief judge of the court of final appeal, consisting of not fewer than three local judges. Additionally, the appointment or removal of principal judges (i.e., those of the highest rank) shall be made by the chief executive with the endorsement of the Hong Kong Special Administrative Region legislature and reported to the Standing Committee of the National People's Congress for the record. The system of appointment and removal of judicial officers other than judges shall be maintained.

The power of final judgment of the Hong Kong Special Administrative Region shall be vested in the court of final appeal in the Hong Kong Special Administrative Region, which may as required invite judges from other common law jurisdictions to sit on the court of final appeal.

A prosecuting authority of the Hong Kong Special Administrative Region shall control criminal prosecutions free from any interference.

On the basis of the system previously operating in Hong Kong, the Hong Kong Special Administrative Region Government shall on its own make provision for local lawyers and lawyers from outside the Hong Kong Special Administrative Region to work and practise in the Hong Kong Special Administrative Region.

The Central People's Government shall assist or authorise the Hong Kong Special Administrative Region Government to make appropriate arrangements for reciprocal juridical assistance with foreign states.

IV

After the establishment of the Hong Kong Special Administrative Region, public servants previously serving in Hong Kong in all government departments, including the police department, and members of the judiciary may all remain in employment and continue their service with pay, allowances, benefits and conditions of service no less favourable than before. The Hong Kong Special Administrative Region Government shall pay to such persons who retire or complete their contracts, as well as to those who have retired before 1 July 1997, or to their dependents, all pensions, gratuities, allowances and benefits due to them on terms no less favourable than before, and irrespective of their nationality or place of residence.

The Hong Kong Special Administrative Region Government may employ British and other foreign nationals previously serving in the public service in Hong Kong, and may recruit British and other foreign nationals holding permanent identity cards of the Hong Kong Special Administrative Region to serve as public servants at all levels, except as heads of major government departments (corresponding to branches or departments at Secretary level) including the police department, and as deputy heads of some of those departments. The Hong Kong Special Administrative Region Government may also employ British and other foreign nationals as advisers to government departments and, when there is a need, may recruit qualified candidates from outside the Hong Kong Special Administrative Region to professional and technical posts in government departments. The above shall be employed only in their individual capacities and, like other public servants, shall be responsible to the Hong Kong Special Administrative Region Government.

The appointment and promotion of public servants shall be on the basis of qualifications, experience and ability. Hong Kong's previous system of recruitment, employment, assessment, discipline, training and management for the public service (including special bodies for appointment, pay and conditions of service) shall, save for any provisions providing privileged treatment for foreign nationals, be maintained.

V

The Hong Kong Special Administrative Region shall deal on its own with financial matters, including disposing of its financial resources and drawing up its budgets and its final accounts. The Hong Kong Special Administrative Region shall report its budgets and final accounts to the Central People's Government for the record.

The Central People's Government shall not levy taxes on the Hong Kong Special Administrative Region. The Hong Kong Special Administrative Region shall use its financial revenues exclusively for its own purposes and they shall not be handed over to the Central People's Government. The systems by which taxation and public expenditure must be approved by the legislature, and by which there is accountability to the legislature for all public expenditure, and the system for auditing public accounts shall be maintained.

VI

The Hong Kong Special Administrative Region shall maintain the capitalist economic and trade systems previously practised in Hong Kong. The Hong Kong Special Administrative Region Government shall decide its economic and trade policies on its own. Rights concerning the ownership of property, including those relating to acquisition, use, disposal, inheritance and compensation for lawful deprivation (corresponding to the real value of the property concerned, freely convertible and paid without undue delay) shall continue to be protected by law.

The Hong Kong Special Administrative Region shall retain the status of a free port and continue a free trade policy, including the free movement of goods and capital. The Hong Kong Special Administrative Region may on its own maintain and develop economic and trade relations with all states and regions.

The Hong Kong Special Administrative Region shall be a separate customs territory. It may participate in relevant international organisations and international trade agreements (including preferential trade arrangements), such as the General Agreement on Tariffs and Trade and arrangements regarding international trade in textiles. Export quotas, tariff preferences and other similar arrangements obtained by the Hong Kong Special Administrative Region shall be enjoyed exclusively by the Hong Kong Special Administrative Region. The Hong Kong Special Administrative Region shall have authority to issue its own certificates of origin for products manufactured locally, in accordance with prevailing rules of origin.

The Hong Kong Special Administrative Region may, as necessary, establish official and semi-official economic and trade missions in foreign countries, reporting the establishment of such missions to the Central People's Government for the record.

VII

The Hong Kong Special Administrative Region shall retain the status of an international financial centre. The monetary and financial systems previously practised in Hong Kong, including the systems of regulation and supervision of deposit taking institutions and financial markets, shall be maintained.

The Hong Kong Special Administrative Region Government may decide its monetary and financial policies on its own. It shall safeguard the free operation of financial business and the free flow of capital within, into and out of the Hong Kong Special Administrative Region. No exchange control policy shall be applied in the Hong Kong Special Administrative Region. Markets for foreign exchange, gold, securities and futures shall continue.

The Hong Kong dollar, as the local legal tender, shall continue to circulate and remain freely convertible. The authority to issue Hong Kong currency shall be vested in the Hong Kong Special Administrative Region Government.

The Hong Kong Special Administrative Region Government may authorise designated banks to issue or continue to issue Hong Kong currency under statutory authority, after satisfying itself that any issue of currency will be soundly based and that the arrangements for such issue are consistent with the object of maintaining the stability of the currency. Hong Kong currency bearing references inappropriate to the status of Hong Kong as a Special Administrative Region of the People's Republic of China shall be progressively replaced and withdrawn from circulation.

The Exchange Fund shall be managed and controlled by the Hong Kong Special Administrative Region Government, primarily for regulating the exchange value of the Hong Kong dollar.

VIII

The Hong Kong Special Administrative Region shall maintain Hong Kong's previous systems of shipping management and shipping regulation, including the system for regulating conditions of seamen. The specific functions and responsibilities of the Hong Kong Special Administrative Region Government in the field of shipping shall be defined by the Hong Kong Special Administrative Region Government on its own. Private shipping businesses and shipping-related businesses and private container terminals in Hong Kong may continue to operate freely.

The Hong Kong Special Administrative Region shall be authorised by the Central People's Government to continue to maintain a shipping register and issue related certificates under its own legislation in the name of "Hong Kong, China."

With the exception of foreign warships, access for which requires the permission of the Central People's Government, ships shall enjoy access to the ports of the Hong Kong Special Administrative Region in accordance with the laws of the Hong Kong Special Administrative Region.

IX

The Hong Kong Special Administrative Region shall maintain the status of Hong Kong as a centre of international and regional aviation. Airlines incorporated and having their principal place of business in Hong Kong and civil aviation related businesses may continue to operate. The Hong Kong Special Administrative Region shall continue the previous system of civil aviation management in Hong Kong, and keep its own aircraft register in accordance with provisions laid down by the Central People's Government concerning nationality marks and registration marks of aircraft. The Hong Kong Special Administrative Region shall be responsible on its own for matters of routine business and technical management of civil aviation, including the management of airports, the provision of air traffic services within the flight information region of the Hong Kong Special Administrative Region, and the discharge of other responsibilities allocated under the regional air navigation procedures of the International Civil Aviation Organisation.

The Central People's Government shall, in consultation with the Hong Kong Special Administrative Region Government, make arrangements providing for air services between the Hong Kong Special Administrative Region and other parts of the People's Republic of China for airlines incorporated and having their principal place of business in the Hong Kong Special Administrative Region and other airlines of the People's Republic of China. All Air Service Agreements providing for air services between other parts of the People's Republic of China and other states and regions with stops at the Hong Kong Special Administrative Region and air services between the Hong Kong Special Administrative Region and other states and regions with stops at other parts of the People's Republic of China shall be concluded by the Central People's Government. For this purpose, the Central People's Government shag take account of the special conditions and economic interests of the Hong Kong Special Administrative Region and consult the Hong Kong Special Administrative Region Government. Representatives of the Hong Kong Special Administrative Region Government may participate as members of delegations of the Government of the People's Republic of China in air service consultations with foreign governments concerning arrangements for such services.

Acting under specific authorisations from the Central People's Government, the Hong Kong Special Administrative Region Government may:
— renew or amend Air Service Agreements and arrangements previously in force; in principle, all such Agreements and arrangements may be renewed or amended with the rights contained in such previous Agreements and arrangements being as far as possible maintained;
— negotiate and conclude new Air Service Agreements providing routes for airlines incorporated and having their principal place of business in the Hong Kong Special Administrative Region and rights for overflights and technical stops; and
— negotiate and conclude provisional arrangements where no Air Service Agreements with a foreign state or other region is in force.

All scheduled air services to, from or through the Hong Kong Special Administrative Region which do not operate to, from or through the mainland of China shall be regulated by Air Service Agreements or provisional arrangements referred to in this paragraph.

The Central People's Government shall give the Hong Kong Special Administrative Region Government the authority to:
— negotiate and conclude with other authorities all arrangements concerning the implementation of the above Air Service Agreements and provisional arrangements;
— issue licences to airlines incorporated and having their principal place of business in the Hong Kong Special Administrative Region;
— designate such airlines under the above Air Service Agreements and provisional arrangements; and
— issue permits to foreign airlines for services other than those to, from or through the mainland of China.

X

The Hong Kong Special Administrative Region shall maintain the educational system previously practised in Hong Kong. The Hong Kong Special Administrative Region Government shall on its own decide policies in the fields of culture, education, science and technology, including policies regarding the educational system and its administration, the language of instruction, the allocation of funds, the examination system, the system of academic awards and the recognition of educational and technological qualifications. Institutions of all kinds, including those run by religious and community organisations, may retain their autonomy. They may continue to recruit staff and use teaching materials from outside the Hong Kong Special Administrative Region. Students shall enjoy freedom of choice of education and freedom to pursue their education outside the Hong Kong Special Administrative Region.

XI

Subject to the principle that foreign affairs are the responsibility of the Central People's Government, representatives of the Hong Kong Special Administrative Region Government may participate, as members of delegations of the Government of the People's Republic of China, in negotiations at the diplomatic level directly affecting the Hong Kong Special Administrative Region conducted by the Central People's Government. The Hong Kong Special Administrative Region may on its own, using the name "Hong Kong, China," maintain and develop relations and conclude and implement agreements with states, regions and relevant international organisations in the appropriate fields, including the economic, trade, financial and monetary, shipping, communications, touristic, cultural and sporting fields. Representatives of the Hong Kong Special Administrative Region may participate, as members of delegations of the Government of the People's Republic of China, in international organisations or conferences in appropriate fields limited to states and affecting the Hong Kong Special Administrative Region, or may attend in such other capacity as may be permitted by the Central People's Government and the organisation or conference concerned, and may express their views in the name of "Hong Kong, China." The Hong Kong Special Administrative Region may, using the name "Hong Kong, China," participate in international organisations and conferences not limited to states.

The application to the Hong Kong Special Administrative Region of international agreements to which the People's Republic of China is or becomes a party shall be decided by the Central People's Government, in accordance with the circumstances and needs of the Hong Kong Special Administrative Region, and after seeking the views of the Hong Kong Special Administrative Region Government. international agreements to which the People's Republic of China is not a party but which are implemented in Hong Kong may remain implemented in the Hong Kong Special Administrative Region. The Central People's Government shall, as necessary, authorise or assist the Hong Kong Special Administrative Region Government to make appropriate arrangements for the application to the Hong Kong Special Administrative Region of other relevant international agreements. The Central People's Government shall take the necessary steps to ensure that the Hong Kong Special Administrative Region shall continue to retain its status in an appropriate capacity in those international organisations of which the People's Republic of China is a member and in which Hong Kong participates in one capacity or another. The Central People's Government shall, where necessary, facilitate the continued participation of the Hong Kong Special Administrative Region in an appropriate capacity in those international organisations in which Hong Kong is a participant in one capacity or another, but of which the People's Republic of China is not a member.

Foreign consular and other official or semi-official missions may be established in the Hong Kong Special Administrative Region with the approval of the Central People's Government. Consular and other official missions established in Hong Kong by states which have established formal diplomatic relations with the People's Republic of China may be maintained. According to the circumstances of each case, consular and other official missions of states having no formal diplomatic relations with the People's Republic of China may either be maintained or changed to semi-official missions. States not recognised by the People's Republic of China can only establish non-governmental institutions.

The United Kingdom may establish a Consulate-General in the Hong Kong Special Administrative Region.

XII

The maintenance of public order in the Hong Kong Special Administrative Region shall be the responsibility of the Hong Kong Special Administrative Region Government. Military forces sent by the Central People's Government to be stationed in the Hong Kong Special Administrative Region for the purpose of defence shall not interfere in the internal affairs of the Hong Kong Special Administration Region. Expenditure for these military forces shall be borne by the Central People's Government.

XIII

The Hong Kong Special Administrative Region Government shall protect the rights and freedoms of inhabitants and other persons in the Hong Kong Special Administrative Region according to law. The Hong Kong Special Administrative Region Government shall maintain the rights and freedoms as provided for by the laws previously in force in Hong Kong, including freedom of the person, of speech, of the press, of assembly, of association, to form and join trade unions, of correspondence, of travel, of movement, of strike, of demonstration, of choice of occupation, of academic research, of belief, inviolability of the home, the freedom to many and the right to raise a family freely.

Every person shall have the right to confidential legal advice, access to the courts, representation in the courts by lawyers of his choice, and to obtain judicial remedies. Every person shall have the right to challenge the actions of the executive in the courts.

Religious organisations and believers may maintain their relations with religious organisations and believers elsewhere, and schools, hospitals and welfare institutions run by religious organisations may be continued. The relationship between religious organisations in the Hong Kong Special Administrative Region and those in other parts of the People's Republic of China shall be based on the principles of non-subordination, non-interference and mutual respect.

The provisions of the international Covenant on Civil and Political Rights and the international Covenant on Economic, Social and Cultural Rights as applied to Hong Kong shall remain in force.

XIV

The following categories of persons shall have the right of abode in the Hong Kong Special Administrative Region, and, in accordance with the law of the Hong Kong Special Administrative Region, be qualified to obtain

permanent identity cards issued by the Hong Kong Special Administrative
Region Government, which state their right of abode:

— all Chinese nationals who were born or who have ordinarily resided in
  Hong Kong before or after the establishment of the Hong Kong Special
  Administrative Region for a continuous period of 7 years or more, and
  persons of Chinese nationality born outside Hong Kong of such Chinese
  nationals;

— all other persons who have ordinarily resided in Hong Kong before or
  after the establishment of the Hong Kong Special Administrative Region
  for a continuous period of 7 years or more and who have taken Hong
  Kong as their place of permanent residence before or after the
  establishment of the Hong Kong Special Administrative Region, and
  persons under 21 years of age who were born of such persons in Hong
  Kong before or after the establishment of the Hong Kong Special
  Administrative Region;

— any other persons who had the right of abode only in Hong Kong before
  the establishment of the Hong Kong Special Administrative Region.

The Central People's Government shall authorise the Hong Kong Special
Administrative Region Government to issue, in accordance with the law,
passports of the Hong Kong Special Administrative Region of the People's
Republic of China to all Chinese nationals who hold permanent identity cards
of the Hong Kong Special Administrative Region, and travel documents of
the Hong Kong Special Administrative Region of the People's Republic of
China to all other persons lawfully residing in the Hong Kong Special
Administrative Region. The above passports and documents shall be valid
for all states and regions and shall record the holder's right to return to the
Hong Kong Special Administrative Region.

For the purpose of travelling to and from the Hong Kong Special
Administrative Region, residents of the Hong Kong Special Administrative
Region may use travel documents issued by the Hong Kong Special
Administrative Region Government, or by other competent authorities of
the People's Republic of China, or of other states. Holders of permanent
identity cards of the Hong Kong Special Administrative Region may have
this fact stated in their travel documents as evidence that the holders have
the right of abode in the Hong Kong Special Administrative Region.

Entry into the Hong Kong Special Administrative Region of persons
from other parts of China shall continue to be regulated in accordance with
the present practice.

The Hong Kong Special Administrative Region Government may apply
immigration controls on entry, stay in and departure from the Hong Kong
Special Administrative Region by persons from foreign states and regions.

Unless restrained by law, holders of valid travel documents shall be free to leave the Hong Kong Special Administrative Region without special authorisation.

The Central People's Government shall assist or authorise the Hong Kong Special Administrative Region Government to conclude visa abolition agreements with states or regions.

ANNEX II

Sino-British Joint Liaison Group

1. In furtherance of their common aim and in order to ensure a smooth transfer of government in 1997, the Government of the United Kingdom and the Government of the People's Republic of China have agreed to continue their discussions in a friendly spirit and to develop the cooperative relationship which already exists between the two Governments over Hong Kong with a view to the effective implementation of the Joint Declaration.
2. In order to meet the requirements for liaison, consultation and the exchange of information, the two Governments have agreed to set up a Joint Liaison Group.
3. The functions of the Joint Liaison Group shall be:

    (a) to conduct consultations on the implementation of the Joint Declaration;

    (b) to discuss matters relating to the smooth transfer of government in 1997;

    (c) to exchange information and conduct consultations on such subjects as may be agreed by the two sides.

    Matters on which there is disagreement in the Joint Liaison Group shall be referred to the two Governments for solution through consultations.
4. Matters for consideration during the first half of the period between the establishment of the Joint Liaison Group and 1 July 1997 shall include:

    (a) action to be taken by the two Governments to enable the Hong Kong Special Administrative Region to maintain its economic relations as a separate customs territory, and in particular to ensure the maintenance of Hong Kong's participation in the General Agreement on Tariffs and Trade, the Multifibre Arrangement and other international arrangements; and

    (b) action to be taken by the two Governments to ensure the continued application of international rights and obligations affecting Hong Kong.
5. The two Governments have agreed that in the second half of the period between the establishment of the Joint Liaison Group and 1 July 1997

there will be need for closer cooperation, which will therefore be intensified during that period. Matters for consideration during this second period shall include:

(a) procedures to be adopted for the smooth transition in 1997;

(b) action to assist the Hong Kong Special Administrative Region to maintain and develop economic and cultural relations and conclude agreements on these matters with states, regions and relevant international organisations.

6. The Joint Liaison Group shall be an organ for liaison and not an organ of power. It shall play no part in the administration of Hong Kong or the Hong Kong Special Administrative Region. Nor shall it have any supervisory role over that administration. The members and supporting staff of the Joint Liaison Group shall only conduct activities within the scope of the functions of the Joint Liaison Group.

7. Each side shall designate a senior representative, who shall be of Ambassadorial rank, and four other members of the group. Each side may send up to 20 supporting staff.

8. The Joint Liaison Group shall be established on the entry into force of the Joint Declaration. From 1 July 1988 the Joint Liaison Group shall have its principal base in Hong Kong. The Joint Liaison Group shall continue its work until 1 January 2000.

9. The Joint Liaison Group shall meet in Beijing, London and Hong Kong. It shall meet at least once in each of the three locations in each year. The venue for each meeting shall be agreed between the two sides.

10. Members of the Joint Liaison Group shall enjoy diplomatic privileges and immunities as appropriate when in the three locations. Proceedings of the Joint Liaison Group shall remain confidential unless otherwise agreed between the two sides.

11. The Joint Liaison Group may by agreement between the two sides decide to set up specialist sub-groups to deal with particular subjects requiring expert assistance.

12. Meetings of the Joint Liaison Group and sub-groups may be attended by experts other than the members of the Joint Liaison Group. Each side shall determine the composition of its delegation to particular meetings of the Joint Liaison Group or sub-group in accordance with the subjects to be discussed and the venue chosen.

13. The working procedures of the Joint Liaison Group shall be discussed and decided upon by the two sides within the guidelines laid down in this Annex.

ANNEX III

Land Leases

The Government of the United Kingdom and the Government of the People's Republic of China have agreed that, with effect from the entry into force of the Joint Declaration, land leases in Hong Kong and other related matters shall be dealt with in accordance with the following provisions:

1. All leases of land granted or decided upon before the entry into force of the Joint Declaration and those granted thereafter in accordance with paragraph 2 or 3 of this Annex, and which extend beyond. 30 June 1997, and all rights in relation to such leases shall continue to be recognised and protected under the law of the Hong Kong Special Administrative Region.

2. All leases of land granted by the British Hong Kong Government not containing a right of renewal that expire before 30 June 1997, except short term tenancies and leases for special purposes, may be extended if the lessee so wishes for a period expiring not later than 30 June 2047 without payment of an additional premium. An annual rent shall be charged from the date of extension equivalent to 3 per cent of the rateable value of the property at that date, adjusted in step with any changes in the rateable value thereafter. In the case of old schedule lots, village lots, small houses and similar rural holdings, where the property was on 30 June 1984 held by, or, in the case of small houses granted after that date, the property is granted to, a person descended through the male line from a person who was in 1898 a resident of an established village in Hong Kong, the rent shall remain unchanged so long as the property is held by that person or by one of his lawful successors in the male line. Where leases of land not having a right of renewal expire after 30 June 1997, they shall be dealt with in accordance with the relevant land laws and policies of the Hong Kong Special Administrative Region.

3. From the entry into force of the Joint Declaration until 30 June 1997, new leases of land may be granted by the British Hong Kong Government for terms expiring not later than 30 June 2047. Such leases shall be granted at a premium and nominal rental until 30 June 1997, after which date they shall not require payment of an additional premium but an annual rent equivalent to 3 per cent of the rateable value of the property at that date, adjusted in step with changes in the rateable value thereafter, shall be charged.

4. The total amount of new land to be granted under paragraph 3 of this Annex shall be limited to 50 hectares a year (excluding land to be granted to the Hong Kong Housing Authority for public rental housing) from the entry into force of the Joint Declaration until 30 June 1997.

5. Modifications of the conditions specified in leases granted by the British Hong Kong Government may continue to be granted before 1 July 1997 at a premium equivalent to the difference between the value of the land under the previous conditions and its value under the modified conditions.

6. From the entry into force of the Joint Declaration until 30 June 1997, premium income obtained by the British Hong Kong Government from land transactions shall, after deduction of the average cost of land production, be shared equally between the British Hong Kong Government and the future Hong Kong Special Administrative Region Government. All the income obtained by the British Hong Kong Government, including the amount of the above mentioned deduction, shall be put into the Capital Works Reserve Fund for the financing of land development and public works in Hong Kong. The Hong Kong Special Administrative Region Government's share of the premium income shall be deposited in banks incorporated in Hong Kong and shall not be drawn on except for the financing of land development and public works in Hong Kong in accordance with the provisions of paragraph 7(d) of this Annex.

7. A Land Commission shall be established in Hong Kong immediately upon the entry into force of the Joint Declaration. The Land Commission shall be composed of an equal number of officials designated respectively by the Government of the United Kingdom and the Government of the People's Republic of China together with necessary supporting staff. The officials of the two sides shall be responsible to their respective governments. The Land Commission shall be dissolved on 30 June 1997. The terms of reference of the Land Commission shall be:

(a) to conduct consultations on the implementation of this Annex;

(b) to monitor observance of the limit specified in paragraph 4 of this Annex, the amount of land granted to the Hong Kong Housing Authority for public rental housing, and the division and use of premium income referred to in paragraph 6 of this Annex;

(c) to consider and decide on proposals from the British Hong Kong Government for increasing the limit referred to in paragraph 4 of this Annex;

(d) to examine proposals for drawing on the Hong Kong Special Administrative Region Government's share of premium income referred to in paragraph 6 of this Annex and to make recommendations to the Chinese side for decision.

Matters on which there is disagreement in the Land Commission shall be referred to the Government of the United Kingdom and the Government of the People's Republic of China for decision.

8. Specific details regarding the establishment of the Land Commission shall be finalised separately by the two sides through consultations.

Exchange of Memoranda

(A) United Kingdom Memorandum

Memorandum

In connection with the Joint Declaration of the Government of the United Kingdom of Great Britain and Northern Ireland and the Government of the People's Republic of China on the question of Hong Kong to be signed this day, the Government of the United Kingdom declares that, subject to the completion of the necessary amendments to the relevant United Kingdom legislation:

(a) All persons who on 30 June 1997 are, by virtue of a connection with Hong Kong, British Dependent Territories citizens (BDTCs) under the law in force in the United Kingdom will cease to be BDTCs with effect from 1 July 1997, but will be eligible to retain an appropriate status which, without conferring the right of abode in the United Kingdom, will entitle them to continue to use passports issued by the Government of the United Kingdom. This status will be acquired by such persons only if they hold or are included in such a British passport issued before 1 July 1997, except that eligible persons born on or after 1 January 1997 but before 1 July 1997 may obtain or be included in such a passport up to 31 December 1997.

(b) No person will acquire BDTC status on or after 1 July 1997 by virtue of a connection with Hong Kong. No person born on or after 1 July 1997 will acquire the status referred to as being appropriate in subparagraph (a).

(c) United Kingdom consular officials in the Hong Kong Special Administrative Region and elsewhere may renew and replace passports of persons mentioned in sub-paragraph (a) and may also issue them to persons, born before 1 July 1997 of such persons, who had previously been included in the passport of their parent.

(d) Those who have obtained or been included in passports issued by the Government of the United Kingdom under sub-paragraphs (a) and (c) will be entitled to receive, upon request, British consular services and protection when in third countries.

Beijing, 1984

(B) Chinese Memorandum

Translation

Memorandum

The Government of the People's Republic of China has received the memorandum from the Government of the United Kingdom of Great Britain and Northern Ireland dated .... 1984.

Under the Nationality Law of the People's Republic of China, all Hong Kong Chinese compatriots, whether they are holders of the "British Dependent Territories citizens' Passport" or not, are Chinese nationals.

Taking account of the historical background of Hong Kong and its realities, the competent authorities of the Government of the People's Republic of China will, with effect from 1 July 1997, pen-nit Chinese nationals in Hong Kong who were previously called "British Dependent Territories citizens" to use travel documents issued by the Government of the United Kingdom for the purpose of to travelling to other states and regions.

The above Chinese nationals will not be entitled to British consular protection in the Hong Kong Special Administrative Region and other parts of the People's Republic of China on account of their holding the above-mentioned British travel documents.

Beijing, 1984

Index

ONE Country, TWO International Legal Personalities

The Case of Hong Kong

The transition from British to Chinese rule, although widely anticipated, is shaping up as one of the most challenging events in Hong Kong's history. It also constitutes a highly complex exercise in social, political, economic and legal engineering from an international perspective. The intricacies of the transition, both at the analytical and practical levels, have been addressed by scholars in different fields. The international legal dimension of the process, however, has thus far been tackled in a piecemeal fashion.

The purpose of this book is to examine the key relevant issues within a single framework, highlighting the interconnections in as broad as possible a context. The author employs international legal concepts to assess, from a normative standpoint, the underpinnings of the unique 'one country-two systems' formula devised by Britain and China, focusing in detail on questions such as Hong Kong's international legal status, jurisdictional competence, international legal obligations, human rights, pivotal aspects of treaty law and the relationship between Hong Kong's domestic law and international law.

Dr Roda Mushkat is a professor of law at the University of Hong Kong, where she has been teaching since 1979 in the subjects of Public International Law, Jurisprudence, Law & Society, Constitutional & Administrative Law, and Conflict of Laws. She has been affiliated as a visiting scholar with some of the world's leading law schools. Dr Mushkat has published extensively in the areas of international refugee law, international environmental law, international law of war, human rights and legal theory. She is considered to be the principal academic authority in issues pertaining to Hong Kong's international legal status and personality, and has written numerous papers on the topic.

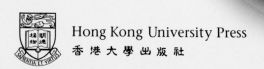

Hong Kong University Press
香港大學出版社

HKU Press
Law Series

ISBN 962-209-427-9

9 789622 094277